THE
GOSPEL-
DRIVEN
LIFE

THE GOSPEL-DRIVEN LIFE

Being Good News People in a Bad News World

MICHAEL HORTON

BakerBooks

a division of Baker Publishing Group
Grand Rapids, Michigan

© 2009 by Michael Horton

Published by Baker Books
a division of Baker Publishing Group
P.O. Box 6287, Grand Rapids, MI 49516-6287
www.bakerbooks.com

Paperback edition published 2012
ISBN 978-0-8010-1319-5

Printed in the United States of America

The Library of Congress has cataloged the hardcover editon as follows:
Horton, Michael Scott.
    The Gospel-driven life : being good news people in a bad news world / Michael
Horton.
       p.   cm.
    Includes bibliographical references.
    ISBN 978-0-8010-1319-5 (cloth)
    1. Christian life. 2. Evangelicalism. I. Title.
    BV4501.3.H677 2009
    248'.5—dc22   2009021356

12   13   14   15   16   17   18   7   6   5   4   3   2   1

To Lisa, for her partnership in the gospel-driven life

CONTENTS

ACKNOWLEDGMENTS

I owe special thanks once again to Robert Hosack and Robert Hand, along with the rest of the Baker team, for their assistance and improvements along the way. I am also grateful to my colleagues and students at Westminster Seminary California as well as to my brothers and sisters at Christ United Reformed Church in San Diego. They offer a consistent source of encouragement, instruction, and joy for my family and me, and provide a concrete expression of the message in this book. Of course, I owe the greatest earthly gratitude to my wife Lisa and my children—James, Olivia, Matthew, and Adam—who are constant sources of inspiration.

INTRODUCTION

The goal of this book is to reorient our faith and practice as Christians and churches toward the gospel: that is, the announcement of God's victory over sin and death in his Son, Jesus Christ. The first six chapters explore that breaking news from heaven, while the rest of the book focuses on the kind of community that this gospel generates in the world. It is not merely that there is a gospel and then a community made up of people who believe it; the gospel creates the kind of community that is even now an imperfect preview of the kingdom's marriage feast that awaits us. The church is its own culture, not only with its distinct story and doctrine, but with its own "politics" and means. Consistent with the message that it proclaims, the church is *receiving* its life, identity, growth, and expansion from above rather than *creating* these for itself and from its own resources.

Distinguished from all religions, spiritualities, and philosophies of life, the Christian faith is, at its heart, a *gospel* (meaning "Good News"). The church originates, flourishes, and fulfills its mission as that part of God's world that has been redeemed and redefined by this strange announcement that seems foolish and powerless to the rest of the world. In other words, every believer—and the church corporately—has passed from death to life by being made a recipient of God's activity.

Following from *Christless Christianity: The Alternative Gospel of the American Church*, this book explores the greatest story ever told and the surprising ways in which God is at work, gathering a people for his feast in a fast-food world. With *The Gospel-Driven Life*, we turn from the crisis to solutions, in the hope that we will see a new reformation in the faith, practice, and witness of contemporary Christianity.

The Good News is not just a series of facts to which we yield our assent but a dramatic narrative that replots our identity. Think of it in terms of a theatrical play. Each week we come to church with our own scripts. If yours is anything like mine, it's "the show about nothing." Yet God descends to give us a new script: a rich plot in which our original character dies and is raised with the lead character. Instead of trying to find a supporting role for God in our play, God writes us into his script as part of a growing cast for his new world. This script does not offer a blueprint for a new creation, if we will only follow certain steps for realizing it. Instead, through this gospel the Spirit sweeps us into the drama, into the new creation that has already been inaugurated. No longer "in Adam," under the reign of sin and death, we are "in Christ."

The book is divided into two sections: *Looking Up, Looking Out* and *Looking Around, Looking Ahead*. I've chosen to use a number of "news" metaphors in this book—"breaking news," "front-page," "headlines"—to emphasize both the urgency of the gospel and the surprising, unexpected means by which God communicates it to us. We don't find the truth about God, ourselves, or the world by looking within, but by being drawn outside of ourselves. Having been turned inside out, we look up in faith toward God and out toward our neighbors in loving service and witness. Surprising news has a way of focusing us on something "out there" in the real world rather than on our own assumptions, experiences, and speculations. Only the Spirit, working through the gospel, has this kind of power to bring about a new creation in the midst of the old. Gradually, we discover that the world outside is more interesting than the inner world of narcissistic preoccupation. It is a liberation that we never expected, much less achieved for ourselves. It's a gift. It is the marriage supper that is promised in the gospel and of which the Spirit gives us a foretaste in this present age. While our consumer culture offers instant gratification in drive-thru spiritualities, the gospel seats us at the table with Abraham, Isaac, and Jacob, as the Triune God serves us with his heavenly gifts.

A new reformation requires both a change in our message and our methods. It's not only our beliefs, but our personal and corporate practices, that must change. If our churches today are focused on our action, piety, and world-transforming agendas, then the crying need of our day is to recover the focus on Christ as the host *and* the meal that delivers forgiveness, new life, and genuine transformation in a world that is literally wasting away.

Like *Christless Christianity*, this book is written for a wide audience of Christians who are burned out on hype and are looking for hope. It especially targets younger laypeople, parents, and pastors who want to see their own lives and their churches become more gospel centered.

LOOKING UP, LOOKING OUT

BREAKING NEWS

1

THE FRONT-PAGE GOD

CHECKING THE HEADLINES

Judging by the success of twenty-four-hour reporting, we are news junkies these days. Besides being informed about the events shaping our world, we long to be a part of something beyond our own cycle of ordinary life. As important as many of these events may be, in most cases they come and go and as weeks, even days—sometimes hours—pass, we have already forgotten the headlines that caught our momentary attention.

The same thing happens in the church world as well. We are so easily distracted from the things that matter most—the commission that Christ gave us to proclaim the gospel and feed his sheep—by fads that come and go. Every party seems to leave a bad hangover: disillusionment, burnout, and fatigue. Yet we are always suckers for The Next Big Thing.

Long before CNN and online journalism, the basic content of the Christian faith was designated "news"—Good News, in fact. In its secular Greek context, *euangelion* (good news) was normally used for the word of victory on the battlefield brought by a herald from the front lines. More than any other designation, this was the term that early Christians borrowed for their message and mission to the world. Sometimes the headlines grab us; sometimes they don't. Often, they become so familiar that we are no longer arrested by them. In *Christless Christianity: The Alternative Gospel of the American Church*, I argued that the basic story line of the Bible, coalescing around Christ and his redeeming work, is being seriously blurred, confused, assumed, and in some cases even denied.[1] In short, the front-page headlines are being sent to the back page, the religion page, or other sections: entertainment, politics, sports, arts and culture. The result is that God becomes a supporting actor in our story instead of the other way around. We become the headliners and the work of the Father, the Son, and the Spirit in history and in our own lives fades into the background.

Part of the problem is that the news industry has become, well, an industry. I haven't been around all that long, but long enough to recall the changing taglines for major news organizations. I remember CBS anchor Walter Cronkite ending each evening broadcast, "And that's the way it is, on this date, _____." But in an era of competing sources, it's sold as "all the news you can use." That shift is not insignificant. It's not so much about what *is* important, but about what I and a decent market share of my fellow consumers *feel* is important *for our own lives today.*

I have become more cynical about the news now, partly because I am not a child anymore and realize that Cronkite had his own point of view, but also because TV news especially has become so unabashedly subsumed under entertainment, marketing, and personal bias. People used to trust Cronkite because he didn't make himself the news, but today we expect our reporters to be celebrities with their own fan base. Too often, it's the same situation in the church.

But here's the pinch for Christianity. On one hand, the gospel is the most reasonable news to believe. That isn't what we are used to hearing these days. Religion is an irrational leap and the more you investigate it intellectually, the more likely you are to outgrow it. This is an assumption that you are as likely to hear in churches as on the street. However, the claim that "Jesus makes me happier" is a purely subjective statement. No one should become a Christian simply because of how helpful you've found it to be in your life. Unique among all religious claims, the gospel is an announcement about certain historical events. At its heart, then, Christianity is not a resource for spirituality, religion, and morality, but a dramatic story at the heart of which is the claim that during the reign of Tiberius Caesar, Jesus was crucified for our sins and, after three days, was raised bodily from the dead. As we will see, the arguments for his resurrection are eminently reasonable—more reasonable, in fact, than alternative explanations. The apostle Paul told the Corinthians that if Christ was not raised, then we are not saved. No other religion makes its validity wholly dependent on a historical fact.

On the other hand, the gospel is "foolishness to those who are perishing" (1 Cor. 1:18). Religion and philosophy—that which the Greeks consider "wisdom"—are there to help us with our inner soul and practical questions about daily living. All of this talk about the incarnation, life, crucifixion, and resurrection of a Jewish rabbi seems beside the point when you do not really think of yourself as a sinner under the wrath of God.

To the extent that we remain pilgrims in this life, the gospel will remain strange even to us. Until the day we die, we will struggle to believe the bad news and Good News that God announces to us. We do not just naturally think that we are born in sin, spiritually dead, helpless, and unable to lift a finger to save ourselves or impress a holy God. As a result, it does not just occur to us that our greatest need is to be redeemed, justified, regenerated, sanctified, and glorified by God's saving work in his Son and by his Spirit. If the "Good News" that we proclaim is determined by what we already know—or think we know—and experience, it isn't really *news*. Limited to whatever we already think is relevant, practical, and useful, the message will never be surprising, disorienting, and troubling. It can never throw us off balance or cause us to reevaluate our priorities and interpretations of reality.

You know real news when you hear it. Think of Saul, the archpersecutor of the church, on his way to Damascus for another purge of Jesus followers. Thrown off his horse by a blinding encounter with the risen and ascended Christ, he was reeling with confusion. Acting out of honest loyalty to his deepest convictions about God and his unfolding plan in history, Saul came to see that his whole take on God, himself, Israel and the Gentiles, and confidence in his moral zeal was wrong. He had totally misunderstood what God was doing in Jerusalem. The revolution was so powerful in his life that he changed his name from Saul to Paul. As the apostle to the Gentiles, Paul told the Philippian Christians that even though his whole identity had been wrapped up in his strict Jewish outlook—"a Pharisee of Pharisees," more zealous than his colleagues in his commitment to the Law—he had now come to see his "righteousness" as "dung." Everything that he had accumulated by his own zeal and effort he now moved over to the debit column, "in order to be found in Christ, not having a righteousness of my own that comes from the law."

For this breaking news Paul was willing to suffer the same persecution that he had inflicted. The news changed everything. And Paul was no longer the headliner; he had a supporting role in God's story. It was Paul who said that the gospel is "foolishness to Greeks and a stumbling block to Jews, but to those who are being saved, it is the wisdom and the power of God."

Paul and his fellow apostles knew that they were by nature—like the rest of us—bent in on themselves. And picking up on a phrase from Augustine, the Protestant Reformers said that as fallen sinners we are all "curved in on ourselves." Born with a severe case of spiritual scoliosis, our spines are twisted so that all we can see are our own immediate felt needs, desires, wants, and momentary gratifications. But the gospel makes us stand erect, looking up to God in faith and out to the world and our neighbors in love and service. Not every piece of news can do that, but the gospel can.

It is interesting that the biblical writers chose the word "gospel." The heart of most religions is good advice, good techniques, good programs, good ideas, and good support systems. These drive us deeper into ourselves, to find our inner light, inner goodness, inner voice, or inner resources. Nothing *new* can be found inside of us. There is no inner rescuer deep down in my soul; I just hear echoes of my own voice telling me all sorts of crazy things to numb my sense of fear, anxiety, and boredom, the origins of which I cannot truly identify. But the heart of Christianity is Good *News*. It comes not as a task for us to fulfill, a mission for us to accomplish, a game plan for us to follow with the help of life coaches, but as a report that someone else has already fulfilled, accomplished, followed, and achieved everything for us. Good advice may *help* us in daily direction; the Good News concerning Jesus Christ *saves* us from sin's guilt and tyranny over our lives and the fear of death. It's Good News because it does not depend on us. It is about God and his faithfulness to his own purposes and promises.

The average person thinks that the purpose of religion is to give us a list of rules and techniques or to frame a way of life that helps us to be more loving, forgiving, patient, caring, and generous. Of course, there is plenty of this in the Bible. Like Moses, Jesus summarized the whole law in just those terms: loving God and neighbor. However, as crucial as the law remains as the revelation of God's *moral* will, it is different from the revelation of God's *saving* will. We are called to love God and neighbor, but that is not the *gospel*. Christ need not have died on a cross for us to know that we should be better people. It is not that moral exhortations are wrong, but they do not have any power to bring about the kind of world that they command. These exhortations and directions may be good. If they come from the Word of God, they are in fact *perfect*. But they are not the gospel.

Imagine a movie with two reels: the first covers the plot from creation to the fall, while the second contains the rest of the story, from the promise of a Savior in Genesis 3:15 to the new heavens and earth in Revelation's closing chapters. Everyone has seen the first reel—or various version of it—hundreds of times. However, the second reel is completely unknown apart from local showings. To bring it back to the biblical metaphor, the law makes sense to us already; the gospel has to be told by heralds.

As Paul explains at the beginning of his Letter to the Romans, the law is written on the conscience in creation. Everybody knows that it is wrong to murder and steal. Idolatry is evidence that everyone knows that there is a God and their attempts to pacify him with their own rites and spiritual duties is reflected in myriad systems of sacrifice. However, this original and universal revelation is law, not gospel. After the original transgression of our first parents, God was not bound in any way to save anyone. Having laid out the condition for entering his Sabbath rest, and the sentence for violating it, Adam and Eve had no reason to expect anything for themselves or their posterity except confirmation in everlasting death. Yet God freely chose to have mercy. *Another* word came from his lips: the Good News of a Savior who will come from Eve's flesh, a new Adam who will crush the serpent's head. From then on, the human race has been divided into two families: the one, represented by Cain and his proud kingdom, and the other, represented by Seth, whose heirs called on the name of the Lord. One kingdom, driven by the craving for domination, aims at temporal prosperity, security, and justice, but falls perpetually into violence and internal collapse. The other kingdom, driven by God's promise, looks to God for salvation and every heavenly blessing in Christ.

So "law" is not *news*. It is what we already know inside of ourselves. Just check the polls that routinely confirm that most people still believe that it is wrong to murder, steal, or otherwise harm the interests of others. They even have some vague sense of responsibility to "God." But the knowledge of God's rescue operation in the death and resurrection of his Son is not something that the average person already knows. When their pastors ask them on their deathbed if they're ready to meet God, they often hear even from lifelong church members, "I hope so. God knows, I haven't done everything right, but I've tried." "Gospel" is the surprise, and it remains a surprise announcement even to believers. Like a branch that has been bent out of shape, we fall back naturally to being curved in on ourselves unless we are being pulled back constantly to raise our eyes up to God in faith as he has clothed himself in the gospel of his Son. We do not need a reporter to announce to us that we need to be better parents, spouses, and friends; that we should have integrity in our relationships; to be less selfish and more giving; get in the game of life instead of standing on the sidelines; and so forth. Give us advice on these matters and we nod. We begin to take notes and resolve to put them into practice next week. Our ears perk up when we hear exhortations to be all we can be. Our self-righteousness springs to its feet when we are told that we have what it takes if we just put the game plan into practice.

As true as a lot of the exhortations might be, the familiarity of law (things to do) can make us wonder why the message of our churches is all that different and why the Christian message is all that radical. Only the radical news concerning Jesus Christ can distract us from all the trivial pursuits and transform us from the inside out. Only the gospel can cause such a radical reevaluation of our core identity that we're willing, like Paul, to throw away what we thought was a great resume in exchange for being found in Christ. In fact, once the gospel reconfigures our whole take on reality, it even opens us up to God's law again as the concrete expression of God's moral will for our relationship to him and to each other. No longer condemning us, it guides us. Thus, even the law itself is given its due when we strip it of our cleverly devised additions and no longer rely on our own obedience. *Trusting in Christ* as he is clothed in his gospel, we are *guided by the law* without any fear of our failures provoking its judgment. Religious programs and outreach strategies might create social centers defined by niche demographics, but the gospel creates a genuine "*cross*-cultural" community that gathers the generations, races, rich and poor around Christ and his feast of grace.

It is no wonder that people become bored with church and assume that they can get along well enough in life without it. We need to see

God as the headliner again, instead of ourselves. It is not we who must find a supporting role for God in our personal and social campaigns for spiritual, moral, and therapeutic well-being. We need to stop and listen to God's surprise announcement about what he has done to save sinners like us. The only thing that the church can provide to the world that is truly unique is the gospel. Only the gospel brings a *new creation* into this present age of sin and death. That is the basic message of this book.

God the Headliner

"You need to get out more." We often hear this—or say it—when we get the impression that someone is a little out of touch with reality. Sometimes it is said when we express surprise at hearing about something that our conversation partner assumes we would have known about already. Focusing narrowly on our own inner thoughts, experiences, feelings, and felt needs, we cut ourselves off from the unfamiliar. Nothing can come to us from outside, disrupting or disturbing our fortress of inner security. Wrapping ourselves in a cocoon of inwardness, we feel cozy in our own personal cult of private piety. We think we're in charge. We imagine that we just follow our heart, that we decide for ourselves what is true, valuable, and useful. In reality, though, our choices are already shaped by the culture of marketing; our preferences have been conditioned by the goods and services, identities and images, possibilities and impossibilities, that have been designed for us in any given moment of this fading age. God's Word comes to release us from this prison that we have mistaken for a palace, as God introduces himself to us and to his world for the first time. God's first word is, "You need to get out more"—out of our cocoon that we have spun for ourselves.

The God of the Bible is a strange God—not the kind of God we can manage, manipulate, accommodate, or domesticate to our familiar experience. We cannot find this God by looking within ourselves. His Word is not the same as our inner voice. He cannot be pared down to our size, measured by our speculations, experiences, or felt needs. Rather, he stands over against us, telling us how things actually are. When God actually confronts us, our speculations are exposed as idols, our experience judged as little more than a projection of ourselves, and our felt needs give way to more pressing needs that we did not even realize that we had. God confronts us, disorients us, and pulls us outside of our comfort zones. If we feel naked and ashamed, then it's a good sign that we are actually in the presence of the God of the Bible.

The idols of the nations make the religion page, but God is a front-page headliner. Repentance and faith are provoked by this encounter. Look outside of yourself to the God who acts in history!

Your Inner Life Is Not the News

Although such a day is not unimaginable at our present pace, it would still be unlikely that major news organizations could survive if they reported their inner longings and hunches as the news. Who would take seriously financial articles that began with the words, "I feel that the economy will improve"? Or the suggestion that the truth of a report on a major disaster depended on how useful it might be for the readers' daily lives. A while back I asked a reporter why U.S. news outlets (especially TV news) routinely omits international stories that I see and hear reported by other news organizations. "It's not judged relevant to the lives of Americans," she told me. Talk about narcissistic! If our criterion for news is whatever we find useful for our daily experience, then given the limitations of that experience, we will miss some of the most important events. News is important not because it sells but simply because it is *news*. It tells us what is going on outside of our own inner experience. Even the sports page with its predictions of division champions is expected to be based on the games that have actually been played, the national standings of each team, injuries, and other factors. We take all of these things very seriously. Yet when it comes to religion, we go soft. It doesn't really matter whether the report is true; the main thing is that it works for me. It helps me create my life plan.

We have accepted the division between the public sphere of facts and the private sphere of values, an outer realm of nature and history and an inner realm of freedom and spirit. However, where religion and spirituality are typically means of driving us deeper into ourselves, following our "little voice within" or our "inner light," the gospel summons us to look outside of ourselves for the truth about our condition and identity and especially for any hope of redemption. It just does not finally matter what we think, feel, do, or want to be true. We need someone to give us the report. Yet this is just what we do not want: an authoritative source—even God—standing outside of us and above us, telling us how things actually are.

At the beginning of the twentieth century, English poet, satirist, and novelist G. K. Chesterton routinely sparred with friends like Oscar Wilde and George Bernard Shaw, who shared the perspective of Friedrich Nietzsche (1844–1900). Nietzsche's legacy has been especially felt in the more extreme forms of existentialism and postmodern thought and it is often identified as *nihilism*. In this sense, nihilism (literally, "nothing-ism") does not mean that there is no point to life, but that there is no point to life *that I don't create for myself*. Only the individual's will is sovereign. "That my life has no aim is evident from the accidental nature of its origin," said Nietzsche. "That I can posit an aim for myself is another matter."[2]

From this perspective, Christianity was a party killer: all about managing one's inner life. The soul, not the body; the pious affections, not the world; is the theater of Christianity, they argued. However, Chesterton pointed out that this caricature resulted from elsewhere than orthodox Christianity. "It is commonly the loose and latitudinarian Christians who pay quite indefensible compliments to Christianity," he observed.

> They talk as if there had never been any piety until Christianity came, a point on which any medieval would have been eager to correct them. They represent that the remarkable thing about Christianity was that it was the first to preach simplicity or self-restraint, or inwardness and sincerity. They will think me very narrow (whatever that means) if I say that the remarkable thing about Christianity was that it was the first to preach Christianity. Its peculiarity was that it was peculiar, and simplicity and sincerity are not peculiar, but obvious ideals for all mankind. Christianity was the answer to a riddle, not the last truism uttered after a long talk.[3]

It is not Christian orthodoxy but moralistic liberalism that reduces the surprising news of the gospel to the bland repetition of what people already know.

Chesterton described a newspaper article he had recently read which opined that "Christianity when stripped of its armour of dogma (as who should speak of a man stripped of his armour of bones), turned out to be nothing but the Quaker doctrine of the Inner Light." "Now, if I were to say that Christianity came into the world specially to destroy the doctrine of the Inner Light, that would be an exaggeration," Chesterton responded. "But it would be very much nearer the truth."[4] The Romans of the first century (especially the Stoics) were advocates of the Inner Light. However, Chesterton concludes that "of all horrible religions the most horrible is the worship of the god within."[5] "Christianity came into the world firstly in order to assert with violence that a man had not only to look inwards, but to look outwards, to behold with astonishment and enthusiasm a divine company and a divine captain. The only fun of being a Christian was that a man was not left alone with the Inner Light, but definitely recognized an outer light, fair as the sun, clear as the moon, terrible as an army with banners."[6]

The Bible is not a collection of timeless principles offering a gentle thought for the day. It is not a resource for our self-improvement. Rather, it is a dramatic story that unfolds from promise to fulfillment, with Christ at the center. Its focus is God and his action. God is not a supporting actor in our drama; it is the other way around. God does not exist to make sure that we are happy and fulfilled. Rather, we exist to glorify God and to enjoy him forever. God is not a facilitator of our "life transformation" projects. He is not a life coach. Rather, he is our Creator, Lawgiver, Judge, and Covenant Lord. As we will see, he is also our Redeemer. However, before we can speak of God's saving work in Christ we have to reverse the focus from a human-centered to a God-centered way of thinking. The gospel witnesses not to an inner light within the self, but to the Light that came into the world, shining in the darkness and overpowering it (John 1:4–9).

The Protestant Reformers comforted anxious believers with the assurance that the gospel lies entirely outside of them. It is an "external Word" spoken by another person to me in the name of Christ. The gospel doesn't depend on anything in me at all; it is an objective, completed work. The gospel is entirely outside of you! Has anyone ever told you that? Has it really hit you that no matter what your inner voice, conscience, heart, will, or soul tells you, God's objective Word on the matter trumps it all?

No Religion Page Deity

The God of the Bible is an "outdoor" God. He likes to find us where we least expect it: in the ordinary and especially lowly things that he has made, in everyday history. As biblical faith is not confined to the inner life, it is not restricted to private religious experience. The central context of God's relationship to human beings in the Bible is that of a *covenant*. The whole Bible can be read as one long courtroom trial, with God as the king, judge, and deliverer, and human beings as the covenant servant. In the Scriptures, God adapts the international political treaties of the ancient Near Eastern world to his relationship with creatures. In these ancient political treaties of pagan nations, there were *suzerains* (great kings or emperors) and *vassals* (lesser kings or tribal leaders) and the gods were called upon as *witnesses*. However, only in Israel was the nation's God himself the *treaty maker*: the great King, Lord of the covenant. The gods of the nations were "religion page" deities, but the God of Israel claimed the whole world and its history as his stage.

God is not a mere witness of history. He is not like modern monarchs whose regal splendor is symbolically significant but historically negligible. Israel's God is not a ribbon-cutting deity who presides over patriotic events, symbolizing the proud heritage and military might of his favored nation. Rather, he is the one with whom even Israel had to reckon. If Israel violated the terms of the treaty, God was not a religious witness, but the *offended party* and he would evict the people from his holy land, as he did our first parents from Paradise. God unilaterally gave his treaties to his people; he did not negotiate them.

It is within this context of Israel's covenant with God that the Bible opens. In fact, the creation narrative in Genesis 1 and 2 is the prelude and historical prologue for the covenant of humanity with God, which Israel's oath at Sinai echoes. The suzerain is *God*. Israel's Lord is not simply a powerful Near Eastern ruler, but the Creator of the heavens and the earth. "The earth is the Lord's and the fullness thereof" (Ps. 24:1). Not only Israel, but all nations, and not only human beings but all creatures, were brought into existence in order to serve his universal reign. God does not sit on the sidelines as a witness, occasionally dabbling in political affairs but mainly keeping himself to the religion page. He is the front-page God who created all that exists for himself, rules history for his own purposes, and reserves the right to disturb the status quo whenever his wisdom dictates.

In this covenantal context, God gave Israel his name. In this formal act God binds Israel to himself and himself to Israel. There are "names" and "*the* Name": "How excellent is your name in all the earth" (Ps. 8:1); "As is your name, O God, so is your praise" (Ps. 48:10); "His name is great in Israel" (Ps 76:2). It is this name that Jesus called us to hallow in our prayers (Matt. 6:9). God has many titles, but only one name. In our English Bibles the difference between the title

(*Adonai*) and God's personal name (*Yahweh*) is distinguished by the use of lowercase (Lord) and uppercase (LORD) letters, respectively.

The ancient political treaties included the provision for calling on the name of the great king in a time of crisis and in this treaty the Covenant Lord gives his name to his people so that they may call upon him in distress. God reveals his name not to satisfy our insatiable quest for intellectual ascent into heavenly secrets, but in order to reconcile us to himself and to each other. God's goal is not simply to be understood, much less to be used, but to dwell in the midst of his people in everlasting peace. Like the places (land and temple) and times (sabbaths and festivals) that God sanctifies, he reveals his name in order to create a community gathered around him in faith, hope, and love.

God takes up a variety of titles already in use among the pagan nations for their gods to refer to himself as the only true God. Yet it is his personal name, *Yahweh*, that Israel is allowed to invoke for rescue from its enemies. The event of this revelation in Exodus 3 bears striking features of its covenantal context (a *suzerain* treaty). Pharaoh is lord (*suzerain*) of Egypt, even an object of worship, at the time when Yahweh's children are under the heavy hand of oppression. God gives Moses his personal name to invoke as the covenant Lord who will liberate his people from Pharaoh's cruel suzerainty. From now on, Yahweh's people are to know him by this personal name (Exod. 3:4–15).

When Moses's appeal to Pharaoh to let God's people go provokes severe hardship in retaliation for this demand, Moses (invoking the proper name) protests, "O LORD, why have you done evil to this people? Why did you ever send me? For since I came to Pharaoh to speak in your name, he has done evil to this people, and you have not delivered your people at all" (Exod. 5:22–23). To this Yahweh reiterates his pledge, adding, "I am the LORD. I appeared to Abraham, to Isaac, and to Jacob, as God Almighty, but by my name the LORD I did not make myself known to them." God made a covenant with them and has remembered and will remember to keep it. "Say therefore to the people of Israel, 'I am the LORD, and I will bring you out from under the burdens of the Egyptians, and I will deliver you from slavery to them, and I will redeem you with an outstretched arm and with great acts of judgment'" (v. 6).

The Lord Yahweh declares war on the lord Pharaoh in order to liberate his people and bring them to his holy land. Begun with Pharaoh's massacre of the firstborn Hebrew sons, Yahweh strikes the firstborn sons of Egypt. Each plague is a judgment that manifests God's sovereignty over each of the principal deities of the Egyptian pantheon.

In sharp contrast with paganism, therefore, the revelation of God's name is not a secret password for manipulating the cosmic forces for one's own pleasure. Rather, it is a covenantal guarantee. Just as Egypt's satellite states could call on the name of their imperial lord for liberation from invading forces, God reveals his personal name to his people as a pledge of redemption and to his enemies as a pledge of judgment. On the basis of this liberation, Israel is not to invoke any other gods or lords: "I am the LORD [Yahweh] your God, who brought you out of the land of Egypt, out of the house of slavery; you shall have no other gods before me" (Exod. 20:2).

In Isaiah 45, God declares, "Turn to me and be saved, all the ends of the earth! For I am God, and there is no other. By myself I have sworn; from my mouth has gone out in righteousness a word that shall not return: 'To me every knee shall bow, every tongue shall swear allegiance. . . . In the LORD all the offspring of Israel shall be justified and shall glory' " (vv. 22–23, 25). In this context, it is significant that the Father handed over this exclusive name to his Son who was born of our flesh and became "obedient to the point of death, even death on a cross." "Therefore God has highly exalted him and bestowed on him *the name that is above every name*, so that *at the name of Jesus every knee should bow*, in heaven and on earth and under the earth, *and every tongue confess that Jesus Christ is Lord*, to the glory of God the Father" (Phil. 2:8–11, emphasis added). Salvation comes by calling on the name of Jesus Christ alone (Acts 2:21; 5:41; Rom. 10:13; Eph. 1:21; Heb. 1:4).

As the story unfolds, the identity of the one God in three persons becomes clearer. All things are done by the Father, in the Son, through the Spirit. In the covenant, God binds himself to specific people, places, and things. He is not an abstract deity, worshiped by some as Yahweh and by others as Allah, the Great Spirit, or the Benign Providence mentioned by many of America's founders. Rather, he is the God of Abraham, Isaac, and Jacob, the God of Israel, the God who dwells in Zion—and the God who became flesh in the virgin's womb.

Does our worship focus on this unfolding historical drama of the Triune God? Are we being constantly directed outside of our inner experience and our own felt needs to the real newsmaker in history? Are we perpetually drawn outside of ourselves, "looking to Jesus, the founder and perfector of our faith, who for the joy that was set before him endured the cross, despising the shame, and is seated at the right hand of the throne of God" (Heb. 12:2)? Is our corporate and private worship centered on "human will or exertion" or "on God, who has mercy" (Rom. 9:16)? Is the main point trying to see how God fits into our existing plot or to hear God tell us how we fit into his unfolding drama of redemption? Like the Old Testament feasts, the great events celebrated by Christians have to do with God's mighty acts: the Son's becoming flesh (Christmas), the crucifixion (Good Friday) and resurrection (Easter), Christ's exaltation to the right hand of the Father (Ascension Day), and the sending of the Spirit (Pentecost). There is no room in the Christian calendar for celebrating our own works.

Competing for the Headlines

We come to know God only insofar as he is pleased to reveal himself and he reveals himself through his actions in history. Yahweh and Israel are both "on trial" in the covenantal drama. Ever since the fall, however, humanity has been trying to replace God as the newsmaker. When the tactic of subtle distortion did not work, Satan went for the more direct approach: "You will not surely die. For God knows that when you eat of it your eyes will be opened, and you will be like God, knowing good and evil" (Gen. 3:5). Why should they listen to every word that comes from the mouth of God when they could determine for themselves how things really are, the nature of good and evil, truth and falsehood, and the best way to happiness?

Many readers will remember the reports of the tragic last days of Howard Hughes, the extraordinary tycoon who rose to international fame as an industrialist, aviator, and filmmaker. Tall, dark, and handsome, he had the world at his feet, moving from resort to resort—often purchasing each and occupying the penthouse floor. In his later years, he became increasingly neurotic and reclusive. When the management of the Desert Inn in Las Vegas could no longer handle their idiosyncratic guest, he bought the hotel—along with several others. An insomniac, he also bought the local TV station so he could watch programs around the clock. Living out his last four years in the Bahamas at his Xanadu Resort, Hughes would only speak to his top lieutenants and his now-alienated wife by phone. Never leaving his room, which was lined with sanitary plastic, he urinated in jars and left them neatly placed throughout his suite. His hair and fingernails grew long and wild and, in sharp contrast to his previous six-foot-four stature, he weighed ninety pounds at his death and his body could only be identified by fingerprint analysis. The man who had boasted that he was born on Christmas Eve and attracted the gaze of the world's public for decades became a sideshow for prurient gossip magazines.

The tragic story of Howard Hughes echoes in my mind as I read the story of the king of Babylon, Nebuchadnezzar II—also known in history as Nebuchadnezzar the Great—in the book of Daniel. In chapter 4, the king calls for Daniel to interpret his latest dream. The proud ruler who had built an empire around his own glory, including the world famous Hanging Gardens, and had reduced Jerusalem and Judah to rubble, lost everything. The dream was fulfilled:

> All this came upon King Nebuchadnezzar. At the end of twelve months he was walking on the roof of the royal palace of Babylon, and the king answered and said, "Is not this great Babylon, which I have built by my mighty power as a royal residence and for the glory of my majesty?" While the words were still in the king's mouth, there fell a voice from heaven. "O King Nebuchadnezzar, to you it is spoken: The kingdom has departed from you, and you shall be driven from among men, and your dwelling shall be with the beasts of the field. And you shall be made to eat grass like an ox, and seven periods of time shall pass over you, until you know that the Most High rules the kingdom of men and gives it to whom he will." Immediately the word was fulfilled against Nebuchadnezzar. He was driven from among men and ate grass like an ox, and his body was wet with the dew of heaven till his hair grew as long as eagles' feathers, and his nails were like birds' claws. (Dan. 4:28–33)

Far closer than the life of an American mogul is the biography of Saddam Hussein, who frequently invoked the long-celebrated legacy of Nebuchadnezzar in Iraq's history and considered himself as the great king's obvious successor. Indeed, he was.

However, whereas Hussein was found hidden in a hole on a farm and was eventually executed in 2006 for crimes against humanity, the book of Daniel indicates that Nebuchadnezzar had a change of heart:

> At the end of the days I, Nebuchadnezzar, lifted my eyes to heaven, and my reason returned to me, and I blessed the Most High, and praised and honored him who lives forever, for his dominion is an everlasting dominion, and his kingdom endures from generation to generation; all the inhabitants of the earth are accounted as nothing, and he does according to his will among the host of heaven and among the inhabitants of the earth; and none can stay his hand or say to him, "What have you done?" (vv. 34–35)

Faith in God is generally treated by the powerful of the earth as a crutch for the weak and foolish. As Nebuchadnezzar admired his accomplishments from his lofty penthouse, he was doubtless of this opinion. However, he literally lost his mind. It is not foolishness, but sanity that recognizes the way things really are. God is Creator and Lord; we are all nothing more than ants pretending to conquer the earth when we merely crawl on top of our own anthill. Together with his sanity, Nebuchadnezzar's counselors and nobility returned to him and he was again "established in my kingdom," with even greater esteem. "Now I, Nebuchadnezzar, praise and extol and honor the King of heaven, for all his works are right and his ways are just; and those who walk in pride he is able to humble" (vv. 36–37).

At last, the great king of Babylon had learned the hard way that God is not a golden statue in a royal temple symbolizing the sovereignty of the king and his empire, but the Lord of heaven and earth. Far from a "religion page" deity, the God of Israel is the only God and he grabs the headlines every day:

> Why do the nations rage and the people plot in vain? The kings of the earth set themselves, and the rulers take counsel together, against the LORD and against his anointed [messiah], saying, "Let us burst their bonds apart and cast away their cords from us." He who sits in the heavens laughs; the Lord holds them in derision. Then he will speak to them in his wrath, and terrify them in his fury, saying, "As for me, I have set my King on Zion, my holy hill." . . . Now therefore, O kings, be wise; be warned, O rulers of the earth. Serve the LORD with fear, and rejoice with trembling. Kiss the Son, lest he be angry, and you perish in the way, for his wrath is quickly kindled. Blessed are all who take refuge in him. (Ps. 2:1–12)

Masters, Tourists, and Pilgrims

Nobody cares if your god generates religion stories. It might be vaguely interesting that families that pray together stay together or that people who follow biblical principles can have their best life now. There are enough mass movements in religion to justify an editor and perhaps a few writers to cover the latest "revival" or political election in which "values voters" played a key role.

However, as Paul told the philosophers in Athens, "The God who made the world and everything in it, being Lord of heaven and earth, does not live in temples made by man, nor is he served by human hands, as if he needed anything, since he himself gives to all mankind life and breath and everything" (Acts 17:24–25). It is he who has determined where each person would live—and how long (v. 26). Pagan religion is certainly a form of superstition (Paul uses a term that is two-toned, meaning "religious" and "superstitious" in v. 22). However, the God of Israel plays on the stage of world history, not in a private corner. "The times of ignorance God overlooked, but now he commands all people everywhere to repent, because he has fixed a day on which he will judge the world in righteousness by a man whom he has appointed; and of this he has given assurance to all by raising him from the dead" (vv. 30–31). As a datable event in our own history, the resurrection cannot be shoved into a closet of personal piety. Everyone has to deal with it. This isn't just another religion story. It's *the* international headline.

Like Adam, we have preferred to write our own script and to create our own plot. In the modern age, it was thought that we had finally matured from the dregs of superstition into the enlightened era of universal reason. Enlightenment philosopher Immanuel Kant argued that the individual is "meant to produce everything out of himself."[7] No external authority—no Word outside of us—can be allowed to judge or save us. However, under the banner of autonomous reason we unleashed more devastation, oppression, violence, and genocide than in all of the centuries combined.

Reacting against rationalistic arrogance, our age is drifting into irrational skepticism disguised as humility. Chesterton spoke of the "dislocation of humility" in modern thought and it works as well as a description of what many people are calling postmodern:

> By asking for pleasure, he lost the chief pleasure; for the chief pleasure is surprise. Hence it became evident that if a man would make his world large, he must be always making himself small. . . . But what we suffer from to-day is humility in the wrong place. Modesty has moved from the organ of ambition. Modesty has settled on the organ of conviction, where it was never meant to be. A man was meant to be doubtful about himself, but undoubting about the truth; this has been exactly reversed. Nowadays the part of a man that a man does assert is exactly the part he ought not to assert—himself.[8]

Today what we doubt is not ourselves but God's Word. Chesterton's friends had assumed, with Nietzsche, that Christian orthodoxy was a blight on humanity, a curse upon life and happiness. However, it is nihilism that has despair at its heart. Because its chief article is that life has no transcendent meaning or purpose, Chesterton added, "It cannot hope to find any romance; its romances will have no plots."

> One can find no meanings in a jungle of skepticism; but the man will find more and more meanings who walks through a forest of doctrine and design. Here everything has a story tied to its tail, like the tools or pictures in my father's house; for it is my father's house. I end where I began—at the right end. I have entered at least the gate of all good philosophy. I have come into my second childhood.[9]

It is not a particularly "postmodern" reaction that finds talk of orthodoxy arrogant and narrow-minded.

The new humility paralyzes people from actually moving in any direction, despite all the talk of progress, innovation, and forward-looking excitement. "We are on the road to producing a race of men too mentally modest to believe in the multiplication table. . . . Scoffers of old time were too proud to be convinced; but these are too humble to be convinced."[10] Chesterton adds, "An imbecile habit has arisen in modern controversy of saying that such and such a creed can be held in one age but cannot be held in another. . . . You might as well say that a certain philosophy can be believed on Mondays, but cannot be believed on Tuesdays."[11]

If the concept of the modern self was that of a *master* of all it surveyed, the postmodern self is best described as a *tourist*. There is no destination; just personal journeys from nowhere to nowhere in particular. A contemporary disciple of Nietzsche, Mark C. Taylor, says that we can only aspire to be "aimless drifters" toward no particular destination except the one or ones that we choose for ourselves. We still want to write our own script, but, like the *Seinfeld* tagline, it's the show about nothing.

"From the viewpoint of a/theology," Taylor explains, "there never was a pure origin and never will be a perfect end. 'All promise, all future hope and expectation, come to an end in the death of God.' "[12] It is "The Book" (the Bible, that is) which creates the notion of "history," with its promise-fulfillment pattern. "Between the 'tick' of Genesis and the 'tock' of Apocalypse, the history of the West runs its course," Taylor notes in disapproval. "History, as well as self, is a theological notion."[13] The Bible assumes that meaning is discovered in the historical events themselves, but Taylor complains that this leaves no place for the individuals to create meaning for themselves.[14] "The death of the sovereign God now appears to be the birth of the sovereign self," Taylor observes, but this has only led to the death of the self as well.[15] "There is no Logos, there are only hieroglyphs."[16]

So we saunter through the carnival, on our way to nowhere. Like tourists, we are not really seeking the truth as much as we are spectators of new experiences, identities, images, and styles that have been marketed to us in the giant mall of Western consumerism. Indeed, we have become "futile in [our] thinking, and [our] foolish hearts were darkened. Claiming to be wise, [we] became fools" (Rom. 1:21–22).

In contrast to modern and postmodern versions of human autonomy (self-rule), the biblical drama celebrates God as the headliner and us as the supporting cast. There is a significant origin and end point to history, within which we ourselves are cast members. It is a courtroom drama in which we are either false or true witnesses, "in Adam" or "in Christ," justified or condemned, alive or dead. Neither masters nor tourists, we become *pilgrims*. Unlike masters, pilgrims have not arrived and they do not presume to inaugurate their own kingdoms of glory. They don't have all the answers and they are not exactly sure what their destination city will be like; they are driven by a promise and by God's fulfillment of his promise along the way. Yet unlike tourists, they are on their way to a settled place and every point along the way is a landmark toward that destination.

Nietzsche and his heirs were right to reject any religious philosophy that caused people to withdraw from the world of flesh and blood, into a cocoon of pious inwardness. They were correct to conclude that a God who liberated the soul *from* the body rather than the soul *with* the body was unworthy of our worship. However, they apparently had no awareness of a Christianity other than this moralistic asceticism. Their only response to a simplistic legalism (confusion of the gospel with law) was an equally simplistic antinomianism (denial of law). They thought that only by wiping away the transcendent realm of God and heaven that reduced this realm of worldly existence to a mere shadow could they affirm life. Yet in the process, they dispensed with the only source of meaning and hope.

Chesterton observed that Christianity's outer ring is dark enough, with its grave view of original sin, judgment, and hell, "but inside that inhuman guard you will find the old human life dancing like children, and drinking wine like men; for Christianity is the only frame for pagan freedom. But in the modern philosophy the case is opposite; it is its outer ring that is obviously artistic and emancipated; its despair is within."[17] For the unbelieving world a kind of superficial happiness and general well-being full of entertainments but lacking any real plot hides the fear of death. Apart from God's grace, we cannot come to terms sufficiently either with our mortal wound nor enter into the genuine revelry and mirth of God's kingdom. Denying our sin (not just *sins*, but our sinful condition), we're too silly for a funeral; finding the gospel foolish, we are too serious for a party.

Ironically, the distorted version of Christianity that Nietzsche and his disciples rejected and their own alternative share much in common. Both are oriented toward turning within rather than receiving reality and its proper interpretation by looking outside of oneself. Both are determined to create a story from individual experience, willing, and effort, rather than to receive judgment and salvation from a transcendent God through his external Word. The one is too pious and the other is too lawless to be judged and saved by someone else and to be gathered with the wretches of the earth at the wedding feast of God's kingdom.

Throughout this book, I will be exploring the ways in which the Tri-une God draws us out of our inner monologue and gives us a new plot, a new character, and new lines in his saving script. Through Zephaniah God prophesied to Israel of a coming Redeemer who will fulfill all righteousness, offering the "Amen!" to the Covenant Lord's command and commission. He will bring a remnant not only from Israel and Judah, but from the nations into his courts: "For at that time I will change the speech of the peoples to a pure speech, that all of them may call upon the name of the LORD and serve him with one accord" (Zeph. 3:9).

Will we surrender our pretension to being the playwright, producer, and director of our own life movie and become part of the thanksgiving parade of liberated captives in the train of the Redeeming God? Or will we use "god" and "spirituality" for our private and public ends? Will we join the throng of worshipers on their way to Zion or the delirious mutiny against the Lord and his Messiah captured in Psalm 2? Neither having arrived nor merely wandering from booth to booth at Vanity Fair, we are travelers who "seek the city that is to come" (Heb. 13:14). Taylor was right: the Bible did give birth to the notion of history, with its origin and destination. The Creator is also the Consummator, as Jesus declared in his revelation to John: "'I am the Alpha and the Omega,' says the Lord God, 'who is and who was and who is to come, the Almighty'" (Rev. 1:8). Now *that* is a headline.

2

THE REAL CRISIS

We are daily confronted with *crises*: the health care crisis, crisis in the Middle East, financial and educational crises, natural disasters, and so forth. From the perspective of pious inwardness, none of these crises matter at all, since they are merely outward disturbances of the flesh that have nothing to do with the upward progress of the soul. From the perspective of active nihilism, they are the *ultimate* catastrophes, since they weaken and shorten lives that are already inconsequential. In a purely naturalistic and nihilistic worldview, there is neither the threat of anything more terrifying than my worst temporal tragedy nor the hope of anything grander than my best moment in this life.

But when we think of God at the center of things, our evaluations change. The headlines we see every day are not insignificant, but they are also not of ultimate significance. Death is bigger than we can manage; the global market is far from a reliable object of our trust; international hostilities are ultimately grounded in original sin; and ultimate peace is beyond our control. It is not only that our enemies have us in their sights; *our own hearts* are full of hatred, violence, and injustice. "It takes two to tango," as they say.

We are not really prepared for life until we are prepared for death. In California, at least, people are not really allowed to die. They just "pass away." Unlike the crosses in the churchyard that were once visible through the glass windows as people heard God's Word and invoked his name for rescue, the sentimental and anonymous cemeteries (with euphemistic names like Forest Lawn) hide death from view. We do not like to talk about it and we are uncomfortable hanging out with relatives and friends on their deathbed. Focusing on ameliorating temporal stress, insecurity, problems in our marriages and families, and general "well-being," the church often misses its opportunity to raise people's eyes to heaven, where earthly things fall into their proper perspective.

As Stanley Hauerwas has observed, it wasn't September 11, 2001, that changed everything, but Good Friday, AD 33.[1] As debilitating as failing schools are for future leadership in the world, the greater crisis is whether the gospel is being passed from one generation to the next. Horrifying floods, earthquakes, storms, and fires threaten temporal security, but have we forgotten the ultimate crisis that will rivet the world's attention when Christ returns to judge?

In the 1950s, Yale's H. Richard Niebuhr described the so-called "gospel" of Protestant liberalism poignantly: "A God without wrath brought men without sin into a kingdom without judgment through the ministrations of a Christ without a cross."[2] Each clause is telling. First, more like Mr. Rogers than the judge of all the earth, the sentimental deity of many Americans is incapable of wrath. Since he exists for us and our happiness, this heavenly friend may be disappointed and sad when we hurt ourselves, but he never sees sin as an offence primarily against himself and his perfect justice. Second, we may make mistakes—pretty bad ones, from time to time—but it would be wrong to call ourselves *sinners*, much less to imagine that we were captive to sin, helpless to do anything to will or work our way out of the mess. So, third, God brings us basically good people into a kingdom without judgment, since there is no law that could condemn and no gospel that could justify. And finally, for this sort of religious therapy you don't need a vicarious, atoning sacrifice if you are basically a nice person; what you really need is a good example.

I have found that the best-prepared audience for the gospel is prisoners. A prison ministry leader once told me that talk of original sin, Christ's substitutionary atonement, and justification by his imputed righteousness were too "ivory tower." Inmates are looking for practical solutions to their problems. The goal of prison, after all, is to reform our neighbors, so that they can become productive citizens upon their release. However, in my experience it is prisoners who get the law and the gospel better than most. They know what it is like to be arrested, to stand trial, to lose the case, and to hear the judge deliver a sentence. It is significant that Jesus did not target religious or morally self-confident folks: "I have not come to call the righteous but sinners to repentance" (Luke 5:32). Of course, the religious leaders were actually unrighteous as well, but they did not acknowledge it. Therefore, they did not run to Christ for forgiveness. He told them, "Truly, I say to you, the tax collectors and the prostitutes go into the kingdom of God before you" (Matt. 21:31).

Wrath just doesn't have any place in a moralistic and therapeutic culture, where being good and feeling good lose any reference to God and his judgment. And that means that the cross cannot really have any place either, except as a weird object lesson, to show us (somehow) how much God loves us.

But the real crisis could be solved by nothing less than God's becoming flesh, fulfilling the law and bearing the sentence for its violations in our place, which is the focus of all of Scripture. We may have problems in our marriage, child rearing, stress at work, low self-esteem, and worries about our health or the financial market. However, the ultimate crisis facing us is summarized in Romans 1:18: "For the wrath of God is revealed from heaven against all ungodliness and wickedness of those who by their wickedness suppress the truth."

Analyzing the Crisis

Although God is the headliner, the biblical drama includes a supporting cast. God did not need to create the world. God didn't have to create us—or anything else. Complete in themselves and fully satisfied in their communion with each other, the Father, the Son, and the Holy Spirit also enjoyed the perpetual worship of the angelic hosts. Yet this Triune God freely chose to create us. It was out of sheer liberality, freedom, love, and extravagant joy rather than lack or need that we were brought into being.

As the Spirit brooded over the unshaped and empty creation, separating the waters so that dry land appeared, a space was made for God—Creator and Lord of the cosmos—to dwell with us. Created in God's image, Adam and Eve were commissioned to rule and subdue the earth—the same verbs used later for the role of the priests in the Temple. Eden was God's temple, the small-scale copy of heaven itself, the footstool of God. Humanity was to be God's kingdom of prophets (declaring his Word), priests (sweeping the whole creation in its train as it led the victory parade into the eternal Sabbath), and kings (reigning as God's viceroys).

Instead, Adam—as our representative head—led creation in a detour from the promised land, away from the stands where the great King waited in pleasure for the passing review of his creatures behind the royal image bearers. Recall the splendor of the Olympics' opening ceremony, with each nation parading with its banner. That is the picture. Created in God's image, Adam and Eve were already crowned with glory and honor, but our representative head had not yet won the gold for his race. Instead, Adam headed for the exit, on his own mission, his own parade, looking for his own glory and happiness apart from God. Not wanting to be dependent on every word that he heard from God, Adam wanted to be guided by his own inner light. Not content to bask in the reflected glory of his Creator, he wanted to be the sun instead of the moon. Quickly, the beauty with which God had adorned our first parents faded and they were ashamed of their nakedness; the glory with which he had crowned them was now transformed into pride, and the power that he had given them to rule would soon be exercised in a tyrannical march of terror across the landscape of history.

There is no happiness without holiness. Created in God's image "to glorify God and to enjoy him forever,"[3] our fulfillment, meaning, and pleasure are found in friendship with God. As the church father Augustine expressed it in the form of a prayer, "You have made us for yourself, and our heart is restless until it rests in you."[4] This restlessness exhibits itself in the feverish craving for domination, in greed, in countless distractions and amusements that promise in vain to numb our conscience to the undeniable fact that we are God's enemies.

The history of Israel is in many ways an echo of this creation narrative. Once again separating the waters in order for his people to walk through the "darkness and void" on dry land, Israel was God's "firstborn son." Nevertheless, Israel too had a trial to endure as God led her to his promised land. Would they heed God's Word, as a faithful covenant servant, or try to put God on trial instead and claim the right to determine their own destiny for themselves? Would they glorify and enjoy God or renounce their office as God's image bearers? Would they drive out the serpent from the garden of God and inherit the land flowing with milk and honey or would they allow themselves to be seduced by the idolatrous nations and become traitors to the covenant?

So our identity as human beings takes shape in the context of a courtroom trial, where we are summoned to the witness stand. This is the script within which our own lives find their plot. "The heavens declare the glory of God, and the sky above proclaims his handiwork. Day to day pours out speech, and night to night reveals knowledge" (Ps. 19:1–2). But will God's *image bearer* declare God's glory as well, taking the stand as God's lead witness? Will the leading character in this supporting cast—the one designated to direct the choir in its procession to the Tree of Life—fulfill his calling? Will he lead the parade into immortality and glory? Or will he lead a detour in his own name, under his own banner, toward his own city?

What Does God Expect of You?

Sounds like a pretty grand story—far removed from our daily lives of working, shopping, and carting our kids around to school and soccer practice. What does the regal destiny of being created in God's image have to do with me and my hectic schedule this week? Already, in asking this question, we exhibit our tendency to get so caught up in the tyranny of the urgent—even valuable aspects of our ordinary vocations—that we are distracted from the big picture. Looking away from God and his purposes for us, we define ourselves by the narrow horizon of our own immediate needs. When we get the big picture right, the other things have their proper place. We're not just hauling our children around town, but raising a dynasty of prophets, priests, and kings who bear God's image. As spouses, we are not merely negotiating our personal schedules and desires, but coordinating our energies in fulfilling our Creator's mandate to "be fruitful and multiply," to serve him and each other in caring for the world that he has made.

Adam was a public representative, not just a private person. Like Adam and Eve, you are created in God's image, to glorify and enjoy God forever. This is not an abstract concept. It is defined by God's law. And law is not the opposite of love, but its concrete expression. Love certainly involves feeling, but it is more than that; it's a commitment to take delight in others that leads us to commit ourselves to them. Often, the feeling of love *follows* the commitment to love as a responsibility, rather than the other way around.

Early in my marriage, I learned a hard lesson about love—a lesson that I am still trying to learn. Saturated with the crazy American idea of love as a spontaneous feeling that I wanted to express in my own way, I routinely gave my wife gifts at Christmas and her birthday that she did not want. As an act of kindness, she told me what she wanted, but I bristled. I wanted to give her what I thought she would like, not what she told me she liked. My "giving" was actually a form of selfishness. I was greedier for my own self-satisfaction at having my choices vindicated than I was at bringing delight to my wife. That's how deep our sin goes: even doing things for and giving things to others become opportunities for us to assert our pride.

It is sort of like the sacrifice that Cain brought to God, which was not the sacrifice that God commanded. When God rejected Cain and his sacrifice in favor of Abel and his offering of a lamb, jealousy turned to murder. Later in the story, the sons of Aaron—priests in God's tabernacle—offered an unauthorized fire in God's worship. They were just being "spontaneous," adding their own personal touch to God's worship, but God had not appointed it and therefore he took their lives then and there.

My wife is a sinner, as I am, so she tends to be more lenient. God, however, is holy and will not greet our "spontaneous" offerings of creative and self-authorized worship with the indulgent shrug, "Well, it's the thought that counts." It's the *thought* that is *perverse*. Even if I occasionally got lucky and my desire coincided with my wife's, it was from the same motive that led me to buy the gift that she *didn't* like! We want to make the world and everyone in it revolve around us: our likes and dislikes, our comfort zones, and our felt needs. God demands that we acknowledge what is simply the fact of the case: namely, that he is the one by whom, in whom, for whom, and through whom all things exist.

As the father of four, I am fairly used to the excuse, "I didn't *hear* you" or "I would have done that if *you* had *told me clearly*." Satan wormed his way into the reasoning of our first parents by questioning the clarity of God's Word: "Has God *really* said . . . ?" It is a lot easier to rewrite the script after convincing ourselves that God's version of reality is a little vague. After the fall, we justify our detour from the thanksgiving parade in the same way: Has God really said that we are under his wrath, dead in sins, helpless even to believe in his Son apart from his sovereign gift of grace? Has God really said that there is a judgment of all people at the end of history and that some will be sentenced to everlasting judgment? Surely hell is not a real place; it's just a subjective experience of loneliness and unhappiness that people encounter when they don't follow God's path. How can the wicked be declared righteous on the basis of someone else's performance, credited to them through faith alone? Has God really said that we must die to ourselves and be raised with Christ?

Over and over again, Israel put God on trial. Micah reports that the people were wondering what they could do to make God happy and to turn away his anger. Just tell us what to do and we'll do it, Israel frequently responds, as if it had *done* everything that God commanded and their punishment must be due to some fine print that God needed to make clearer. "He has told you, O man, what is good; and what does the LORD require of you but to do justice, and to love kindness, and to walk humbly with your God?" (Mic. 6:8).

What *haven't* we done? That is the question raised repeatedly in the prophets—not unlike the query of the rich young ruler to Jesus in Matthew 19: "Teacher, what good deed must I do to have eternal life?" When Jesus replies that it is to keep the whole law, the ruler asks, "Which ones?" as if there might be one he was missing. After Jesus simply repeats the second table of the law (love of neighbor), the man replies, "All these I have kept. What do I still lack?" So Jesus presses him: "If you would be perfect, sell what you possess and give to the poor, and you will have treasure in heaven; and come, follow me." This is what true kingdom living looks like.

The rich young ruler thought he had kept the law because he had not been even remotely involved in murder or theft. He had never perjured himself in court. He had honored his father and mother and never slept with a woman outside of marriage. So what's missing? Yet, as Jesus had explained in his Sermon on the Mount (Matthew 5), anger toward one's neighbor is tantamount to murder (vv. 21–26), lust equals adultery (vv. 27–30), divorce "except on the ground of sexual immorality" makes an adulterer of one's new spouse (vv. 31–32), oaths presume that you have control over things that you don't (vv. 33–37), all forms of retaliation are forbidden (vv. 38–42), even enemies must be loved (vv. 43–48), and giving to the poor must be done with pure motives, in secret rather than in public displays of charity (Matt. 6:1–4).

By this standard, of course, the rich young ruler did not have just a few moral hairs out of place. It was not a matter of identifying some *additional* law that he had not fulfilled to push him over the edge into eternal life. Let's not be too hard on this fellow. In terms of public sins that made a Jew an outcast on the basis of Israel's law, he *was* a fine, upstanding citizen. Yet Jesus presses him to realize that he had not *truly* fulfilled the law at *any* point, in terms of its real intention. If he truly loved his neighbor, he would have sold everything and given it to the poor. "When the young man heard this he went away sorrowful, for he had great possessions" (Matt. 19:22). As James writes, "For whoever keeps the whole law but fails in one point has become accountable for all of it" (James 2:10). God does not grade on a curve, and his holy justice cannot be adjusted to suit us.

So what does God expect of you—and of all of us? He expects us to be what he created us to be: the covenant partner in whom he takes delight, his image bearer commissioned to lead a parade of thanksgiving from the center of worship (Eden, and later the temple) out to the ends of the earth, with the whole creation in humanity's train. God created us in ethical splendor and strength, capable of fulfilling our destiny of completing the commission of bringing his kingdom of glory to the ends of the earth.

The Royal Procession from Work to Everlasting Rest

The first two chapters of Genesis group together the rulers and the ruled in each domain: day and night ruled by sun and moon, the waters ruled by the fish, the skies ruled by birds, and the earth—filled with flourishing vegetation—ruled by land mammals. And then, at last, when the stage was set with such abundance,

> God said, "Let us make humanity in our image, after our likeness. And let them have dominion over the fish of the sea and over the birds of the heavens and over the livestock and over all the earth and over every creeping thing that creeps on the earth." So God created humanity in his own image, in the image of God he created him; male and female he created them. (Gen. 1:26–27)

Having fulfilled his own trial of work, deeply satisfied with his achievement, God entered in conquest into his Sabbath rest, taking his throne over the works of his hands. Now it is creation's turn to follow him in this pattern of creative work leading to a triumphal entrance into the everlasting Sabbath day, the heavenly rest. As the Creator sat in royal splendor, the creature rulers paraded before his review under the leadership of his chief prophet, priest, and king (Gen. 2:1–3).

As Jewish as well as Christian scholars have pointed out, this pattern of working (trial) and rest (conquest) is echoed throughout the history of Israel. For example, Psalm 68 is a hymn that recites God's parade of victory, led by Israel, a royal march from exodus to Canaan, cleansing the garden from the serpent's corrupting influence and arriving in triumph to Zion, the Lord's mountain at the center of the world.

Our daily grind seems like a long way from the royal march of Psalm 68 which echoes the parade of the creature kings before the great King on their way into his everlasting Sabbath. Wake up, dash out the door, return home, watch a little TV, and do it all over again the next day. In between it all we try to fit in the gym, friends and family, and maybe dabble in a hobby every now and then. It is ironic that we have more technology to make our lives more efficient, ostensibly reducing our workload, and we work harder than we ever have. I was dragged into email kicking and screaming. On most issues technological I'm wrong, but I think I had this one nailed. Given the way emails come like baseballs from a machine in a batting cage, I spend more time responding to them than I spent manually opening and responding to letters. My friends from England write beautiful letters: bonded correspondence paper, elegant penmanship, and prose that reads like poetry. I shoot back an email. To the equivalent of a well-prepared feast I reciprocate with the equivalent of a bag of chips.

In this context, efficiency threatens quality; depth, breadth, deliberate reflection, thoughtful regard for things that matter (including other people) are driven out by the tyranny of the urgent. These values show up in our faith and practice as well. This seems evident not only in our own reluctance to spend time with our Lord in reading his Word, prayer, and meditation, but in public worship: the often superficial and half-prepared sermons that we hear, in the substitution of a fast-paced and noisy choreography for a well-conceived liturgy, and in the routine concentration on efficiency in our everyday lives with little exposition of a biblical text and teaching for all ages. The Christian Sabbath is no longer the weekly source of Christian formation, as the values of the marketplace—if not the mall itself—crowd out the holiness of the day.

Busyness does not equal a rich life. We hear increasingly from the medical community that stress is literally killing us. We like to stay busy, but busy doing *what*? What is the point of it all? Why are we here and what are the goals toward which we so feverishly strive? Stress is not alleviated by more techniques for relieving it, but by changing our values. The problem is that when we stop and smell the roses, we also begin to get to know ourselves better. And that can create *more* stress than we ever imagined. The roses are not always sweet. To be sure, we spend a lot of time on ourselves, but it is usually on improving ourselves in various ways rather than on evaluating our lives in a serious and big picture kind of way. We often assume that the question, "How can I be happy?" can be successfully answered without reference to the love of God and our neighbors. And the irony is that if our biggest question is our own happiness, we can never know the God in whom we find our ultimate joy and rest.

The great church father Augustine pointed out that sin is not necessarily loving bad things, but loving good things *inordinately*. In other words, it is turning God's gifts into idols. It is our "enlightened" way of fulfilling the apostle's description of ungrateful living in Romans 1: "Claiming to be wise, they became fools, and exchanged the glory of the immortal God for images. . . . [T]hey exchanged the truth about God for a lie and worshiped and served the creature rather than the Creator, who is blessed forever!" (vv. 22, 25).

Can you really say that you love God more than anyone or anything else? Is your life characterized by gratitude to God and service to your neighbor or do you find yourself, like me, grumbling and complaining about even the slightest setbacks? Is your work a divine vocation or just a job? Do your daily habits, schedule, and interests testify in your defense? Are your neighbors, relatives, and co-workers—even people you don't necessarily like that much—beneficiaries of your daily concern and acts of generosity? Do you evaluate your relationships (with God and other people in your life) on the basis of their usefulness to your own interests and needs? Or do you drop everything when you see someone who needs your help—even if you've never met the person?

On the very day that I wrote these questions, my seven-year-old son asked me to play with him. Even though I was at a good stopping place, I told him I was busy. It's especially easy to justify my decision, since I am after all working on a book to help people understand God's claim on our lives. Yet I missed a moment to love and serve my nearest neighbor. Not only as a general evaluation, but in a concrete instance, I fell short of the glory of God.

A few people may say some really nice things about you at your funeral, but when you are lying on your deathbed, evaluating your life, what regrets will you have? What will be the overall verdict on the investments that you made in time and treasure? These are some of the questions that help us to take inventory not only of what we say we are all about, but who we *really* are and what we *really* count most important in life.

What's *God's* Problem?

Israel fared no better than Adam in leading the royal procession from its creation at Sinai to its rest in the land. "Like Adam, they broke my covenant . . ." (Hosea 6:7). When Israel failed its trial, leading God's people in mutiny rather than celebration of God's goodness and grace, the recurring irony is that the nation put *God* on trial. *They* had turned God's new paradise into a howling wasteland, and yet they wondered why God had failed to fulfill his promise. I thought God promised to be our God. I thought we were the apple of his eye, his favorite people in the world. Where is God amid the threat of captivity, torture, and the destruction of Jerusalem? Like their forebears in the wilderness, the Israelites in the land centuries later "put God to the test," demanding their rights. This penchant for shifting blame from ourselves to others—and ultimately, to God—goes all the way back to our first parents. Even God's people are compared to sheep that go their own way, blaming God when they get lost. We want to be autonomous individuals, but we point fingers at God when this impossible dream turns into a nightmare.

One of the great courtroom scenes is reported in Isaiah 59. Israel had contested God's faithfulness. Similar to the usual conundrum we encounter when the question of evil is raised, the people charged that either God did not care or he was not powerful enough to save them from the threat of invading armies. Through Isaiah, his covenant attorney, God turns the tables: "Behold, the LORD's hand is not shortened, that it cannot save, or his ear dull, that it cannot hear, but *your* iniquities have made a separation between you and your God, and your sins have hidden his face from you so he does not hear" (v. 1, emphasis added).

Israel had tried to domesticate God. God may sometimes have "issues" with us, but the threat of his *wrath* was not even on the radar. Jeremiah reminds us there were plenty of lying prophets around who told the people whatever they wanted to hear. It was unthinkable that any harm should come to *Jerusalem* or the holy temple, and the false prophets lulled the people into false security by their upbeat message of health, wealth, and happiness: "They speak visions of their own minds, not from the mouth of the LORD. They say continually to those who despise the word of the LORD, 'It shall be well with you'; and to everyone who stubbornly follows his own heart, they say, 'No disaster shall come upon you' " (Jer. 23:16–17). Is God really a locker-room pal? Or, to put it in biblical terms, "Am I a God at hand, declares the LORD, and not a God afar off? Can a man hide himself in secret places so that I cannot see him?" (v. 23). But Israel was in fact taken into exile by Assyria and Judah was carried off in chains to Babylon. It did not matter what the false prophets and their cheerful followers thought was true, helpful, uplifting, or morally justifiable. God proved his faithfulness to the covenant precisely by evicting his unfaithful tenants.

The trial in Isaiah 59 continued, with the judge prosecuting his case through his prophet. People and priest alike are like vipers, hatching offspring filled with venom when they are still in the egg, or like spiders weaving cobwebs to cover their guilt. "Their webs will not serve as clothing; they will not cover themselves with what they make. Their works are works of iniquity and deeds of violence are in their hands" (vv. 3–6). After the judge brought out the damning evidence in the trial, the people finally confessed that the calamity that had befallen them was due to their own sin:

> We hope for justice, but there is none; for salvation, but it is far from us. For our transgressions are multiplied before you, and our sins testify against us, for our transgressions are with us, and we know our iniquities; transgressing, and denying the LORD, and turning back from following our God, speaking oppression and revolt, conceiving and uttering from the heart lying words. Justice is turned back, and righteousness stands afar off; for truth has stumbled in the public squares, and uprightness cannot enter. Truth is lacking, and he who departs from evil makes himself a prey. (vv. 11–15)

The problem was not a lack of zeal, pious phrases, and spiritual enthusiasm. Apparently, the churches were filled every Sabbath, but given the corruption of their doctrine, worship, and their daily lives, God could only reply,

> I hate, I despise your feasts, and I take no delight in your solemn assemblies. Even though you offer me your burnt offerings and grain offerings, I will not accept them; and the peace offering of your fattened animals, I will not look upon them. Take away from me the noise of your sons; to the melody of your harps I will not listen. But let justice roll down like waters, and righteousness like an ever-flowing stream. (Amos 5:21–24)

In all of these passages, the real crisis is not that the people are unhappy, nor that they are faced with imminent threats from foreign powers, but that they are unrighteous and God is their enemy.

The apostle Paul offers the same indictment in Romans 10: "I bear them witness that they have a zeal for God, but not according to knowledge. For, being ignorant of the righteousness that comes from God, and seeking to establish their own, they did not submit to God's righteousness. For Christ is the end of the law for righteousness to everyone who believes" (vv. 2–4).

There is a lot of zeal today for religion, spirituality, and moral crusades. Yet when we are ignorant of the righteousness that God demands in his law and the righteousness that he gives in the gospel, we are farther from his kingdom than the prostitutes and tax collectors (Matt. 21:32). This is the message that the prophets brought and that Jesus proclaimed in his ministry.

No More Crisis Management

There is a place for crisis management. Victims of natural disasters are served by governmental and private sector relief. We are grateful to those busily at work developing vaccines, economic plans, and hospitals. However, the one crisis that we cannot manage—which is in fact the root of all other crises—is sin and its eternal consequences.

Pastors have increasingly become experts in crisis management. Some of that is simply part of shepherding a flock, but a lot of it is due to the fact that we expect our pastors to be personal coaches, therapists, and life managers rather than faithful prophets who diagnose our condition and heralds of the Good News that actually solves our deepest crisis. We may be a little more sophisticated in our spiritual technology, but the pattern is familiar. We will gladly follow preachers who tell us that everything is fine, that there is no wrath to fear, that either God is too nice or we're too good for any final judgment to land on our heads. We will even pay a lot of money to spiritual designers who will help us weave cobwebs to hide our guilt, assisting us in shifting the blame to our parents, our circumstances, society, our spouse, and ultimately God. As false prophets, we lie to ourselves, to others, and to God about who we really are. As false priests, we offer whatever pitiful sacrifices we think might buy God off for a while. As false kings, we seek to dominate rather than serve, expecting everyone—including God—to assume their role in our supporting cast.

However, the problem is not God's unfaithfulness to his covenant, but ours. And because we are the ones at fault, *God is our problem*, and this is one we cannot manage. In fact, God's Word calls us to face the crisis at its root and to give up our strategies for self-salvation. When the righteousness *of* God no longer disturbs (much less terrifies) us, we feel no need to cry out for the righteousness *from* God that is a gift in Christ Jesus. No longer "sinners in the hands of an angry God," as in Jonathan Edwards' famous sermon, we are more like somewhat dysfunctional but well-meaning victims who need to be "empowered." Nobody today seems to think that God is *dangerous*. And that is itself a dangerous oversight.

The holiness of God obscured, the sinful human condition is adjusted, first, to the level of *sins*. That is, instead of recognizing that sin is the universal condition of bondage, death, and condemnation from which we cannot extricate ourselves, we reduce it to particular actions or habits that we can be scolded or cheerfully encouraged out of repeating. Symptoms are mistaken for the illness. Second, we treat them primarily as negative behaviors that adversely affect fellow human creatures or our own well-being. For many, especially in our pampered culture, the only law left—and it is a relentless command that generates enormous anxiety—is to take care of oneself. The vertical relation—that makes sin truly sinful—is almost entirely forgotten. Now they are no longer sins—offences against God—but mistakes: failures to live up to our potential or to improve our world. In fact, they need not even be defined by God's law, but reflect our own inner lights: that which we personally find morally offensive. Third, we deflect these sins to "outsiders," defining them as things that *other* people do. Depending on your ideology, "sinners" become either Republicans or Democrats, gays or social conservatives, socialists or capitalists, Muslims, Jews, Christians, or secular humanists. In this reconstruction of the problem, sins are deflected to others. Even when we discover them in ourselves, they are easily treated merely as self-destructive behavior that can be managed with the proper strategies.

However, in the biblical perspective, that which makes sin *sin* is not first of all the unhappiness or shame that it brings to us and those around us, but the objective offense that it is before God. No one is eternally condemned for failing to find meaning, purpose, or fulfillment in life. But when sin is first defined vertically—that is, in reference to

God—our nagging sense of unworthiness and guilt finally finds a real source and object. Only real sins can be really forgiven. We cannot forgive ourselves. Even the forgiveness of other people cannot erase the debt and give us a righteous status. Only if our sins are first of all offenses against God can they be objectively, fully, and finally forgiven. There is no way of avoiding the biblical insistence that God's wrath is real and is being stored up for judgment day. At the heart of Christ's work on the cross is his propitiation of God's wrath, but this makes no sense when we worship our own idolatrous projection of a domesticated deity who thinks we are basically good people who need a little help to be better. If "people today" find the preaching and teaching of sin and the cross irrelevant, it is only because we, like Israel, have dulled their sense of God's holiness and righteousness.

When theology dispenses with propitiation (the satisfaction of God's wrath) as a theme, it must eventually surrender forgiveness as well. We see this connection between a denial of God's wrath and forgiveness in Don Henley's song, "The Garden of Allah":

> Because there are no facts, there is no truth, just data to be
>   manipulated . . .
> Because there is no wrong, there is no right, and I sleep very
>   well at night.
> No shame, no solution, no remorse, no retribution
> Just people selling T-shirts. . . .

A Person, Not a Principle

Jewish theologian Michael Wyschogrod contrasts the modern notion of "ethics" with the biblical concept of law.[5] Like an error in arithmetic, a violation of a principle may be a mistake but it is hardly something that demands forgiveness from an offended party. In other words, it is a mistake against a principle rather than an offense against a person. Yet, Wyschogrod notes, the Bible speaks of sin as an offense "with a high hand," equivalent to a certain familiar gesture in popular culture. It is not a mistake but a personal offense. "But precisely because this is so, forgiveness is possible," as it cannot be from principles and problems.[6] How do you ever receive objective forgiveness from a standard, a vague sense of well-being, or one's own aspirations for moral decency? Purposelessness cannot forgive, but God can. We cannot be condemned for failing to live up to our own standards, and consequently we cannot forgive ourselves. It is not ultimately to ourselves or our spouses or our neighbors that we are accountable, but to God.

"The atonement is not high on the contemporary agendas of either Catholics or Protestants," Yale theologian George Lindbeck observes.[7] This is as true for evangelicals as for liberal Protestants.[8] And that is because we do not really believe that the ultimate crisis facing us is the wrath of God. We understand neither God and his holiness, nor ourselves and our depravity. We may not think that we can save ourselves by meritorious works, but at least God will take notice of our good intentions. At least we had the decency to exercise our free will properly, deciding to "make Jesus our Savior and Lord." "Where the cross once stood is now a vacuum," Lindbeck concludes.[9] Similarly, George Hunsinger notes, "The blood of Christ is repugnant to the Gentile mind, whether ancient or modern. This mind would prevail were it not continually disrupted by grace."[10] Where God's wrath is no longer a problem, Christ's cross is no longer the solution. "The social or horizontal aspect of reconciliation . . . eclipses its vertical aspect."[11] Hunsinger is justified in his observation: "The idea that in his suffering Jesus bore the sins of the world is a motif that has been almost completely abandoned in the modern period."[12]

The doctrine of justification—that is, God's act of declaring the wicked righteous by imputing our guilt to Christ and Christ's righteousness to us through faith alone—is only irrelevant or incomprehensible for our society today because God and sin have become irrelevant or incomprehensible for the church. "Justification is an understandably strange doctrine to those who have substituted self-realization for salvation," as Episcopal bishop C. Fitzsimons Allison reminds us.[13] In fact, Allison points to the history of theology to demonstrate that Pelagianism (the belief that people are basically good and can save themselves by their works) always leads to a denial of Christ's sacrificial atonement and, finally, to the necessity of his divinity. Although this type of religion advertises itself as liberation from guilt, "the pastoral cruelty of scolding people in bondage who are not properly 'using' their freedom (a freedom they do not possess until graced by the word) has been largely ignored."[14] All of this points to the irony that prophets who specialize in eliminating guilt and divine wrath—and therefore Christ's saving work—are actually purveying a kind of legalism. People still *feel* guilty (because they *are* guilty), only now they're also supposed to feel guilty *for feeling guilty*.

Without Excuse: How God Silences Our Spin

Whether we admit it or not, the *ultimate* source of our guilt, anxiety, depression, and stress is God's wrath and we cannot wish this problem away by denying it or by numbing our sense of it by focusing on the more manageable symptoms. There is only one way to be liberated from the condemnation of God's law. We have to stop rationalizing our lives, questioning God's Word, and defending ourselves. We were created to be talkers, answering God's speech with our own "Amen!" However, as false prophets we have become masters of spin. We use the very gifts of wisdom and communication that God gave us to mount our assault against him. Instead of reciting God's story, we make up our own verbal equivalent of fig leaves to try to cover our nakedness. We talk ourselves—and each other—into nonsense. The first thing that God has to do to save us is to get us to be quiet.

In Romans 1:19–32, Paul explains that God's wrath is being revealed from heaven against the wicked and that this is entirely justified. Adam and Eve knew God's law. In fact, they had no need of the gospel in their original condition, since the gospel is the Good News of what God has done to save us. Adam didn't need to be saved; he needed to obey God's commands so that he could lead creation into the Sabbath rest and eat of the Tree of Life. Humanity was originally "wired" for law. God created us for obedience and gave us all of the requisite abilities for fulfilling the commission he had given us to extend his kingdom throughout the earth.

We call this the covenant of works (also called the covenant of creation). After the fall, of course, not only was any hope of winning the right to eat of the Tree of Life foreclosed; we couldn't even get back into Eden. The unexpected happened, though: God announced the gospel to Adam and Eve, and thus began the covenant of *grace*.

But what about those who are outside this covenant of grace, who do not embrace its promises? It is just not true that unbelievers do not have a personal relationship with God. Paul here in Romans 1 says they do! It is not just that God's existence can be discerned by his works, but that everyone already knows God—at least as judge. "So they are without excuse" (Rom. 1:20). It is precisely because unbelievers—even professing atheists—*do* have a personal relationship with God that, as creatures obligated to keep his law, they are under his wrath. So even though there are people who claim to be atheists, the fact is that they are suppressing the truth that they really know to be true, and they do so in order to evade the reality of the wrath of God on account of their sin. This is the ultimate case of "living in denial."

Even apart from the gospel revealed in Scripture, everybody knows God, but only as creator and judge. Our natural knowledge of God extends only as far as that original covenant of creation. The Good News that God delivered after the fall was a *surprise announcement*. God did not have to save anyone. He could have allowed his enemies to go on being his enemies, going their own way, earning their own just condemnation. God's promise of salvation in Christ, therefore, is totally foreign to our consciousness. It makes sense to us that good people go to heaven and bad people go to hell—even if we bend the rules in order to justify ourselves and our loved ones. But the bad news is worse than we think:

> For we have already charged that all, both Jews and Greeks, are under sin, as it is written: 'None is righteous, no not one; no one understands, no one seeks for God. All have turned aside; together they have become worthless; no one does good, not even one. . . . Now we know that whatever the law says it speaks to those who are under the law, *so that every mouth may be stopped*, and the whole world may be held accountable to God. For by works of the law no human being will be justified in his sight, since through the law comes knowledge of sin. (Rom. 3:9–12, 19–20, emphasis added)

In other words, if we think that we can cover our guilt with our own moral zeal, spirituality, free will, and good intentions, we do not realize the seriousness of our condition. We do not seek God. We are not righteous and even our best works are offensive to God even if they are praiseworthy to us and to our neighbors. Finally, God's judgment silences our spin. We are arraigned. No longer protesting our innocence and putting God on trial, we accept the verdict.

Facing the Real Crisis

Solving the health care crisis is hardly unimportant. Not without reason we are concerned about having reliable insurance for regular and catastrophic medical needs. Our attention, sympathy, and support for victims of natural disasters will always be vitally necessary. The health of our marriages, families, and society is not insignificant.

Nevertheless, all of these worries are mere symptoms of a deeper crisis that we prefer not to address.

The apostle Paul tells us that "the wages of sin is death" (Rom. 6:23). Death is not just "the way things are"; it is part of a universal sentence that God has imposed on humanity for transgression of his covenant. And for all who remain "in Adam," this first death is merely the harbinger of the second death: everlasting punishment. "The sting of death is sin, and the power of sin is the law" (1 Cor. 15:56). We Americans spend billions of dollars on health care, billions more on spiritual, psychological, and physical makeovers to improve our self-image and relationships. We try very hard not to die, but die we will and the root cause of these symptoms is *sin*.

Sin is first of all a *condition* that gives rise to particular *actions*. One day, Jesus and his retinue passed a blind man and those who were following him asked, " 'Rabbi, who sinned, this man or his parents, that he was born blind?' Jesus answered, 'It was not that this man sinned, or his parents, but that the works of God might be displayed in him' " (John 9:1–3). All of us participate in this condition. Each of us dies, as part of the sentence that God pronounced on us as Adam's heirs. The religious leaders of Jesus's day, much like our own, had reduced sin to actions—particularly, acts that *other* people commit. Surely this blind person—or at least his parents—must have done something terrible.

In *The Sound of Music*, Maria, overwhelmed by her good fortune in being the object of the captain's affection, sings, "Nothing comes from nothing; nothing ever could. So somewhere in my youth or childhood, I must have done something good." Pelagianism—the belief that we are good people who can save ourselves—is our natural theology. No one has to be taught this idea. In the West it may be called "getting what's coming to you," and in the East it may be called *kharma*, but it is the same concept. In this episode in John 9, Jesus's followers were just assuming the other side of the coin: Good things happen to good people and bad things happen to bad people.

Even if this does not quite work out in this life, surely it will turn out this way in the next life, we reason. Evil deeds or bad kharma will come back to bite us and good deeds will be rewarded with the favor of God or the Universe.

All of this is true apart from the gospel. It is how God set things up: You reap what you sow. God warned Adam that death would be the curse for breaking the covenant, with enmity against God and each other. Our natural sense of moral justice is due ultimately to our being created in God's image. The New Testament consistently affirms that humanity will be judged by works, weighed in the scales of God's holy justice. Those who seek to be justified by their personal performance of the law's stipulations (love of God and neighbor) will be weighed by that law (Rom. 2:12). And the standard will not be how hard we tried, or how tenaciously we defended biblical morality in our public and private lives. "For it is not the hearers of the law who are righteous before God, but the doers of the law who will be justified" (v. 13).

However, from Genesis to Revelation there is *another word* that is odd and far from familiar to our moral consciousness. *It is the gospel.* Jesus disrupts this corrupted common sense in this episode in John 9 with the blind person. Those who appeared to be righteous are condemned and the wicked are acquitted—more than acquitted, justified: that is, actually declared by God to be righteous on the basis of Christ's obedient life and death. This particular blind man suffered this particular handicap not because of the particular sins that he or his parents committed, but because he shared in the common curse of fallen humanity and God chose him as the subject of his dramatic display of mercy in Jesus Christ. He was chosen not to be an active coagent in his deliverance or a great moral example but a passive recipient of free grace. He came to Jesus to be healed of his physical blindness, but received that and much more besides. The arrival of this healer from heaven was the answer to the prophet's prayer: "O LORD, I have heard the report of you, and your work, O LORD, do I fear. In the midst of the years revive it; in the midst of the years make it known; in wrath remember mercy" (Hab. 3:1).

Don't Believe Your Own Press: Yellow Journalism

There's a time to look within, to take stock. The problem is that we are not our own best judges. Our own feet smell just fine. I used to think that I was a sleuth at directions until I got married. Come to find out, I cannot even read a map properly. I did not really know this until I had some "objectivity" in the car with me.

As we have seen, the Bible indicates that we "suppress the truth in unrighteousness." We either let ourselves off the hook, making excuses, or hide from the world in despair of ever being able to face it because of our failures. The "journey within" that characterizes so much of contemporary spirituality, even in our own Christian circles, easily becomes just another way of running from God as he summons us to appear in his courtroom. We need God's Word, standing outside of us, to pass judgment on our lives, calling us out of our optimism and pessimism to hear things as they really are. If our introspection leads us to greater self-confidence, we have only deceived ourselves. The false prophets in Israel and in the church today are engaged in "yellow journalism." Born out of a rivalry between New York newspapers at the end of the nineteenth century, yellow journalism came to refer to the practice of preferring entertainment and sensationalism to serious news in order to sell newspapers. Paul warned Timothy,

> But understand this, that in the last days there will come times of difficulty. For people will be lovers of self, lovers of money, proud, arrogant, abusive, disobedient to their parents, ungrateful, unholy, heartless, unappeasable, slanderous, without self-control, brutal, not loving good, treacherous, reckless, swollen with conceit, lovers of pleasure rather than lovers of God, having the appearance of godliness, but denying its power. (2 Tim. 3:1–5)

During such times, false teachers will easily "creep into households" and seduce the weak (v. 6).

A lot of church marketing experts describe a similar condition in American society and the church itself today. Yet where they typically prescribe various strategies of accommodating this narcissistic orientation, Paul tells Timothy, "But as for you, continue in what you have learned and have firmly believed, knowing from whom you learned it and how from childhood you have been acquainted with the sacred writings, which are able to make you wise for salvation through faith in Christ Jesus" (vv. 14–15). Unlike the yellow press of days past, "All Scripture is breathed out by God . . ." and is therefore totally sufficient for faith and practice (v. 16). The apostle adds,

> I charge you in the presence of God and of Christ Jesus, who is the judge of the living and the dead, and by his appearing and his kingdom, preach the word; be ready in season and out of season; reprove, rebuke, and exhort, with complete patience and teaching. For the time is coming when people will not endure sound teaching, but having itching ears they will accumulate for themselves teachers to suit their own passions, and will turn away from listening to the truth and wander off into myths. (2 Tim. 4:1–4)

We all have "itching ears." The question is whether we will allow ourselves to hear the truth about our condition, so that we are ready for the Good News in Jesus Christ.

Yellow journalism is like medical quackery. I come from a long line of self-diagnosing patients. My grandmother swore by her "remedy," which was her own concoction—consisting mostly of cheap bourbon (for medicinal purposes, of course). I resist doctor's appointments like the plague, pleading to my wife that I know my issues and how best to treat them. The offensiveness of the inevitable checkup begins with being weighed. I'm always several pounds heavier than I am when I weigh myself at home—and the nurse never allows me even to empty my pockets or take off my belt.

Whether in our physical or spiritual health, we need someone to stand outside of us and tell us the truth about our condition. Diagnosing myself, I can say, "Well, I may not do everything I should—and I'm sure I make mistakes every day. But deep down, I'm a pretty good person. At least my heart is right." But then I come to church and someone stands up front in Christ's name, giving me the true diagnosis. My heart is even more corrupt than my outward actions—at least the ones people see—might suggest. I am like the rich young ruler, asking Jesus to give me the "one thing" to do that I haven't done yet. Yet it is here, sitting under God's Word, where I hear and realize that I have not done *anything* the way it was meant to be done. Sin does not lie on the surface; "deep down" it is even messier. Our hearts have committed sins that our hands haven't gotten around to yet. It is from the heart that our perversity ascends to God and out to our neighbors (Matt. 12:33–37). "The heart is deceitful above all things and desperately wicked—who can know it?" (Jer. 17:9).

Forced to face the facts presented to me after my medical exam, I know that ignorance is not bliss; it can lead to serious problems down the line. And we need physicians, both of the body and the soul, who are willing to ruin our day. Accumulating teachers who will tell us whatever our itching ears want to hear is even more dangerous than finding a doctor who will make us feel good even when we shouldn't. We cannot diagnose ourselves. When we hear someone who is commissioned by God to deliver his Word after careful preparation and deliberation, our defense mechanisms break down. Our excuses lose their saliency as we are weighed on true scales. What does God expect of you? He doesn't expect you to steal into his private chamber and go through his secret files in order to discern his will for your life. We are not responsible for knowing things that God has not revealed: like where we should live, whom we should marry, which job we should take. It is not a question of *finding the place* where God wants you to be, but *being the person* he wants you to be where you are. He has *told* you everything for which he holds you responsible. It is all there, in black-and-white. He has revealed his purpose for your life. Are you fulfilling it? Is your chief goal each morning to glorify God and to enjoy him or to glorify and enjoy yourself, taking God as seriously as his services justify in your pursuit of happiness? Regardless of our protestations to the contrary, God's objective verdict answers us all with a resounding, *No!*

After Adam sinned, God descended in judgment. Adam and Eve had no right to expect anything other than a death sentence. "Adam, where are you?" God called—as he still calls all of us as his fallen children (Gen. 3:9). Adam replied, "I heard the sound of you in the garden, and I was afraid, because I was naked, and I hid myself" (v. 10). No precious robes could supplement the beauty with which God had adorned the human body, but now its nakedness was a visible testimony to the nakedness of man's corrupt heart before God. Adam blamed Eve, Eve blamed the serpent, and everybody blamed God. Talk about reversing the charges! Putting God on trial even in their own transgression of the covenant, Adam and Eve could not accept their role as servants rather than lords. Yet God did try them in his court, and pronounced them guilty. Although he executed the sanctions of the covenant for violation, he kept open the door to the Tree of Life—not for Adam to fulfill this time, but for a second Adam who will crush the serpent's head (Gen. 3:15). As a visible pledge of this promise, "The LORD God made for Adam and for his wife garments of skins and clothed them" (v. 21).

God comes to each of us now and asks, "Where are you?" drawing us out of the shadows, out of the stream of excuses, qualifications, alibis, and pretensions of self-righteousness. He sees your nakedness. He knows that you cannot cover it up—that the garments of morality and spirituality that you weave are like "cobwebs" that cannot hide your shame (Isa. 59:6) and that not only our sins but "all our *righteous* deeds are like a polluted garment" (Isa. 64:6, emphasis added).

Paul tells the Roman Christians, "None is righteous; no, not one; no one understands; no one seeks for God" (Rom. 3:10–11). Can that really be true? Is Paul exaggerating here? What about all those people around the world devoting their lives to the search for God, and the many decent people who give their lives to serve humanity? Surely God will judge the world on the basis of whether we have done our best with the light that we have been given. But Paul's whole point in these first three chapters is to convince us that regardless of how much light we have been given, we always do the same thing with it. We suppress the truth, whether it is the light of nature (God's existence and moral will known to unbelieving Gentiles) or the light of grace (God's revelation of the gospel in the Scriptures). There is enough revelation to render a guilty verdict. Regardless of our own evaluation, before God's bar no one is good and no one seeks God.

This does not mean that no one is morally decent before fellow human beings, since Paul has affirmed that even Gentiles without the written law sometimes follow their conscience (Rom. 2:14–15). Nor does it mean that nobody seeks a god; indeed, Gentiles as well as Jews are very religious. However, we systematically distort this revelation of God's moral will in order to justify ourselves and keep God's truth about us and his righteousness at bay (Rom. 1:21–2:11). Natural religion, spirituality, and morality are in fact our chief means of running away from God.

God's law is not a tool that we can use; it is the rod by which God measures us. God's law says, "Be perfect." God's gospel says, "Believe in Christ and you will be reckoned perfect before God." The law tells us what must be done if we are to be saved; the gospel tells us what God has done to save us. Both of these seem too extreme to our fallen hearts. Jesus pointed out that the religious leaders of his day found John's somber preaching of the law too pessimistic and Jesus's preaching of the gospel too good to be true (Luke 7:31–35). The same is true in our day.

The proper preaching of God's demands will first of all drive us to despair rather than encourage us in our attempt to ascend to glory. We are frequently told that the church is in the business of "life transformation." However, both the problem and God's solution are greater than we ever imagined. God does not come to improve our life, but to end it; not to transform the "old Adam," but to kill it and to raise us together with Christ in newness of life. *Our transformed life will never be transformed enough to pass through God's judgment safely, but "salvation is from the LORD"* (Jon. 2:9, emphasis added).

3

THE BIG STORY

Many of the headlines that grab our attention are related to important courtroom dramas. Often, the airtight defense seems impenetrable. The defendant apparently has a solid alibi. And then a piece of evidence is revealed that unmistakably exposes the charade and the criminal confesses.

This is exactly what happens in Isaiah 59, as we have seen: the evidence is brought forward and the people, instead of trying God, accept their guilt. But what now? This is when the episode usually ends. Justice is served. However, in the biblical drama, this is right where the surprising reversal occurs. The prophet continues, "The LORD saw it, and it displeased him that there was no justice. He saw that there was no man, and wondered that there was no one to intercede" (vv. 15b–16a). If God were merely just, righteous, and holy, he could simply wipe out the human race and start over. Without a mediator, how could there be any resolution in Israel's favor? Moses had interceded for Israel after the "golden calf" episode and God relented, but now he saw no one offering to take Israel's place of judgment or even to plead her cause. But this is just where the plot becomes really interesting: "Then *his own arm brought him salvation*, and *his* righ-

teousness upheld him" (v. 16b, emphasis added). The Judge himself
descended in judgment, but also in deliverance: "'And a Redeemer
will come to Zion, to those in Jacob who turn from transgression,'
declares the LORD" (v. 20). This is just the news that Israel did not
expect, but received anyway.

God turned everything around. The trial began with Israel's suit
against God; God turned the tables and put Israel on trial, bringing
conviction, with no one to save the people from their just sentence.
Nevertheless, God himself became the Savior. The judge became the
deliverer. In fact, the judge became the judged. God's love did not
overwhelm or overrule his justice, but fulfilled it. Justice and love,
righteousness and mercy, wrath and peace embraced at the cross. This
is the big story. It broke first in Eden, after the fall, and God kept the
promise alive through Israel's darkest days.

In Romans 3:9–20 Paul summarized his argument thus far: The
law condemns everyone, Jew and Gentile alike, shutting every mouth
before God's tribunal. The righteousness of God leaves no one standing. Everyone is guilty. One may not be guilty before a human court,
or before the court of public opinion, or in the eyes of neighbors,
spouses, or friends. One may not be convicted in one's own sight.
Nevertheless, the only verdict that really matters is God's, and it is
unambiguous. If the only revelation that we had were that which is
gleaned from our natural knowledge of God's existence, power, and
righteousness, we would have no hope.

Just then, as in Isaiah 59, a new word is announced by Paul:

> But now the righteousness of God has been manifested apart from the
> law, although the Law and the Prophets bear witness to it—the righ-
> teousness of God through faith in Jesus Christ for all who believe. For
> there is no distinction, for all have sinned and fall short of the glory of
> God, and are justified by his grace as a gift, through the redemption
> that is in Christ Jesus, whom God put forward as a propitiation by his
> blood, to be received by faith. (Rom. 3:21–25)

The Old Testament ("the Law and the Prophets") anticipated this
day, when God would be vindicated as "just and the justifier of the
one who has faith in Jesus" (Rom. 3:26). Our real crisis is the righteousness *of* God, but the solution is the righteousness *from* God
that is a free gift. Someone wisely offered the following acronym for
GRACE: "God's Riches At Christ's Expense." Jesus Christ, the Lord

of the covenant who gave the law, became the representative servant of the covenant, perfectly fulfilling it and bearing its judgment in our place.

God is full of surprises. Put us at the center of the story, and it is pretty bleak: the story ends with exile and the confession that God is just in his verdict. No less than the pagan nations, Israel too is found guilty. Adam and Eve had no right to expect anything but condemnation, and yet God surprises them with his gift.

Once the spotlight shifts from us to God, the bad news is overcome by the Good News. Paul reminds us, "And you were dead in trespasses and sins. . . . *But God*, being rich in mercy, because of the great love with which he loved us, even when we were dead in our trespasses, made us alive together with Christ—by grace you have been saved—and seated us with him in heavenly places in Christ Jesus" (Eph. 2:1, 4–5, emphasis added). "*But God . . .*" always turns things around. The plot is reversed and begins moving in an unexpected direction.

The Greatest Story Ever Told

In 1949, Dorothy Sayers (1893–1957), celebrated English playwright, mystery novelist, essayist, and poet described "the greatest story ever told": Christ's incarnation, life, death, and resurrection—as the plotline of Scripture—and then wondered why the churches had exchanged this for bland moralism:

> Official Christianity, of late years, has been having what is known as "a bad press." We are constantly assured that the churches are empty because preachers insist too much upon doctrine—"dull dogma," as people call it. The fact is the precise opposite. It is the neglect of dogma that makes for dullness. The Christian faith is the most exciting drama that ever staggered the imagination of man—and the dogma *is* the drama. . . . This is the dogma we find so dull—this terrifying drama of which God is the victim and the hero. If this is dull, then what, in Heaven's name, is worthy to be called exciting? The people who hanged Christ never, to do them justice, accused Him of being a bore—on the contrary; they thought Him too dynamic to be safe. It has been left for later generations to muffle up that shattering personality and surround Him with an atmosphere of tedium. We have very efficiently pared the claws of the Lion of Judah, certifying Him

"meek and mild," and recommended Him as a fitting household pet for pale curates and pious old ladies.

Sayers contrasts the biblical drama with the usual fare:

> That God should play the tyrant over man is the dismal story of unrelieved oppression; that man should play the tyrant over man is the usual dreary record of human futility; but that man should play the tyrant over God and find Him a better man than himself is an astonishing drama indeed. Now, we may call that doctrine exhilarating or we may call it devastating; we may call it revelation or we may call it rubbish; but if we call it dull, then words have no meaning at all.[1]

In the biblical drama, all of our expectations, assumptions, and cherished ideas are thrown into question. God the judge bears the sentence that his own justice demands. The offended party becomes the redeemer, even as he is subjected to further acts of the most heinous violence from those he redeems. The outcasts become royal heirs, the outsiders become insiders and the insiders outsiders, those who thought they were righteous are in fact condemned and those who were beyond any hope of moral recovery are declared righteous. A strange story, indeed.

"*God justifies the wicked*" (Rom. 4:5, emphasis added). As counterintuitive as it is simple, that claim which lies at the heart of the Good News has brought immeasurable blessing—and trouble—to the church and the world. Be nice, take out the trash, stop nagging your spouse, try to spend more time with your children, don't get into credit card debt, lose some weight, and get some exercise. Every one of these exhortations might be valid. Some of them may even find a legitimate application in a handful of biblical passages. However, it is not the big story. No wonder people—especially younger folks—are bored if this is the "news" that the church has to bring to the world. This kind of news need not come from heaven; there are plenty of earthly sages who can communicate it better than most preachers.

In the usual stories of religion and spirituality, we hear of heroic individuals who did something over and beyond the call of duty. Their example is intended to inspire us, or perhaps to shame us into failing to transform ourselves into noble creatures. But in the story that Jesus tells, it is not the Pharisee, confident in his own righteousness, who went home justified, but the despised tax collector who could not even raise his eyes to heaven but cried out, "Lord, be merciful to me, a sinner" (Luke 18:9–14). It was this simple claim that caused the apostle Paul to look back on all of his zealous obedience as "a Pharisee of Pharisees" and to call it "dung . . . in order that I may gain Christ and be found in him, not having a righteousness that is of my own that comes from the law, but one that comes through faith in Christ, the righteousness from God that depends on faith" (Phil. 3:8–9).

The righteousness *of* God is a command that condemns us all, but the righteousness *from* God is a gift that saves all who believe. This gospel announces that sinners "are justified by his grace as a gift, through the redemption that is in Christ Jesus, whom God put forward as a propitiation by his blood, to be received by faith" (Rom. 3:24–25). God imputes (credits) our sin to Christ and Christ's righteousness to us. "Therefore, since we have been justified by faith, we have peace with God through our Lord Jesus Christ" (Rom. 5:1). This is the simplest news to grasp and yet the most difficult news to accept. Paul considered this doctrine to be so central that he regarded its explicit denial as "anathema"—that is, an act of heresy that the Galatian church was on the verge of committing (Gal. 1:8–9). For Paul, a denial of justification was tantamount to a denial of grace and even to a denial of Christ, "for if justification were through the law, then Christ died for no purpose" (Gal. 2:21).

So God justifies the *wicked*—not those who have done their best yet have fallen short, who might at least be judged acceptable because of their sincerity, but those who at the very moment of being pronounced righteous are in themselves unrighteous. "And to the one who does not work but trusts him who justifies the ungodly, his faith is counted as righteousness, just as David also speaks of the blessing of the one to whom God counts righteousness apart from works . . ." (Rom. 4:5–6). This message sounds bizarre to our natural sense of the way religion and morality work. Isn't the point of religion to get people to try to be better people, to improve their lives, and to please God? How can you say that the only way to be righteous before God is to *stop* working and trust in a God who declares the *ungodly* to be *righteous*? Surely such a message would lead to moral chaos.

As we have seen from the statistics, most Americans—including the majority of those who claim to be Christians—believe that good people go to heaven when they die. The most commonsensical, intuitive, natural conviction of the average person on the street is that God justifies the *godly*. We may have to redefine "godly," of course, to get the bar low enough for generous entry. God's righteousness, justice, and holiness may need to be relaxed a bit, but judging by the polls most Americans think they can make it to the wedding feast dressed in their own righteousness.

"Jesus Christ Is Lord!": The Resurrection as Historical Fact

The crucifixion is not the end of the story; Jesus was also raised from the dead. Jesus Christ "was crucified for our sins and was raised for our justification" (Rom. 4:23). Therefore, we are not only *forgiven*; we are *declared righteous*. The resurrection is not simply an amazing miracle to which we yield our assent; it was the event that secured the objective justification of every sinner who is identified with Christ by faith. So the gospel is not what happens inside of us, which varies from person to person and from week to week, but the news of an objective accomplishment by God that cannot be diminished, altered, improved, or completed by us.

The main thing for generic religion has always been universal, timeless principles. Even in popular culture, a figure like Santa Claus is an important icon at Christmas because the mythology surrounding him teaches a good lesson. If we could only give back some of the love that we are given on a regular basis, there would be peace on earth. Santa, Jesus, Ghandi, and Mother Theresa can be used to make this point. The principles of the major religions would be true, according to many of their adherents, even if the myths surrounding the lives of their famous teachers were not. However, Christianity is not centrally concerned with good lessons and timeless principles that are known, deep down, by everybody. It rivets our attention to an unfolding plot, where God makes promises and fulfills them in spite of human opposition.

Recently, I had several conversations with a network news producer who was intrigued by a passing comment I had made about Christianity standing or falling on the basis of certain historical events. "Isn't religion about the 'magical' aspect of life anyway? Who's to say that one interpretation is right and another is wrong? They're all attempts to wrestle with the realm of mystery." It is a common assumption, especially since the Enlightenment, that faith belongs to the realm of irrationality. It serves an important therapeutic function, but it's not like history or science, where there are right and wrong interpretations. After I went through the historical claim of and evidence for the resurrection, the producer—I'm not making this up to fit the theme of this book—replied, "Interesting. Now that's *news!*" Whether one believes it or not, it is not in the realm of haunted houses and self-help therapies. It is a public claim that requires a response from our minds as well as our hearts, and from everybody, not just from people looking for spirituality and inner peace. Reporting on people's spiritual habits and hobbies is different from reporting historical events of epochal and universal significance.

I had a similar conversation with the late Richard Rorty, a leading philosopher famous for (among other things) his insistence that religious arguments should not be admitted into debates over public policy. While I agreed with him that the Bible is often used by liberals and conservatives to justify ideologies that it does not actually address, I asked him if it would make a difference if Christianity were articulated not on the basis of personal, subjective feeling or pragmatic usefulness but on the basis of its historical claims. After a while, he concluded, "Yes, aside from the question of whether the claims are true, it would make a big difference if one were making public claims that invite public investigation." Of course, no one is neutral in these investigations, I realize. And no one realized that more than Rorty, who said that knowledge is "interpretation all the way down." However, the nature of the Christian claims as public truth removes them from the realm of irrational, subjective, and private mysticism and brings the conversation into the public sphere. In their testimony to Christ, the apostles therefore routinely pointed to the events to which they—and others—were eyewitnesses.

At its heart, Christianity is a gospel—an announcement—that Jesus Christ "was delivered up for our offences and was raised for our justification" (Rom. 4:25). As the head of his body, Christ's resurrection secured the justification of all who trust in him. Only when our conscience is persuaded that God is favorable toward us in Christ can the announcement, "Jesus is Lord!" be greeted as Good News rather than the threat of imminent judgment. He is Lord over death and hell, sin and condemnation.

It is certainly Good News that because of the gospel Christ has sent his Spirit to indwell us as a deposit guaranteeing our final salvation. Nevertheless, the gospel is not that Jesus lives in our heart; it is that he lived for us, died for us, rose for us, reigns for us, and will return for us at the end of the age. The gospel indeed transforms us, but precisely because it is an objective historical fact about what someone else has accomplished for us. It is the news about what happened to *Jesus Christ* as our mediator and representative, in his obedience, sacrifice, and resurrection from the dead.

Even the most skeptical of scholars acknowledge that Christ died on the cross under Roman authority, particularly since this is reported by non-Christian officials and historians at the time. Here is what early Jewish and Roman officials agreed on: (1) Jesus was crucified as a blasphemer under Jewish law and as a troublemaker under Roman law; (2) Jesus died, confirmed by the strict procedures of Roman crucifixion; (3) he was placed in a tomb with Roman and Jewish guards posted (to guard against theft of his body by followers); (4) three days after his death Jesus's tomb was empty; and (5) a widespread commotion broke out in Jerusalem over his whereabouts. These can be pieced together by first century statements from Roman rulers and historians, rabbinical writings, and the Jewish historian Josephus.

From there, theories varied. Jewish leaders (Pharisees) argued that the body had somehow been stolen in spite of the double regiment of Sanhedrin police and Roman soldiers. Romans, treating the whole matter as a troublesome intra-Jewish affair, were so provoked by the empty tomb that they began rounding up anyone and everyone who claimed to have known Jesus. Disappearing bodies did not bode well for the deterrent force of Roman crucifixion. And since we know that the penalty for soldiers abandoning their post was capital punishment, whatever happened on Easter morning so frightened the guard that they gave no thought to their fate at the hands of their generals.

Those who had the means, the motive, and the opportunity to produce Jesus's body—or at least some plausible explanation other than the resurrection—failed to do so. Hence, the uproar. By their own account, not even the disciples greeted the resurrection report with faith. In fact, in his postresurrection appearances Jesus expressed frustration with their slowness in understanding and believing what the prophets had prophesied and he had himself told them to expect concerning his crucifixion and resurrection on the third day. The disciples were not at all disposed to believing, much less creating, a resurrection story.

Of course, the early followers of Jesus came to believe that Jesus had been raised and had appeared to them for forty days, explaining how his death and resurrection were promised throughout the Old Testament. They saw him ascend to the right hand of the Father in glory where he will remain until he returns to judge the living and the

dead. The disciples, who, by their own accounts, had shown themselves to be cowards after Jesus's arrest, were now willing martyrs
for their testimony to the risen Christ and this Good News spread
rapidly, just as Jesus promised, "from Jerusalem to Judea to Samaria
to the uttermost parts of the earth."

As the apostles were brought before Roman authorities, they said
nothing about how Jesus had helped them put their marriages back
together or how they found the gospel helpful and useful in daily living.
There may well have been stories like that to report. However, that was
not their gospel. Rather, they testified to datable events, which they
assumed to have been well-known to their judges. It was not a "religion story," but an international headline of immense world historical
significance. (People aren't persecuted for having an invisible friend
who helps them through personal crises.) They referred the secular
rulers to eyewitnesses who were still living to back up their claim. If
the witnesses only offered good advice, spiritual and moral therapy, or
defended their "product" for its pragmatic usefulness, Rome would have
had no trouble adding another cult to the soup of imperial religion.
However, the claim was that Jesus alone is Lord of the cosmos and
Savior of the world (both titles that Caesar claimed for himself).

Vindicating his claim to be God incarnate, the one by whom the
Father created the world and in whom all things continue to hold
together, Jesus's resurrection from the dead means that the only real
Lord of history—of our own lives—is not only the supreme judge of
all the earth, but the redeemer who invites, "Come to me, all you who
are weary and I will give you rest" (Matt. 11:28). As the last Adam, who
fulfilled the trial and entered God's Sabbath glory as our conquering
head, he alone could offer himself as our everlasting rest.

Think of all the other "lords" to whom we surrender our destinies:
the invisible hand of the market, the government, pharmaceutical
companies and hospitals, and so on. Yet none of these is personal,
benevolent, merciful, or compassionate. Nor are any of these powers
truly sovereign over the personal and impersonal forces that threaten
our ultimate safety. As we have seen especially over the last few years,
the market is not a rational provider; it does not think about us,
plan our lives, work all things together for our salvation, or send us
redemption. The government is a bureaucracy, not a loving shepherd.
It fulfills important responsibilities, but it is hardly worthy of our
ultimate trust. And regardless of how much we invest in vaccines and
medical technology, we will die anyway.

In this context, the announcement that Jesus is Lord means everything and its meaning is determined by the fact that the one who is
enthroned in heaven above all principalities and powers is the same
one who died for our sins and was raised for our justification.

If Jesus Is the Answer, What Is the Question?

I took this subheading from a bumper sticker I have seen a few times.
We throw around slogans that we are often hard pressed to explain
if someone asked us, like, "Are you saved?" "Jesus is the answer" is
meaningless apart from the biblical story. Judging by the standard
diet in churches, popular Christian books, and broadcasts, Jesus is the
answer to *everything*. He fixes broken lives, marriages, relationships;
helps us recover from addictions; relieves stress; teaches us how to
raise positive kids in a negative world; improves our self-esteem; and
boosts our optimism about life.

I am not denying that there are remarkable consequences of belonging to Christ. We are indeed liberated from the bondage as well
as the guilt of our sin. As Christians we have heard amazing cases of
radical conversion and transformation. However, similar accounts can
be found in every religion and even in secular programs. Transformed
lives certainly witness to the power of the gospel, but precisely because the gospel itself is not our imperfect transformation but Christ's
perfect work on our behalf.

Furthermore, Christians continue to fall short of God's glory—
even in their best moments. Christ's saving ministry is sufficient even
to save Peter, who denied Christ three times in the early morning
hours of Good Friday. It is enough to save a believer whose marriage crumbles or who has fallen into serious immorality, as much
as those who have destroyed someone's reputation through gossip, mistreated an employee, robbed an employer, or turned away
a friend in a time of crisis. No less in the middle and at the end
than at the beginning, the believer clings to Christ's righteousness
as the only appropriate attire in the presence of a holy God. The
gospel is not about us or what we do, feel, experience, or think is
important. It affects us at all of these levels, in varying degrees at
various times, but the gospel is always an announcement concerning unrepeatable, unique, and unalterable facts. It is an objective
announcement about that which God has done for us in his Son.

The gospel solves a problem that we do not even know we have apart from the law.

Gentiles do not naturally get the story of redemption, in part because they are not part of the history of Israel. They do not have the sacrifices and the temple, much less the prophecies that directed God's people to the Messiah who will bear the sins of the people. So it comes as news, but the most counterintuitive news possible. Gentiles, by nature, think that they can save themselves by discovering the right principles for overcoming pain, suffering, unhappiness, and immoderate behavior. That was the essence of Greek philosophy: finding the best path to "the good life." Wisdom was basically ethics. They are not looking for a gospel, because they do not believe that they are lost. They are not looking for reconciliation with God, because they do not feel that they are enemies. They are offended by the message of Christ and him crucified, Paul argues in the first two chapters of his letter to the Corinthians. It is not just the answers that Gentiles found (and find) irrelevant, but the questions that provoke them. The gospel had become assimilated to law among Jesus's Jewish contemporaries also, but in the expectation of a revived national theocracy. That is why Paul said that the gospel is a stumbling block to Jews and foolishness to Greeks.

The gospel is unintelligible to most people today, especially in the West, because their own particular stories are remote from the story of creation, fall, redemption, and consummation that is narrated in the Bible. Our focus is introspective and narrow, confined to our own immediate knowledge, experience, and intuition. Trying desperately to get others, including God, to make us happy, we cannot seem to catch a glimpse of the real story that gives us a meaningful role.

From a Christian perspective, we can see this as narcissistic, right? The only problem is that the gospel is usually told today as if the big story were already determined by "this fading age." In the New Testament perspective, there are two ages: "this present age," whose time is running out, and "the age to come," inaugurated by Christ's resurrection and consummated at his return (Matt. 12:32; 24:3; 1 Cor. 2:6; Gal. 1:4). Whatever great or trivial events that form "our world," they take place, as the Preacher would say, "under the sun" (Eccles. 1:3). That is, they are the world as it is, taken as a given rather than a gift, as a fate to be endured as best as possible, with whatever accoutrements—including religion and spirituality—we need in order to cope. But God's story introduces a vertical dimension, raising our eyes from our despair as well as the "high places" that we have erected "to make a name for ourselves," as the infamous architects of the Tower of Babel imagined.

But what if the gospel does not answer our questions—at least the ones that we automatically come up with in the context of our life movie set in this present age under the sun? It is the job of the one presenting the gospel to place people in the biblical setting, provoking questions that they never knew they had before. God's Word gives us the right questions, not just the right answers.

Located in God's story, the problems, anxieties, hopes, aspirations, and plans that we imagined are no longer the most important, although they have a new relative importance in the grand scheme of things. We suddenly find ourselves, as Isaiah did, confronted with a holy God before whom we are "undone"—literally, coming apart at the seams, without any defense. In this situation, we are at God's mercy. He must act if there is going to be genuine resolution to this dilemma. Confronted by the God who is actually there, instead of imagining an idol that we can manage by the right spiritual technology, we begin to ask different questions and have different concerns, experiences, and needs.

No doubt, the passengers on board the *Titanic* would have had a lot of needs, experiences, interests, and plans just minutes before the luxury ship struck an iceberg. Yet on the other side of that fateful event, everything changed. No longer wondering if the stewards would pass by with another glass of champagne or whether it would be too cold to take an evening stroll on the deck, they rushed frantically to their loved ones and looked beyond the narrow horizons of their immediate felt needs for someone to rescue them. It is not surprising that the ship's orchestra, which a short time before was entertaining passengers with "Alexander's Ragtime Band," concluded with "Nearer, My God to Thee," as the luxury liner sank. Why do we wait until the end to take the most important things seriously? The gospel not only addresses *my* guilt, corruption, death, and judgment, but the sheet of death, violence, injustice, and hatred that has been pulled up over the whole creation.

If we try to make the gospel "relevant" and "accessible" to people who are still judging stories, problems, and resolutions in terms of their own life movie, it will never rise above moralistic therapy. It is amazing how stubbornly we deny the reality of death and facing God's judgment even when we are faced with it. Whether facing the death of loved ones or our own "near death" encounters, often we pass quickly from deeper reflection on ultimate issues to return to the cozy familiarity of our self-enclosed cocoon. In this respect, at least, this characteristic of our captivity is not uniquely American. "For the word of the cross is folly to those who are perishing, but to us who are being saved it is the power of God" (1 Cor. 1:18). Greeks consider it foolishness because they are looking for "wisdom," but for those who are being saved, he adds, *Christ* is the epitome of God's wisdom (1 Cor. 2:30–31). When we are placed in God's courtroom, the definition of wisdom—that which is useful for us to know in life—changes. God has a way of creating his own publicity.

So God justifies the wicked—not those who have done their best yet have fallen short, who might at least be judged acceptable because of their sincerity, but those who are at the very moment of being pronounced righteous are in themselves unrighteous. "And to the one who does not work but trusts him who justifies the ungodly, his faith is counted as righteousness, just as David also speaks of the blessing of the one to whom God counts righteousness apart from works . . ." (Rom. 4:5–6).

The claim that God justifies the *wicked* was not only "foolishness to Greeks and a stumbling block to Jews"; it brought enormous controversy to the apostolic church and has continued to do so throughout the history of the church. This surprising truth was officially declared heretical, in fact, by the Roman Catholic Church at the Council of Trent (1545–63). Hopefully, this is not the end of the story. Through continued study of God's Word together, it is hoped that all of us who profess Christ's name will together discern the Good News that God justifies the wicked. "But if it is by grace, it is no longer on the basis of works; otherwise grace would no longer be grace" (Rom. 11:6).

However, Protestants are just as likely today to assume that the gospel gives us something to do rather than an announcement of something that has already been fully, finally, and objectively accomplished for us by God in Jesus Christ. Like the Council of Trent, many Protestants will affirm the *necessity* of grace, but deny its *sufficiency*.

The difference between Roman Catholic and evangelical doctrines of salvation can be summarized as follows: *infused righteousness leading to a process of justification* versus *imputed righteousness leading to a process of sanctification*. According to the former interpretation, justification is a process of becoming righteous. The first justification occurs at baptism, which eradicates both the guilt and corruption of original sin. Due entirely to God's grace, this initial justification infuses grace into the recipient, who then must cooperate with this inherent grace in order to acquire (merit) an increase of this justifying righteousness. The more one cooperates, the more one grows in justification and, if dying in a state of grace, hopes to be accepted before God. This is final justification. So while initial justification is by grace alone, final justification depends on the merits of the believer. If one has cooperated well, there will be fewer punishments to endure in this life and the next; if poorly, there will be greater. God's justice requires satisfaction—not only Christ's, but our own—before we can be welcomed into heaven.

The Good News, however, is that in Jesus Christ our elder brother, God has received the perfect obedience that his law requires. There is nothing left to merit! He has earned every penny in the heavenly estate. We are indeed saved by works—and not by good intentions—but by works that are perfect, complete, and perpetual to every command. However, it is *Christ's* works, not ours, that have secured the eternal inheritance for us.

Paul was not inventing this gospel, which he received directly from the risen Christ; he supports his arguments by appealing to the examples of Abraham and David (especially in Romans 4 and Galatians 2–4). In fact, the familiar prophecy of Isaiah 53 describes this imputation or exchange. The suffering servant bears our sins, suffers in our place, and by his righteous act "will make many to be accounted righteous, and he shall bear their inquities" (v. 11). Our sins are credited to him, and his righteousness to us. In Zechariah 3, there is the prophecy of Joshua the high priest in the heavenly courtroom, with Satan as the prosecuting attorney and the angel of the Lord as his defender. Although condemned in himself, Joshua's filthy clothes are removed and instead he is arrayed in a spotless robe. All of these passages flood the New Testament's testimony to Jesus Christ as "the LORD Our Righteousness" (Jer. 23:5–6; 33:16, with 1 Cor. 2:30–31; 2 Cor. 5:21). "There is now no condemnation for those who are in Christ Jesus" (Rom. 8:1). Nothing remains to be done; all has been accomplished for us by Christ and in him we are already holy and blameless before the Father.

Do we believe that Christ's death and resurrection are the sufficient ground of our acceptance before God and our title to his estate as children and heirs? Or do we think that grace got us started but now we have to do "our part" to remain in God's favor? I often hear believers say that it was wonderful when they first believed. Then and there they were promised forgiveness, God's favor, and eternal life. But over time the message changed. Now it's time to get busy. The gospel is for unbelievers, but Christians need a constant stream of exhortations to keep them going. Yet this is far from the way that the Bible itself reasons. Not only in the first instance, but throughout the Christian life, faith is born and fed by the gospel alone. Christ is sufficient even for the salvation of weak and unfaithful Christians.

The great divide, then, is between an objective, complete, perfect, and finished justification by God alone in Christ alone received through faith alone and a subjective, progressive, incomplete, and unfinished justification by the believer's cooperation with grace.

Don't Follow Your Heart

Faith is not the same as religious experience or pious activity. Rather, it is turning away from both in order to cling to Christ as he is clothed in his gospel. We live in a "follow your heart" culture, where it is simply assumed that this will get us to the right destination. It is this philosophy that yields infidelity in marriage and friendships, because it is simply another way of following our immediate desires without any obligation to God or our neighbors. "Follow your heart" equals "Believe and do whatever you want, no matter what." This idea that the deeper we go into ourselves the cleaner, purer, and truer things get is just a fantasy. If, as Jeremiah, Jesus, and the rest of Scripture teaches, our corrupt hearts are the wellspring of sinful actions, relationships, and structural systems that make us simultaneously victim and perpetrator, then this sentimental greeting card theology of "follow your heart" will just not do.

It is a good thing that we are not allowed to follow our heart as often as we would like, and that there are courts and police officers to back it up. This might sound a little extreme. Surely there are a lot of nice people out there: true enough, and my point is not that people are as terrible as they could possibly be. Rather, it is that we are thoroughly corrupt in every aspect of our existence, and that our hearts are the seat of our thoughts, desires, and actions. If our whole person is born in bondage to sin, then our hearts are in love with that which will ultimately destroy us. There were a lot of otherwise sweet and decent people who purchased, held, and even abused slaves and justified the extermination of other people on the very romantic assumption that their own race was superior. In fact, the Romantic movement was at its peak during the rise of German, English, and American nationalism.

It is not the heart itself that is evil. Rather, it has been *corrupted*. Our hearts simply follow that which they desire. The problem is that ever since the fall we desire that which brings death. Our minds are fallen, too. The question is not whether we follow our minds rather than our hearts, but whether simply following the path that comes naturally to us is in fact in our best interest. Of course, there is such a thing as falling in love and romance, but we wouldn't even fall in love with someone else unless the other person held some surprises. If we really followed our heart, we would try to find someone totally compatible—in other words, satisfying the instincts, life plans, goals, dreams, and preferences that *we* think are most important. This is the essence of narcissism and it does not mean that we are always as bad as we could possibly be, but that we are enslaved to the myopic interest in what we already know, experience, feel, believe, and do. Most people who fall in love do so after they have had to get used to a personality quite different from their own and have been introduced to a whole new set of ideas about a good life other than what they would have chosen for themselves. Genuine romance requires being opened up to a shared life with others who challenge us to think, feel, and do things that would not even have occurred to us before.

If truth is whatever suits us, we will never actually bump into anything interesting. What's the point of searching, investigating, hoping, or even living if there is nothing to find except one's own reflection in the mirror? Imagine if the real world were nothing but billions of subjective worlds that were created by each person's act of will? Sounds like an episode of *Twilight Zone*, doesn't it? Like kids imagining a holiday without their parents, we think that it would be nice to inhabit a world of the individual, by the individual, and for the individual, but it would be its own hell. Left to ourselves, nothing will ever come to us from outside our own head, heart, experience, or relationships. We will never be disrupted from our dull, banal life. We will never be disoriented or reoriented to something grand, either called on the carpet or led through an undiscovered door into a new creation. We will never find out we were wrong or be amazed at something we never knew before or even dreamed possible. In short, if we just follow our heart we will in truth be led along by the vain images and aspirations of this fading age. Why resign ourselves to a walk-on role in a movie with car chases, sex, and pyrotechnics but without any real plot when there is a role in God's drama? If we are looking for a real drama, we need to follow God's script, not our heart. God is the creator and infallible interpreter of reality, not us. We know that we have really connected with reality when we are surprised by it. We know that we have actually encountered the God who is there when he is not who we thought he was and eludes captivity to our own idolatrous imagination.

The Gospel Transforms

The gospel transforms us in heart, mind, will, and actions precisely because it is not itself a message about our transformation. Nothing that I am or that I feel, choose, or do qualifies as Good News. On my best days, my experience of transformation is weak, but the gospel is an announcement of a certain state of affairs that exists because of something in God, not something in me; something that God has done, not something that I have done; the love in God's heart which he has shown in his Son, not the love in my heart that I exhibit in my relationships. Precisely as the Good News of a completed, sufficient, and perfect work of God in Christ accomplished for me and outside of me in history, the gospel is "the power of God unto salvation" not only at the beginning but throughout the Christian life. In fact, our sanctification is simply a lifelong process of letting that Good News sink in and responding appropriately: becoming the people whom God says that we already are in Christ.

While we can change our outward behavior through various techniques, programs, and principles, we cannot change our hearts. If there is to be a new creation, it must be—like the first one—a word spoken by the Triune God *ex nihilo*—out of nothing. In that first creation, God did not work with any preexisting material. His approval ("and it was very good") was not his first word, but followed from his declaration, "Let there be . . . ! And there was . . ."

In the same way, God does not find anything in the ungodly to warrant his justifying verdict, but the verdict *creates* the state of affairs. When God declares us righteous while we are still unrighteous (justification), he immediately—by this same word—begins that process of inner renewal that actually makes us righteous (sanctification). "For God, who said, 'Let light shine out of darkness,' has shone in our hearts to give the light of the knowledge of the glory of God in the face of Jesus Christ" (2 Cor. 4:6). But the *verdict* comes first! First God declares us righteous, on the basis of Christ's obedience, death, and resurrection, and then he begins to conform us to Christ's image. This is what we find so counterintuitive. Shouldn't it be the other way around? A judge *declares* someone to be righteous after he or she has been *found* innocent. In this case, however, God finds us innocent—and more than innocent, perfectly righteous—because someone else's record has been credited to us.

"Spirituality" is as successful as materialism in feeding our narcissism. Keeping us preoccupied with our inner self and its experiences, morality, and activity, the "search for the sacred" is as godless as atheism. There are plenty of resources on the market to feed our culture's anxiety over self-improvement. But they are all different ways of dressing up the old Adam. Furthermore, their moralistic prescriptions never actually reduce stress but pile more expectations upon us to try to make ourselves acceptable to God.

We are not sick, but spiritually dead. We are not good people with room for improvement, but the ungodly. We are not children who need a little direction, but lost. The gospel comes not to help us get our act together, fixing us up for a night on the town, making us more respectable to ourselves or to others. Rather, it comes to kill us and make us alive as completely new creatures. Not a new and improved self, but a self buried and raised with Christ, is the gospel's message of genuine transformation.

Moralistic, therapeutic spirituality is part of that narcissistic complex about which Paul warned Timothy that makes us "lovers of self . . . , having an appearance of godliness, but denying its power" (2 Tim. 3:2, 5). And the power that it denies is the announcement of free justification in Christ, apart from works. The power of God does not lie in programs, strategies, self-help formulas, seven steps to a better life, or political reform. Like someone trapped in a burning building, we cannot rescue ourselves. *There is no hope inside of us!* There are no inner resources or possibilities—no Archimedean point at which we might pry ourselves open to God and begin to climb the stairway to heaven. Our whole nature is in bondage to sin, so we cannot even repair our condition by an act of will. *Our only hope lies outside of us, from the God who rescues us in his Son!* Paul said that he was "not ashamed of the gospel, for it is the power of God for salvation to everyone who believes . . ." (Rom. 1:16).

As counterintuitive as it seems, embracing the gospel as God's free justification of the ungodly, apart from works, is the only possible source not only for our legal acceptance before God but for the good works that are its fruit. Only when we know that we are condemned in ourselves but righteous in Christ are we free for the first time to love God and our neighbors. Responding to both out of gratitude for a free gift, we are truly freed to love and enjoy them instead of using them for our own ends.

This gospel—the Good News of God's justification of sinners in Christ—is not a means to a greater end. It is not one theme among many. It is not something we use in order to go on to something more important, more relevant, and more practical. It is the ocean that we swim in, the air that we breathe, the identity that defines us. Marxists may apply their doctrines in different ways depending on new circumstances and contexts, but they always return to the story of class warfare, just as capitalists respond to every economic crisis by invoking the invisible hand of the market. So why shouldn't Christians return again and again to the biblical drama as their defining narrative regardless of changing times? The gospel story does not change, not because it is timeless but because it reports historical events that have already happened. Like the Battle of Waterloo, they cannot be undone. Christ's work of redemption is a completed fact in the past, with continuing effects in the present.

The Bible's "big story" does not *make* a point; it *is* the point. It is interesting that when Jesus converses with Martha at the tomb of her brother and Jesus's dear friend, Lazarus, Jesus says to her, "Your brother will rise again" (John 11:23). Martha treated it simply as a doctrinal claim about the resurrection of the dead at the end of the age, a belief that she shared with many Jews of her day. "I know that he will rise again in the resurrection on the last day," she replied (v. 24). Martha may have wondered if this was a good time for a theological discussion or perhaps she thought that Jesus was offering the kind of faithful condolence that we appropriately offer to grieving friends and relatives. However, Jesus was pressing her to confess something more: "Jesus said to her, 'I *am* the resurrection and the life. Whoever believes in *me*, though he die, yet shall he live. . . . Do you believe *this*?" (vv. 25–26, emphasis added). Understandably, Martha's focus was on Lazarus and her own grief, but Jesus put it back on himself precisely because in doing so Martha's *greatest* need (and her brother's) was addressed. As a result, Martha confessed Jesus as the resurrection and the life—and was justified.

The gospel is not a general belief in heaven and hell or hope for a better life beyond; it is not even confidence in a resurrection at the end of the age. It is the announcement that Jesus Christ himself is our life, for he is our peace with God. He does not merely *show* us the way; he *is* the way, the truth, and the life (John 14:6).

Saved from What?

A lot of different answers are given to this question today. For some Christians, it means that in Jesus Christ God has triumphed over the powers of evil, death, and hell, liberating captives from the oppression and violence that especially stalk the poor and weak in this age. As we have seen—and will especially see in the next chapter—there are a lot of biblical passages to support this view. Another prominent interpretation, especially in the early church, was that Christ saved us by becoming flesh and undoing Adam's corruption of our nature in his obedient life, death, and resurrection. Again, this is an important aspect of Christ's mission, as I have already suggested. Another dominant view understands Christ's work primarily as a payment to God's offended dignity, like the penance paid to a king after having reproached his honor in public. This view (associated with the medieval theologian Anselm) properly focuses attention on the objective offense of sin against God, which requires satisfaction, but the Bible speaks of the cross as a satisfaction of God's justice, not of his dignity. For others, Christ's death reestablished God's moral government in the earth, demonstrating his righteousness and discouraging sin. Many see Christ's work chiefly as a moral example that shows us how much God loves us and inspires us to love each other. All of these answers have a certain degree of plausibility in particular passages in Scripture. That's why each is identified with a distinct theory of the atonement in the history of theology.

However, Christ's work is completed in the context of the sacrificial system of the Old Testament. He is the "Lamb of God who takes away the sin of the world"; the kinsman-redeemer who purchases his brothers and sisters out of the slave market; the Lord who bears the servant's curse, propitiates the Father's wrath, and reconciles us to God. *Because he died as the vicarious sacrifice for sinners*, he has conquered the evil powers, undone Adam's transgression and fulfilled his mission, demonstrated God's righteous government and inexpressible love, and vindicated his honor in history. *Yet all of these other important aspects of Christ's saving work can only be true if in fact his vicarious, substitutionary sin-bearing lies at its heart.* What are we saved from? *God!* We are saved from God's wrath by God himself, because God is love.

Christ's vicarious death as a subsitute for sinners pulls everything else in its wake. Because Christ has borne our curse—the sentence imposed by the law—death's sting is removed. "The sting of death is sin, and the power of sin is the law. *But thanks be to God, who gives us the victory through our Lord Jesus Christ*" (1 Cor. 15:56–57, emphasis added). "For the wages of sin is death, *but the free gift of God is eternal life in Jesus Christ our Lord*" (Rom. 6:23, emphasis added). Even the view of Christ's work as victory over the evil powers is grounded in his legal satisfaction of God's justice: God has "*forgiven* us all our trespasses, by *canceling the record of debt* that stood against us with its *legal demands*. This he set aside, nailing it to the cross." But only in performing this legal act can it be added that Christ thereby "*disarmed the rulers and authorities* and *put them to open shame by triumphing over them in him*" (Col. 2:13–15, emphasis added). In going to the root of the crisis—the curse of sin and death—Christ's sacrifice accomplished everything that is necessary for the new creation.

The cross of Christ is not "cosmic child abuse," as some have suggested, precisely because it was not only a demonstration of God's righteousness and love or a satisfaction of his offended dignity but the full satisfaction of his just and holy law. If it is *only* a demonstration of God's love, then Christ's death could be considered more of an object lesson in divine cruelty than love. Yet the wonder of the cross is that the same God whose holy character requires justice also paid the price himself. Now *that* is love! Furthermore, it means that his self-sacrifice is not repeatable. We may be called to sacrifice our own interests—perhaps even our own life—for the temporal *good* of our neighbors, but we will never be called to sacrifice our lives for the *sins* of others. God's gift of his Son is the sacrifice to end all such sacrifices.

The Father did not take his frustration out on his Son, but sent the Son of his love because of his love for a world of enemies. Fur-

thermore, Jesus was not a passive victim, but the willing party to
the eternal covenant he made with the Father to save his people. "I
am the good shepherd. The good shepherd lays down his life for the
sheep" (John 10:11). His life is his own to give up. "No one takes it
from me, but I have authority to lay it down, and I have authority to
take it up again" (v. 18). The big story is the triumph of God's love
over our hatred, his mercy over our guilt, his life over our death, and
his glory over our pride. *God outloves our hatred!*

The goal of the cross was not simply to punish but to restore. If we
dig beneath all the symptoms of our troubled lives and our distressed
world, the root of it all is a broken covenant. That is the wound of the
cosmos that we cannot heal, but that God has healed by establishing
peace through the cross of his Son. We will never exhaust the richness
of this gospel because it reverberates into every nook and cranny of
our lives, our history, and our world.

The Good News is that "salvation is of the Lord" (Jonah 2:9). "So
then it depends not on human will or exertion, but on God, who has
mercy" (Rom. 9:16). "And those whom he predestined he also called,
and those whom he called he also justified, and those whom he justified he also glorified" (Rom. 8:30). There is no link in that golden
chain that has our fingerprints on it. God chose us before we chose
him; God saved us while we were enemies; God justifies us while we
are ungodly; God makes us alive together with Christ even while we
are dead—and he even gives us the faith to receive all of this! Paul
can therefore only exclaim,

> What then shall we say to these things? If God is for us, who can be
> against us? He who did not spare his own Son but gave him up for us
> all, how will he not also with him graciously give us all things? Who
> shall bring any charge against God's elect? It is God who justifies.
> Who is to condemn? Christ Jesus is the one who died—more than
> that, who was raised—who is at the right hand of God, who indeed
> is interceding for us. Who shall separate us from the love of Christ?

Paul's answer is as clear as it is astonishingly wonderful: *nothing*
"will be able to separate us from the love of God in Christ Jesus our
Lord" (Rom. 8:31–35, 39). Whatever else is happening in our lives or in
the daily headlines, the news just does not get any better than that.

4

GETTING
THE STORY STRAIGHT

The better newspapers have a staff of fact-checkers. Of course, that does not eliminate all of the errors, but it helps—and it strengthens the paper's credibility. Just a little sloppiness in reporting, a little misunderstanding here or distortion there and the story becomes misleading. If credibility is important for reporting daily events, then it is even greater when it comes to the big story. We not only have to get the gospel *out*; we have to get it *right*.

Knowing all the names, events, and a battery of Bible verses does not mean that we understand the plot. In this chapter, we will accompany the disciples along the route of the Last Adam in his trial and victory parade into God's Sabbath rest. As we will see, the disciples thought that they had their facts straight. They thought that they knew what the journey from the backcountry of Galilee to Jerusalem meant. But they didn't—at least until, by God's grace, they did.

On the Way to Jerusalem

It's not quite California, but there are a lot of highways in the Bible. There is the highway that the forerunner of the Messiah would build, for example. The message and ministry of John the Baptist are prophesied in the last two chapters of the Old Testament (Malachi 3–4). But when Jesus arrives, nobody seems to be really waiting for him. Sure, a lot of people are *preparing* for him, especially the Pharisees, busying themselves with serious rules upon rules for getting Israel's act together so that Messiah can appear. But preparing is different from *waiting*. The prophets had done their job as covenant prosecutors. The trial was over. God was vindicated in his judgment to send Israel into exile, as a landowner evicting tenants, and the Pharisees themselves recognized that the nation was still in exile under Roman oppressors, a half-hearted people, and a tragicomic usurper of the Davidic throne—Caesar's lapdog, Herod.

Israel's national covenant with God at Sinai in which they promised, "All this we will do" (Exod. 19:8), was in tatters. In view of the obvious facts of the case, the religious leaders should not have encouraged a moral rearmament campaign ("all this we will *really* do this time"), but repentance: a radical rethinking of the whole journey. They should have taken a different highway at the turnoff that appeared with Jesus's advent. This is the intersection that meets at the Jordan River when John the Baptist, highway-builder for the Messiah, points away from himself to "the Lamb of God who takes away the sin of the world" (John 1:23–34). Aside from a few others (Mary, of course, but also Elizabeth, Anna, and Zacharias—after he had a run-in with an angel), it seems that this rather odd and austere prophet was the only one who was really waiting for Jesus Christ. He knew, as Jeremiah prophesied, "the new covenant . . . will not be like the covenant that I made with your fathers at Sinai, which you broke even though I was a husband to you" (Jer. 31:31). This covenant would be based on the faithfulness of God alone, through the work of his Messiah for his people.

But from then on, Jesus gathers fellow travelers whom he will lead to Zion (which is none other than himself) and the people he calls were not waiting for him. Isn't that striking? He is always a stranger who calls: "Adam, where are you?" But now he is also the covenant servant who finally answers back in our name, "Here I am."

First, there are the unlikely folks who will become the twelve apostles: uncouth fishermen, thieving tax collectors, and the like. Second, there are the real outsiders—promiscuous women (one a Samaritan to boot), "publicans and sinners," as well as the lame, sick, blind, and diseased—all of whom were forbidden from entering the temple precincts. Jesus calls the disciples while they were doing something else: their daily routine. In fact, in one of his parables, he said that a lot of people who were invited to the wedding feast offered as their regrets that they were too busy with "life" to actually become recipients of true life (Matt. 22:1–14). Jesus's parables point to the rejection of Christ and his kingdom by Israel's religious leaders and its being given to sinners and outsiders instead. It is interesting that whenever Jesus tells his parables of the kingdom the religious leaders change the subject. In this instance, for example, instead of asking Jesus for further explanation of this profound invitation to the wedding feast, they try to trap him in a legal question about tax policies (vv. 15–22). They moved the big news to the back page and put the supposedly more pressing and relevant issues of daily life in the headline. The kingdom that Christ was inaugurating was not as interesting, relevant, and useful as the one that they had come to expect.

In his *Heidelberg Disputation*, Martin Luther contrasted the "theology of the cross" with "theologies of glory"; the former embraces God as he is clothed in the humility of Golgotha while the latter looks for a direct sight of God in his blinding majesty.

Even the disciples assumed that Christ was going to Jerusalem in order to inaugurate a kingdom of glory, restoring the old covenant theocracy by driving out the pagan overlords and their corrupt servants among the Jewish establishment. Like aids to a political candidate on the bus from the backwoods to the big city, they thought that Jerusalem meant power, glory, and the inauguration of the kingdom of the Messiah with fanfare.

Even when Jesus prepared them for his sacrificial death, they changed the subject and Peter even rebuked Jesus for being a negative thinker. After Jesus fed the five thousand as the Bread of Life from heaven Peter offered that marvelous confession of Jesus: "You are the Christ of God" (Luke 9:20). On the heels of this confession, Jesus foretells his crucifixion and resurrection (vv. 21–22). In Mark's account we read, "And he said this plainly. And Peter took him aside and began to rebuke him" (Mark 8:32). Evidently, "Christ of God" did not mean for Peter—at least at this point—the sin-bearing Lamb. For Peter, the goal of the journey was glory rather than shame. "But turning and seeing his disciples, he rebuked Peter and said, 'Get behind me, Satan! For you are not setting your mind on the things of God, but on the things of man'" (Mark 8:33). Echoing Satan's temptation to get Jesus to go around the cross instead of through it to glory—in other words, the opportunity to have his best life now—Peter was unwittingly trying to distract Jesus from his mission. Jesus went on to indicate to his disciples that this journey is a cross story, not a glory story, and anyone who wants to follow him must get that story right (vv. 34–38).

Even after Peter (with James and John) beheld the transfiguration of Christ on the mountain, with Moses and Elijah attesting to Jesus Christ (Luke 9:28–36), he does not get the point. Jesus again tells the disciples, this time with greater emphasis, "'Let these words sink into your ears: The Son of Man is about to be delivered into the hands of men.' But they did not understand this saying, and it was concealed from them, so that they might not perceive it. And they were afraid to ask him about this saying" (vv. 43–45, emphasis added). When a Samaritan village rejected their preaching of the Good News, James and John (the "sons of thunder") ask Jesus, "'Lord, do you want us to tell fire to come down from heaven and consume them?' But he turned and rebuked them. And they went on to another village" (vv. 51–56).

Do you see a pattern here? In spite of the fact that Peter has offered a marvelous confession of Jesus as the Christ of God, and his repeated reference to his crucifixion, they are theologians of glory. They do not expect danger, suffering, and peril up ahead, but the inauguration of the King of the Jews, in regal splendor. In his second coming, Jesus will come in glory and power, judgment and wrath, but now he comes in weakness, suffering, humiliation, and a sin-bearing death.

In fact, a dispute broke out among the Twelve over cabinet posts (Luke 22:24). In Mark's account, James and John vie for the honor of being enthroned on Jesus's left and right, but Jesus replies, "You do not know what you are asking. Are you able to drink the cup that I drink, or to be baptized with the baptism with which I am baptized?" Imagining that Jesus was referring to an inaugural ball, they answered eagerly, "We are able" (Mark 10:35–39). Sure, it will be challenging; there is a lot to fix, after all. Caesar is powerful and the priests and most powerful rulers in Jerusalem are in cahoots with his corrupt and oppressive regime. It will take strategy and dependence on God, but we can do it—with Jesus at the helm. This is their thinking as they near Jerusalem. Jesus appears befuddled by their utter confusion concerning his mission. James and John did not know what they were asking: namely, to drink the cup of the Father's wrath and to be baptized in the fury of his justice. They missed the point, so Jesus added, "For even the Son of Man came not to be served but to serve, and to give his life as a ransom for many" (v. 45). Still, blank stares. It is as if Jesus was speaking gibberish.

Whenever Jesus tells them about the cross that they will bear, they are all ears: not really knowing what he is talking about, they nevertheless responded affirmatively. They thought they could handle their own burdens. "What Would Jesus Do?" is something that they thought they were ready to answer if anyone asked. It is the work that Jesus alone could do *for them*—his death and resurrection—that they found beside the point.

After entering Jerusalem, Jesus tells the Twelve of his impending death for a third time: " 'See, we are going up to Jerusalem, and everything that is written about the Son of Man by the prophets will be accomplished. For he will be delivered over to the Gentiles and will be mocked and shamefully treated and spit upon. And after flogging him, they will kill him, and on the third day he will rise.' But they understood none of these things" (Luke 18:31–34). They saw Jesus as a character in their story of Israel, rather than seeing themselves—and Israel—as characters in the story of Jesus.

Surely everything would fall into place in the upper room, as Jesus instituted the Last Supper, inaugurating his last will and testament that will make them beneficiaries of heaven's riches upon his death. With the bleating of thousands of sheep in the Jerusalem streets for Passover in the background, surely now they would recognize the purpose of Christ's mission. Yet even in this room, Jesus tells Peter,

> "Simon, Simon, behold, Satan demanded to have you, that he might sift you like wheat, but I have prayed for you that your faith may not fail. And when you have turned again, strengthen your brothers." Peter said to him, "Lord, I am ready to go with you both to prison and to death." Jesus said, "I tell you, Peter, the rooster will not crow this day, until you deny three times that you know me." (Luke 22:31–34)

At the arrest of Jesus, one of his disciples drew his sword and cut off the ear of the high priest's servant. "But Jesus said, 'No more of this!' And he touched his ear and healed him" (Luke 22:51). Right to the end, the disciples imagined that they were characters in an unfolding drama of geopolitics, not realizing that Jesus's mission in his first coming was to give his own life for everlasting redemption. It was a war, to be sure, but not the kind of military conquest that they had envisioned. And, of course, Peter did deny his master three times before daybreak (vv. 54–65).

Even after the cross, the disciples did not understand the road they were on. Just as Jesus was a stranger when he first called the disciples away from their daily chores, he met up with them on the Emmaus road after the resurrection and they were kept from recognizing him (Luke 24:13–16). God is never *found*; he *finds* us. As the Good Shepherd, "The Son of Man came to seek and to save that which was lost" (Luke 19:10 with Ezek. 34:16). Although "no one seeks for God" (Rom. 3:11, quoting Pss. 14:1–3 and 53:1–3), Paul quotes Isaiah 65:1: "I have been found by those who did not seek me; I have shown myself to those who did not ask for me" (Rom. 10:20). Christ calls those who are not prepared, are not waiting, do not get it, and are busy doing other things.

In this case, the disciples on the road to Emmaus were busy mourning their master's death and trying to pick up the pieces of their lives in the wake of their disillusionment. They told the stranger, "But we hoped that he was the one to redeem Israel" (Luke 24:21). They had fixed their hopes on the right person, but they did not understand what "redeem" really means. Jesus responded, "O foolish ones, and slow of heart to believe all that the prophets have spoken! Was it not necessary that the Christ should suffer these things and enter into his glory?" (vv. 25–26). It was not glory first, but suffering and then glory, that the prophets foretold. Jesus is the suffering servant of Isaiah 53, who bears the sins of many and justifies the wicked. First the cross, then the resurrection; first suffering in this age and then sharing in Christ's victory as we enter the Sabbath rest in his train. "And beginning with Moses and all the Prophets, he interpreted to them in all the Scriptures the things concerning himself" (v. 27).

We will return to these last days before Jesus's ascension, but for now the important point is that Jesus is not only the central character of the entire biblical drama, but that he was accomplishing our redemption even while the disciples were missing the point. They were not coredeemers. They did not help Jesus to bring in the kingdom. Eventually, they would become *witnesses* to Christ's triumph, but they could not point to any contribution of their own along the way for its fulfillment. Like us, they were recipients of his kingdom labors and like us they entered the Sabbath rest behind him, in triumphal procession. Getting this story right is the key to understanding the Bible. It is the key to becoming Christians, disciples whose eyes have been opened by Christ, through his Spirit, to the marvelous riches of the mission that he has accomplished. The disciples followed Jesus. They sought to learn the wisdom of his ways and imitate his example. However, they missed the most important elements that true discipleship entailed. They had misunderstood the point of the journey. They failed to realize that the most important part of following Jesus was realizing that they could not go everywhere that he was going; could not do everything that he alone could accomplish; and could not even understand why he had come, apart from the work of the Spirit opening their hearts to recognize Christ in all the Scriptures. The most important things that had to be done for the establishment of this kingdom Jesus had to do by himself. In fact, the disciples had fled for their own lives.

Yet Christ came to them, as he comes to us, tenderly healing our blindness and deafness, leading us not only by his example but *to himself* as the source of forgiveness and everlasting life. Only when we see Christ's person and work at the center of this unfolding drama can we read the map of redemptive history right side up. And with those disciples along the Emmaus road, we say to each other each time we gather to hear God's Word, "Did not our hearts burn within us while he talked to us on the road, while he opened to us the Scriptures?" (Luke 24:32).

Close, but Not Quite: Popular Misconceptions of the Gospel

Like the Old Testament, the New Testament proclaims the mighty acts of God and then tells us what they mean in the grand scheme of things. The Gospels tell us what Jesus did; the Epistles flesh out the meaning and significance of his ministry for our faith, worship, and practice. Just as the disciples needed Jesus to reinterpret the unfolding drama of his mission, the churches addressed by the apostles needed to have their doctrinal misconceptions corrected. And so do we.

In the light of everything I've said so far, the Good News is that God has fulfilled his promise that he made to Israel and to the world by sending his Son for the forgiveness of sins and the inauguration of his new creation. We have seen how Jesus interpreted the Old Testament with himself at the center and in his postresurrection instruction (especially in Luke 24), he deepened this approach as he prepared his disciples to be his witnesses to all nations. In their transition from disciples to apostles, Jesus's students seem finally to have understood the gospel, since all of the examples of apostolic preaching that Luke records in the book of Acts exhibit a promise-fulfillment pattern with Christ at the center. Jesus Christ is the sin-bearing substitute for sinners promised in the Law, the Prophets, and the Psalms: crucified and raised on the third day.

This constitutes the gospel that spread rapidly from Jerusalem to Judea, Samaria, and the uttermost parts of the earth. This is Peter's message (Acts 2:1–41; 3:11–26; 4:5–12), provoking the Jewish council to forbid speaking "in this name" of Jesus (4:13–17). Yet when Peter and the others reported this decision, the church erupted with praise to God and repeated back with even greater boldness the Good News of Christ's fulfillment of God's promise (vv. 23–31). Finding themselves once more on trial before the council, the apostles again openly declared the gospel concerning Christ's death and resurrection for salvation (Acts 5:22–32). "And every day in the temple, and in every house, they did not cease teaching and preaching Jesus as the Christ" (v. 42).

This was the content of Stephen's sermon at his execution, as he recounted the history from Abraham to the exodus to Israel's rebellion in the wilderness, all the way to Jesus Christ as the true tabernacle of God (Acts 7:1–53). It was the content of Philip's witness to the Ethiopian treasurer who was reading Isaiah 53 concerning the suffering servant (Acts 8:26–40).

The Good News of Jesus Christ as the fulfillment of the Scriptures was the content of Paul's first sermon in Acts 13, recounting Israel's history that led to the Son of David in whom there is now "forgiveness of sins." "And by him everyone who believes is justified from all things from which you could not be justified by the law of Moses" (Acts 13:13–39). Gentiles, in fact, "begged that these words might be preached to them the next Sabbath" (v. 42). "Now when the Gentiles heard this, they rejoiced in the word of the Lord. And as many as had been ordained to eternal life believed" (v. 48). Example after example confirms the point that the heart of apostolic preaching was that God had fulfilled his promise to the patriarchs and prophets in his Son's death and resurrection.

Although there are allusions to this remarkable story in popular preaching and evangelism today, one wonders if it can be said that it forms the central content. Even in conservative Protestant circles today, the gospel is popularly summarized with formulas, definitions, and phrases that are not even implied in the New Testament. In fact, these phrases shift the focus from Christ back to us. I will mention a few examples. What they all share in common is a tendency to identify salvation (hence, the gospel) with our own experience of conversion rather than with the news of Christ's objective work in history. "Getting saved" comes to mean "what happened to me when I said yes to Jesus," rather than the announcement of God's triumph at the cross. Remembering the day that I "got saved" was meant to anchor my assurance more than the actual event that secured my salvation. I recall as a teenager sharing my enthusiasm for the truths I was learning especially in Paul's Letter to the Romans. "Son, when were you saved?" my pastor asked, as if he was worried that I might not be converted. I don't think I was being cavalier in my response; it just came to me: "Two thousand years ago."

Of course, we are justified through faith and conversion is the reality of every believer (as I explain below). However, the gospel is not how we become Christians; it is the message *about Christ* that brings about conversion. Here are a few examples of how the gospel is often defined in our circles today.

1. "A personal relationship with God"

Nowhere do we find the apostles proclaiming the gospel as an invitation to have a personal relationship with God. After all, they presupposed that *everyone* has a personal relationship with God already. In fact, our major problem is that we *do* have a relationship with God: the relationship of a guilty defendant before a just judge.

Offering the gospel as a personal relationship with God assumes that one is currently in a neutral situation, lacking the joy of knowing God. Or perhaps, if not neutral, this condition is thought of in terms of separation, a breaking off of communication. However, we have seen that all people know God, but suppress this truth in unrighteousness. Our problem is not that we are not on speaking terms with God (or vice versa), but that God is declaring his righteousness and we are shaking our fist in his face. As Paul points out in Ephesians 2:1–9, the problem that the gospel addresses is the fact that we are born into the world "dead in trespasses and sins," "children of wrath," and enemies of God.

So the gospel does not offer the *possibility* of a personal relationship with God, but announces a *different* relationship with God based on Christ! Instead of enemies, we have been reconciled through Christ's sacrifice (Rom. 5:8–11). "Therefore, having been justified by faith, we have peace with God through our Lord Jesus Christ" (Rom. 5:1).

2. *"Asking Jesus into your heart"*

God has used the truth contained in such formulas, especially the confession of God's holiness, our sin, and faith in Christ's saving work. However, to equate salvation with Jesus's taking up residence in one's heart is, at best, a half-truth. The gospel is that Christ has borne our guilt and has been raised for our justification and life, interceding now at the Father's right hand. It is this objective work of Christ outside of us, even now defending us in heaven from every accusation of Satan, that makes the gospel truly Good News even for us as we struggle in the Christian life. "Asking Jesus into your heart" simply does not answer the problem identified in the Scriptures.

My main crisis is not that Jesus is not in my heart, but that I am— with the rest of humanity—"in Adam," and the gospel is that through faith in the gospel I am—with my coheirs—now "in Christ." I am the one, rather than Jesus, who needs to be relocated! The New Testament does indeed teach that the *Holy Spirit* is sent by the Father and the Son to indwell believers. However, this indwelling of the Spirit is saving only because it unites us to Christ, the incarnate Son who reigns in heaven.

Salvation by asking Jesus into your heart typically assumes that the Good News is merely something that God offers, but the hearer is then commanded to do something—however small—in order to actually make this salvation effective. As with the previous misconception, there is some truth here: We are justified *through faith*. However, even this faith is a gift of God (Eph. 2:8–9). When people are given the impression that they are saved by praying a prayer, we can easily forget that it is the Spirit who gives us the faith to desire, much less to pray for, God's mercy. The focus shifts from the gospel itself, through which the Spirit gives us faith, to the act of faith itself.

The most important criticism of this definition of the gospel is that it is not found in Scripture. No one is called in the New Testament to pray "the sinner's prayer," asking Jesus to come into his or her heart. Especially in Acts, this is the pattern: God's judgment is announced on all people; the gospel is proclaimed as Christ's fulfillment of the Scriptures, and many, convicted of their sins and the Good News of salvation in Christ, believe, are baptized, and are thereby added to the church.

3. *"Making Jesus your personal Lord and Savior"*

This is another expression that is not found in Scripture. In fact, the Good News is so good precisely because it is simply an announcement of *what is already in fact the case*: "This Jesus God has raised up, of which we are all witnesses. Therefore being exalted to the right hand of God, and having received from the Father the promise of the Holy Spirit, he poured out this which you now see and hear. . . . Therefore let all the house of Israel know assuredly that *God has made this Jesus*, whom you crucified, *both Lord and Christ"* (Acts 2:32–33, 36, emphasis added).

We all want to be and to do something rather than to be made and to receive our identity from above. It is a blow to our spiritual ego to be told that everything has already been done. Yet that is the glory of the gospel! That is why it is Good News. Imagine what would have happened if God had waited until Israel made God Lord and Savior before he liberated them from Egypt! It was because he had elected Israel, set his love on her, and had mercy on her as he heard her cries under severe oppression—in other words, *because he was already Lord and Savior*—that he fulfilled his promise. "Lord and Savior" is simply who God is, not something that we make him to be for us. In fact, he was reigning and saving us while we were "ungodly," "while we were still sinners," even "while we were enemies" (Rom. 5:6–10).

Faith *receives*; it does not *make*. Only God's declarative word creates. When God created the world, he did not say, "Let it be possible!" He said, "Let there be light! And it was so." It is certainly true that we must receive Christ. Yet it is because he has first received us. "But as many as received him, to them he gave the right to become the children of God, to those who believe in his name, who were born not of blood, nor of the will of the flesh, nor of the will of man, but of God" (John 1:12–13).

To be sure, there is more to the gospel than salvation from hell. The cross is not simply God's way of forgiving sinners, but of conquering the demonic forces and structures that yield oppression and violence. And it's certainly true that the gospel has often been reduced to a simplistic and individualistic message that misses the sweeping grandeur of Christ's redemptive historical achievement. It is not just "fire insurance," but the way in which the Triune God fulfills his promise of a new creation in spite of human rebellion. However, this broadening of the gospel extends today, to include not only the fuller aspects of Christ's work, but the works of believers as somehow redemptive. We hear a lot these days about our being "coredeemers," completing Christ's work of redeeming love in the world. As the meaning of "gospel" expands to anything and everything that flows from the gospel (and perhaps many things that do not), the meaning of "the ministry" expands to include virtually any activity of Christians conducted under the auspices of the church or in the name of Christ.

In this case, Christ becomes primarily a moral example rather than a Savior. Whereas the gospel makes us receivers who then become actors, this emphasis on making Christ master and extending his redeeming work in the world renders us agents of rather than witnesses to God's reconciling act in Jesus Christ.

The Story behind the Stories: The Plot's Central Character

It has sometimes been said that the Bible is more like a library than a book. Sometimes we are bewildered by the diversity of its writings, wondering how Leviticus or Esther bears any relation to the Gospel of Matthew or Romans. What is the thread that pulls together all of the narratives, laws and wisdom, prophecy, poetry, instruction, and exhortation? There really is a unifying message from Genesis to Revelation and it is Christ who brings all of the threads together. When we read the Bible in the light of its plot, things begin to fall into place. Behind every story, piece of wisdom, hymn, exhortation, and prophecy lies the unfolding mystery of Christ and his redemptive work.

Jesus himself told us how to read the Bible—all of it. The Pharisees were the guardians of the Bible. For their followers, they were its authoritative interpreters. Yet for them the Bible was primarily a story about Sinai: the covenant that Israel pledged to fulfill all of the commands of his Law. It was not the subplot—the "schoolmaster" leading to Christ, as Paul described—but the main thing. When the Messiah finally arrived, he would drive out the Romans and reinstitute the Jewish theocracy. The Messiah was a means to an end, not, as Paul called Christ, "the end of the law."

Jesus himself told the religious leaders, "You search the scriptures, because you think that in them you have eternal life; and it is they that bear witness about me, yet you refuse to come to me that you may have life" (John 5:39). Jesus taught his disciples to read the whole Bible (at that point, the Old Testament) in terms of promise and fulfillment, with himself as the central character (Luke 24:25–27, 44–45). No matter how well they had memorized certain Bible verses or how quickly they could recall key moments in Israel's history, the Bible was a mystery to them before Jesus explained it as *his* story.

Christ is the thread that draws together all of the various strands of biblical revelation. Apart from him, the plot falls apart into a jumble of characters, unrelated stories, inexplicable laws, and confusing prophecies. The disciples finally seemed to have understood this point, since the gospel went from Jerusalem to the Gentile world through their witness. Even Peter, who had denied Christ three times, was able later to write as an apostle,

> Concerning this salvation, the prophets who prophesied about the grace that was to be yours searched and inquired carefully, inquiring what person or time the Spirit of Christ in them was indicating when he predicted the sufferings of Christ and the subsequent glories. It was revealed to them that they were serving not themselves but you, in the things that have now been announced to you through those who preached the Good News to you by the Holy Spirit sent from heaven, things into which angels long to look. (1 Peter 1:10–12)

God's eternal Son is present at the beginning of the story at creation (John 1:1–3; Col. 1:15–20). He was the Rock struck in the wilderness for Israel's sins (1 Cor. 10:4). And in the Bible's closing book he is God's last Word, too: "Fear not, I am the first and the last, and the living one. I died, and behold I am alive forever more, and I have the keys of Death and Hades" (Rev. 1:17–18). In the heavenly scene only the Lamb was able to open the scroll containing the revelation of all of history: "And they sang a new song, saying, 'Worthy are you to take the scroll and to open its seals, for you were slain, and by your blood you ransomed people for God from every tribe and language and people and nation, and you have made them a kingdom and

priests to our God, and they shall reign on the earth.'" And everyone
in heaven fell down before the Lamb in worship (Rev. 5:9–14). And
that is the goal of God's Good News.

Drama, Doctrine, Doxology, Discipleship

It is often asserted today that postmoderns are looking for a good story
and a community that exhibits it rather than a good argument. This
makes sense to me on many counts, but especially for those reared
in a generation in which the story was taken for granted—even by
conservatives.

It is the story that gives rise to doctrines, so without the former, the
latter become abstract and timeless principles. Take the resurrection,
for example. What difference does it make that someone rose from
the dead long ago in Jerusalem? The doctrine of Christ's resurrection
belongs to an unfolding plot. We might nod when it is asserted that
by this act God brought justification and life to sinners, but what does
that mean? How can such a remarkable event be responsible for the
end of the old world and the beginning of the new creation?

We need the story to interpret the doctrine, but we also need the
doctrine to interpret the story. Only by working back and forth between them do we increasingly come to understand what God was
doing and its significance for our lives today. The dramatic narrative
provides the context for the doctrines, but the doctrines explain its
meaning. We can no longer take the story for granted, but we also
should not overreact by downplaying the importance of doctrine.

Christian faith and practice do not end at the drama and the doctrine. The goal of the doctrine is to give us the faith to trust in Christ
and to raise our hearts to him in praise. Only then can there be genuine
discipleship as the fruit of faith.

I know it's a gross oversimplification, but it might be a useful generalization to suggest that a couple of generations ago in conservative
evangelical circles, the emphasis fell on *doctrine*. The fundamentals
of the faith were under attack (and still are), so the understandable
response was to teach the basics. People still understood the main
plotline of the story, but they needed to get the doctrine right (at least
a few "fundamentals"). People knew whether they were Catholics or
Protestants, Arminians or Calvinists, Lutherans or Baptists, Charismatic or non-Charismatic. Growing up in conservative evangelical

churches, I recall lengthy lectures on a single verse, complete with the Greek construction projected on overhead transparencies. Of course, we sang—in fact, the songs were full of emotion, verging on sentimental. Nevertheless, the ambiance was that of a classroom. While pulpits are hardly necessary for true worship, they do fit the expectation that God is going to address us. Proclamation is going to happen from this piece of furniture. But instead of a pulpit there was now a lectern. Teaching, not preaching, was going to be the focus. Furthermore, at least in the churches I remember, there was no baptistery (whether a tank or a font) and there was a small table, but it held flowers and an open Bible: no Communion cup, except on those rare Sundays where the Supper was celebrated. Nature abhors a vacuum and in the relative absence of the drama generated by preaching and sacrament, many in my generation were longing for something more meaningful.

In a relatively short period of time, the emphasis shifted from teaching doctrine to experiential worship: "Let's just praise the Lord, and not get caught up in doctrinal refinements." In public and private worship, the focus was on expressing our feelings about God and his importance in our lives. Teaching became something that we did at times other than the weekly service. So now, the classroom atmosphere was converted into the ambiance of a theater, with a stage and praise band front and center, bathed in carefully designed stage lighting. The accent fell on *doxology* over everything else.

Now, we see a rising generation of conservative Christians who are burned out on what they regard as an individualistic and privatized form of religious experience. They want to recover the story and they want to live it. What are we doing to follow Jesus's example and feed the poor, care for prisoners, and steward the environment? Reacting against the ambiance of slick consumerism and entertainment, as well as doctrinal lectures, many younger Christians prefer an atmosphere that stresses mystery and transcendence. The accent falls on *discipleship* over everything else.

I am not nostalgic for "the good ol' days" of Bible lectures. In my view, we need to go back before the doctrine to the story that justifies it. And this story is not only told from the pulpit, but enacted and ratified in baptism and the supper. We respond to it together in common confession, prayers, and praise. Instead of settling on any one of those points along the way (doctrine, doxology, discipleship), we must keep each of these as coordinates in vital connection with each other. Just as it is God's story and doctrine, not ours, it is God's methods that should determine the shape of our public services. Finding our place in God's story, renewed in our thinking by his instruction, and led by his Word to respond in grateful thanksgiving, we now have the proper content, motivation, shape, and direction for our discipleship in the world. Without God's dramatic narrative framing our worship and the great doctrines defining it, it is *our* story, *our* exuberant zeal, and *our* transformative discipleship that takes center stage. In our public worship, we are like the disciples on their way from Galilee to Jerusalem. We are no more prone to get the point of the journey than were they. We need Christ to reveal himself from all of the Scriptures and to give himself as our food and drink for everlasting life.

It strikes me as significant that even when Paul wrote to well-established churches (like Rome), he began with the story: "The gospel of God, which he promised beforehand through the prophets in the holy Scriptures, concerning his Son, who was descended from David according to the flesh and was declared to be the Son of God in power, according to the Spirit of holiness by his resurrection from the dead . . ." (Rom. 1:1–4).

Then, without leaving the story behind, he interprets its plot through steep and breathtaking doctrinal vistas until finally he is lost in wonder and praise in the doxologies of chapters 9 and 11. It is precisely these steep climbs that we like to avoid. It's a workout. But it's well worth the hike when you look out at the view. We may have been complaining for the last three miles. We may have wondered why we couldn't just have stayed in our warm campsite on the valley floor, visiting with each other, singing, and taking in the scenery, but once we are looking out across the vast landscape of rivers and forests, snow-capped mountains and open glades, the trip is unforgettable. "You can see for miles," as they say. With the apostle, we are gripped by awe and joy, ready to sing not simply to express ourselves and entertain each other, but because the experience of something real like this demands it.

Only then does the apostle extrapolate the appropriate practical response "in view of God's mercies" (Rom. 12:1 to the end of the Epistle). There seems to be this reasoned argument from the story to the doctrine to the practice, yet with no compulsion to draw thick lines between them. Many of the Psalms follow a similar pattern: reciting God's mighty works, teaching us what they mean, and then leading us in the appropriate response of praise and obedience.

A constant diet of exhortations to follow Christ's example or instructions will only drive me deeper into myself, either in self-righteousness or despair (depending on whether I'm honest). But guide me through the Alps and I will gladly go through the hassle of packing, unpacking, and repacking my gear. My comrades will become companions, as we rely on each other's gifts and expertise, and we will have something to talk about and sing about at dinner around the campfire together on our return. The more we receive, the more we are able to give. Discipleship—following Christ—means being called away from our dead-end plots to become a part of his story; to be taught by him so that we find ourselves entrusting our lives to him in growing confidence. Only then can discipleship be something other than a lot of busywork.

We need the story *and* the arguments. Without the narrative, the doctrines become abstract and timeless concepts; without the doctrines, the moral imperatives lose their location as the reasonable response to God's triumphant indicatives. Once the narrative of the Triune God becomes submerged in "my story" of personal conversion and religious experience, and doctrine is reduced to trite slogans that lose their image like worn-out coins, all that is left are the practical exhortations: deeds rather than creeds, discipleship without doctrine, focusing on what Jesus would do rather than on what Jesus has done.

Just think of how we use the word "testimony" today. While the object of the apostles' testimony and witness in the New Testament is always to Christ's person and work, we typically use these words to refer to our own experience, transformation, and improved lives. I am not saying that there is no place for this, but its priority suggests that we have made ourselves the main attraction. Instead of finding ourselves in God's story, we create a supporting role for God in our own narratives of personal and social transformation. But if my generalization about church history is anywhere near the mark, the Good News is that the end of the cycle is often met by God's faithful work of reawakening the church to the treasure it has taken for granted.

Although a rising generation may be prone too easily to dismiss doctrine because of caricatures, its intuitions are right that we need to go back not only to an explicit instruction in the doctrines of the faith but to the narrative of the gospel that stretches from Genesis to Revelation. We also need the kind of doxology (or praise) that is consistent with (and in fact generated by) the drama and the doctrine. Otherwise, our praise will be an exercise in self-expression rather than in genuine worship of the Triune God on the basis of his Word. With God's mercies in view, our hearts are not only filled with praise; our bodies are animated to works of love toward our neighbors. Yet apart from the distinctively biblical drama, doctrine, and doxology, whatever we call "discipleship" will simply be another form of moralistic activism.

Acting Out

From an authoritative script (the Bible), God creates a theater (the church) in which he rewrites our dead-end characters as part of God's supporting cast, and creates the set and the props that reveal *this biblically defined world* as reality: the in-breaking of the enduring "age to come" that renders "this present evil age" nothing more than a fading shadow that is passing away (Gal. 1:4). The Triune God is playwright, central character, and casting director; Word *and* sacrament are the means of God's action, yet with a stage that is more than expansive enough to accommodate an innumerable supporting cast of covenant servants and heirs. It also integrates (without confusing) the unique, completed, once-and-for-all, and unrepeatable events that form the script with the ongoing work of the Spirit, through that script, in drawing us into the growing cast for local performances.

When we enter Christ's community theater, we are not spectators, much less masters, of all we survey, but members of the cast—either as strangers and aliens to God's promises or as "a chosen race, a royal priesthood, a holy nation, a people for [God's] own possession, that you may proclaim the excellencies of him who called you out of darkness into his marvelous light" (1 Peter 2:9). By nature, we come to this drama with our own script, as our own screenwriter as well as central character, finding a supporting role for God. Prepared perhaps to take away useful concepts or morals from the story that might improve the plot, we are surprised to find ourselves as new characters written into God's play. "Once you were not a people, but now you are God's people; once you had not received mercy, but now you have received mercy" (v. 10). Once uncomfortable in God's presence and comfortable in this passing age of sin and death, we now find ourselves "as sojourners and exiles" (v. 11) as we are relocated from identification with Adam to our baptism into Christ. The Good News is not only *about* this reality; it is the means by which the Spirit *creates* the reality of which he speaks.

In this drama, outsiders become insiders and insiders become outsiders, the wicked are justified while the "righteous" are condemned, the winners are losers and the losers are winners, the hungry are filled while the satisfied go away empty. In this drama, the plot reaches its climax in the most amazing of all reversals: right where God seems weakest and most foolish he is actually triumphing in power and wisdom.

Of course, the world has its dramas as well. In the one now playing in North America and in theaters around the globe, it is, as I have suggested, "a show about nothing." According to this narrative, we came from nowhere and are going nowhere, but in between we have the opportunity to create for ourselves a moment of self-chosen glory. It is still too difficult to tell whether this is really a new story or just another chapter in an old one. Regardless, it belongs to the age that is passing away. The world's drama generates its own dogmas as well as its own methods of shaping the identity of its cast.

The News Has Reached Us

The gospel is indeed the nucleus of the greatest story ever told, but it is not just a tall tale. It is history. As Peter reminds us, "We did not follow cleverly devised myths when we made known to you the power and coming of our Lord Jesus Christ, but were eye-witnesses of his majesty" (2 Pet. 1:16).

The apostles did not live the undisturbed lives of sages and story-tellers, but died as martyrs. The Greek word for "witness" is *martus*, from which we also get the word *martyr*. Laying their lives on the line, they did not claim to be superior intellects or to have had superior mystical experiences or even better stories. Rather, they testified in the courtroom of history to the victory of God over the powers of death and hell in the person and work of Jesus Christ. News has reached us that Satan has been cast out of heaven, where he accused the saints day and night forever. "And they have conquered [the dragon] by the blood of the Lamb and by the word of their testimony, for they loved not their lives even unto death. Therefore, rejoice O heavens and you who dwell in them! But woe to you, O earth and sea, for the devil has come down to you in great wrath, because he knows that his time is short" (Rev. 12:9–12). This is the moment in which we find ourselves today. The big news has already reached us. In the great courtroom epic, we have been redeemed by Christ to be witnesses to his conquest and the faithfulness of the Covenant Lord.

5

DON'T JUST *DO* SOMETHING, *SIT* THERE!

FINDING YOURSELF IN THE STORY

Most headlines come and go. They grab our attention for a while, and then a few days pass and they get filed away somewhere in our memories. Every now and again, though, there is a big one that changes our lives. Many people remember where they were when they heard that President Kennedy was assassinated or on September 11, 2001. When it's big enough, news not only informs; it changes our lives.

A while back I came across the famous 1945 cover photo of *Life Magazine* announcing "Victory in Europe!" with a Navy sailor lifting in the air a woman he had never met before in a jubilant embrace that she gladly returned. In the background were perfect strangers doing the same thing. Good News—if it is good enough—can do strange things to people. In that moment, these strangers were not asked to do something; they were simply hearers, recipients, and beneficiaries of the news of what had been achieved by the Allied troops. It was not even their believing the news that made it true, but the announcement of the news that made them believe it.

The gospel is not only *good* in terms of its content; it is Good *News* in the form of its delivery. This is the point that Paul makes in Romans 10. He begins by lamenting the fact that his "brethren according to the flesh"—ethnic Jews—were still seeking to justify themselves by their own righteousness, instead of embracing the righteousness of Christ that God imputes to sinners as a free gift through faith alone.

First, there is the well-known lament concerning the offense of the cross—a lament because so many of Paul's flesh and blood stumble over the Rock. But the Rock cannot be moved. It cannot be softened, broken into pieces, or absorbed into the environment. It cannot be made relevant to the concerns generated by other stories that we happen to be starring in at the moment. It's just there—in the way. God demands a perfect righteousness, which Jews seek by their own lawkeeping rather than by faith in Christ alone. Paul works out the logic of grace quite clearly throughout this Epistle, but especially beginning at Romans 8:29 it becomes a tight logical argument: "Those whom he foreknew he predestined, those whom he predestined he called, those whom he called he justified, and those whom he justified he glorified. What shall we therefore say? If God is for us, who can be against us?"

And now in chapter 10 he laments that his brothers and sisters according to the flesh substitute their own religious zeal for faith in Christ and his perfect righteousness. The "righteousness which is of the law" leads to conclusions which are antithetical to those reached by the "righteousness which is by faith." The logic is most succinctly stated finally in chapter 11: "If then it is by grace, it is no longer of works; otherwise grace is no longer grace." That's the logic of the gospel.

This summary is familiar enough to many of us. To be sure, there are two paths: our way, which leads to death, and God's way, which leads to life everlasting. But what may not be as familiar is Paul's argument in Romans 10; namely, that each road not only has its own destiny and method of redemption, but has its own methods. Works righteousness strives to attain God's righteousness, while faith simply receives it. God not only provides salvation by grace alone in Christ alone; he even delivers the gift to us.

Marketing gimmicks were made with people like me in mind. It took me a while before I wised up to the promotional ads announcing that I had won a free trip. Contacting the company to collect my "free" prize, I learned that there were several hoops I had to jump through in order to get it. A lot of Christians express a similar frustration. At first, they were overwhelmed with the Good News. Salvation in Christ is a free gift. However, the fine print came later. Now they are on a treadmill, trying to find the "higher life," hoping desperately to experience the fullness of their salvation.

Note Paul's argument in chapter 10:

> Moses describes in this way the righteousness that is by the law: "The man who does these things will live by them." But the righteousness that is by faith says: "Do not say in your heart, 'Who will ascend into heaven?'" (that is, to bring Christ down) "or 'Who will descend into the deep?'" (that is, to bring Christ up from the dead). But what does it say? "The word is near you; it is in your mouth and in your heart," that is, the word of faith we are proclaiming . . . for "Everyone who calls on the name of the Lord will be saved." How, then, can they call on the one they have not believed in? And how can they believe in the one of whom they have not heard? And how can they hear without someone preaching to them? And how can they preach unless they are sent? . . . Consequently, faith comes from hearing the message, and the message is heard through the word of Christ. (Rom. 10:5–17)

Do you see the logic of the method which Paul outlines here? Certain methods just go with certain messages, and that is certainly true in this case. We often hear it said that the message of the gospel never changes, but the methods do. However, Paul is saying that the gospel has its own method. It never changes. It always puts us on the receiving end.

The spirit of works righteousness says, "How can I climb up to God and bring Christ down to me, where I am, in my own experience?" Like Ulysses crossing the expansive seas to conquer dragons and finally to arrive at his reward, the logic of works righteousness conceives of salvation by personal conquest. Luther spoke about ladders that people climb in order to steal into God's presence: mysticism, merit, and speculation were the ladders he had in mind.[1] These same ladders are plentiful today: the feverish interest in makeovers, reinventing ourselves, and changing our identity. We are all looking for a plot to make sense of our lives, a script that will make us feel like our lives are not a waste, that they mean something. We all want a new drug, a new experience, a new achievement.

Where do you think you'll find God? Some people speak of finding ultimate peace of mind in Tibet or rock climbing in the Alps. Perhaps it's not surprising that we call spiritual epiphanies "mountaintop" experiences. Others talk about their experience of seeing the Dalai Lama, the spectacle of the Mass, or experiencing "transcendence" at a Hindu ashram or Buddhist temple. Some travel great distances to touch the hem of Jesus's garment: to Lourdes in the hope of experiencing a miracle or at more Protestant venues, like Toronto or Pensacola to "catch the blessing." We are always looking for a revival: something exciting, awe-inspiring, and majestic. *Newsweek* is not likely to send a reporter to your church next Sunday simply because the Word will be preached. That is not where the action is. And yet, Paul tells us, this is exactly where the Spirit is miraculously at work in his grace. It is precisely here where he unites us to Christ and gives us his gifts. Sometimes we make "spiritual disciplines" a way of making our way up the mountain to experience God. However, unless we are going regularly to the Scriptures to find Christ and crying out to him for salvation in prayer, even personal Bible reading and prayer can become methods of idolatry and self-trust.

We don't expect to find God in the feeding trough of a barn in an obscure Palestinian village, much less hanging from an instrument of Roman execution. Yet this is where God meets us. While we are trying to climb higher, he descends lower. Of all our faculties, our natural religious, moral, and spiritual instincts are actually the least likely to find God where he has found us.

Scores of methods abound for pulling God down out of heaven, to manipulate him into doing what we want him to do when we want him to do it. If I follow God's instructions (or the steps and formulas laid out in the latest religious bestseller), he is sort of obligated to heal me, improve my marriage or finances, or give me some intense experience of his glory.

Refusing to receive God at the lowly places he has chosen to meet us, we try to pull him down to us or rise up to him. This is the essence of idolatry, as we see in the "golden calf" episode in Exodus. Terrified by the word that God declared amid lightning and thunder at Mount

Sinai, Israel begged that no further word be spoken. Understandably, they asked for Moses to mediate God's word to them. However, while God was giving his people a written and preached word through his servant Moses at the top of the mountain, they were busy fashioning a golden calf that they could see and touch—and control. Israel was tired of hearing, patiently waiting on God's timetable in hope. Instead, the people wanted to see and experience a silent, manageable deity whose words did not fill them with fear. Later, Israel, wanting to be like the nations, demanded a king whom they could see, rather than the great King whose word they heard. "Seeing is believing."

Throughout Israel's history, the covenant people strayed from God's law and promise, building "high places" instead of worshiping as God had prescribed, at the temple with its sacrifices that pointed faith toward the coming Savior. That is why we will always fall for golden calves, signs and wonders, awe-inspiring religious productions, and sanctification plans that promise measurable progress. But as Paul reminds us, "For in this hope we were saved. But hope that is seen is no hope at all. Who hopes for what he already has? But if we hope for what we do not yet have, we wait for it patiently" (Rom. 8:24–25).

Everything that we possess right now of our salvation has come to us through the ear, not the eye. Even the sacraments are visible confirmations attached to God's verbal promise. We have heard God's justifying verdict in the gospel and his promise to conform us to Christ's image. Yet we are not yet bodily raised and glorified; in fact, our bodies are wasting away even as we mature in our sanctification. God tells us that we are not only justified but are being inwardly renewed, yet often what we actually see and experience in ourselves and in the church seems quite different. The same apostle who said that we are justified (Romans 3–5) and have already been buried and raised with Christ in newness of life (chapter 6) goes on to relate his own experience of persistent failures in the Christian life (chapter 7). Only when he takes his eyes off of himself and gives his ear again to Christ and his Word is the apostle once again cheered (chapter 8).

Sight corresponds to full possession, a complete realization of heavenly reality. By contrast, hearing corresponds to faith in a promise. If we demand our best life here and now we will be particularly susceptible to idolatry, but God calls us to embrace a promise that we hear and believe. This promise is delivered through the broken and not so spectacular vessels of human messengers, and the very common elements of water, bread, and wine. Why are these effective means of grace? Not because of the minister or the elements themselves, but because of God's promise. God has promised to deliver his grace at these humble venues.

It is not that we get one sort of grace in the preaching, another in baptism, and another in the Lord's Supper, but that in these divinely instituted means God offers and gives the same grace: namely, forgiveness and new life. The revival down the street may promise the vision, but God's Spirit calms us down and says, "Give ear to my words"; "Taste and see that the Lord is good." The logic of "the righteousness which is by works" may attract us to the latest method of gaining victory over all known sin or take a trip to some new evangelical "hot spot" of allegedly spiritual activity. But the logic of "the righteousness which is by faith" says that we don't have to cross the seas to find God and "appropriate" his power. Rather, he is as near as the means of grace; in this passage specifically, the preaching of the gospel: "the word of faith that we proclaim" (v. 8), "the Good News" that is preached (v. 15). "So faith comes by hearing, and hearing through the word of Christ" (v. 17), and hearing the word of Christ through messengers sent from the front lines as heralds appointed by Christ himself.

This is great news! It means that God has not only saved us by grace in sending his Son two thousand years ago; he has applied this grace by grace alone in sending his Spirit down to us here and now to make his preached gospel and his administered sacraments means of grace, creating faith and confirming it until the end. The gospel not only *tells us about* a gracious God; its proclamation is the place where this gracious God *finds and forgives* us. Not only its message, but its method seems foolish to us. The outwardly fragile, weak, and foolish means of preaching is a stumbling block apart from faith, but it is Good News for believers precisely because God has so thoroughly accommodated his revelation to our feeble capacity. As Paul says in this passage, God's condescending mercy through preaching puts Christ within reach and makes God truly "haveable" as our saving Lord. *God does not simply create the gift and offer it to us, if we will only climb the stairway to heaven to get it; he brings it down to us, uncurls our ungrateful fingers, and places it in our hands.*

In our native works righteousness, we will always look for methods of pulling God down out of heaven or for bringing Jesus Christ up from the dead. The hardest thing in the world for us even as believers in Christ is to sit down and receive something. However, that is exactly what we have to do. The new covenant is a "sit down for this" kind of covenant. At Mount Sinai, the people heard the Law and responded, "All that the Lord says we will do." It was a legal covenant in which the nation swore obedience and its temporal security in the earthly land was conditioned upon their fulfillment of that oath. However, the new covenant that Jesus ratified in the upper room the night before his crucifixion was of a completely different type. Instead of splashing blood on the Israelites, "in accordance with the words of the covenant" that they swore, the blood was on Christ's head. He was about to drink the cup of wrath, so that the disciples (and we) could drink the cup of forgiveness.

The form of Christ's words and actions at the Last Supper clearly indicate that this new covenant is a last will and testament. It is not conditioned on our performance: "Do this and you will live." Rather, it is an announcement that someone else has performed everything and now gives the inheritance to us as a gift: "This is my body. . . . This is my blood of the new covenant shed for many." Relating Christ's sacrifice to a last will and testament directly, the writer to the Hebrews points out that the benefits are only given to the heirs upon the death of the one who makes it (Heb. 9:16–17). On Good Friday, at about noon, all of those whom God had chosen from every tribe and nation across the millennia of human history became legal beneficiaries of heaven, coheirs with Christ.

You stand up for a "do this" covenant and you sit down to hear the reading of a will telling you what you have inherited from someone else's labors. Directly connecting the new covenant with the Abrahamic covenant in Romans 4, Paul points out that the gospel is not a contract for hire, where workers are paid their due at the end of the day, but is a free gift. In fact, it is only given "to the one who does not work but trusts him who justifies the ungodly . . ." (v. 5).

The riches of this estate that believers inherit are so vast that the will must be proclaimed every week. Christ's attorney must read and expound the will in sections over a lifetime. Not just once, but every day we must renounce our trust in other would-be lords, saviors, providers, and promise makers. We must let go of our anxious grip on our own lives, our sense of being in control, our own integrity and confidence in our religious experience. We must renounce the contracts we have entered that promised to make our life meaningful and say "Amen!" to the will as it is read to us.

Christians still hear the law and are called to obey it, but as "the reasonable service" of their adoption as royal heirs, not as the condition of their receiving it. One becomes a beneficiary of the estate on the basis of another family member's achievements, received through faith, and then follows the "house rules" not as a way of gaining or keeping the inheritance but as a proper way of responding to our new surroundings in a new family. We need to hear both the law and the gospel proclaimed to us from Genesis to Revelation, so that we can become more familiar with God's righteous requirements and be plunged more deeply each week into the benefits secured for us by our Mediator and elder brother.

That *Life* cover photo captured the power of Good News to alter people at the core of their being. If someone had stood on the street corner encouraging people to be more loving, to invest in relationships, and to improve their lives, passersby may have kindly nodded and smiled. But it wouldn't have been *news*. It certainly would not have revolutionized anyone's identity or expectations for the future. It wouldn't have made strangers dance with each other in the streets. Not only in its message but in its form, the gospel is *Good News*. Good News comes to us from outside of ourselves; it doesn't well up from within. A report announces what has happened. Our natural tendency is to be most certain of that which we know (or think we know) inside, deep down in our hearts. However, we must come to see that this is part of the captivity from which the Spirit releases us. The truth comes to us from the outside, turning us inside out. So the content and the form of delivery are inextricably linked. We do not accomplish the victory, but are recipients of the report that it has been achieved. Salvation is not a program for us to follow; it is a gift to be received. That is the simplest and most difficult truth of the Christian faith.

Receiving a New Script

"Makeovers" are all the rage these days. Not only our homes, but our personal identity is always under construction. In fact, our homes become the "sets" for what Neal Gabler has called the "life movie" that each of us is making for ourselves. Gabler has provided a riveting account of how entertainment has conquered reality in the United States (exported globally). Our culture of entertainment makes us think of ourselves as the star of our own show. He writes in *Life, the Movie*, "An ever-growing segment of the American economy is devoted to designing, building and then dressing the sets in which we live, work, shop and play; to creating our costumes; to making our hair shine and our faces glow; to slenderizing our bodies; to supplying our props—all so that we can appropriate the trappings of celebrity, if not the actuality of it, for the life movie." "Drama coaches" such as Martha Stewart help us achieve these images that we have of ourselves in our life movie.[2]

Psychologist Robert Jay Lifton observes that our passion for "reinventing ourselves" is driven by "a nagging sense of guilt" that we cannot quite identify or explain.[3] Like the fig leaves that Adam and Eve designed to cover their sense of shame after the fall, we search frantically for moral, therapeutic, pragmatic, cosmetic, and spiritual ways of making ourselves more presentable and acceptable. Yet it is not until God strips us of our own fig leaves and covers us with his own garments of righteousness in Christ that we find acceptance with God and therefore the source of a stable identity that can evoke the confidence, "If God is for us, who can be against us?" (Rom. 8:31). Everything else is cosmetic; it does not really address the source of our anxieties, stress, depression, and pride.

In Hollywood, scripts lacking a compelling plot can nevertheless become blockbuster movies, playing cheaply "the lust of the flesh, the lust of the eyes, and the pride of life" (1 John 2:16). It is not that we desire too much, but that we settle for too little. We are too easily satisfied (at least for the moment) with the trivial dramas of our own lives and of those other characters we long to be, whose lives we long to live. Our identity is increasingly shaped by a collage of advertising that idealizes the superficial attractions of this fading age.

The working assumption in much of contemporary Christianity seems to be that modern culture—whether sociology, psychology, anthropology, business and marketing, politics, education, and ethics—properly interprets human identity and the ideals of proper human flourishing. However, it lacks some crucial methods for attaining these goals. This is where we typically introduce the Bible as the "answer to life's questions." This is where the Bible becomes relevant to people "where they are" in their experience. Accordingly, it is often said that we must *apply* the Scriptures *to daily living*. But this is to invoke the Bible too late, as if we already knew what "life" or "daily living" meant. The problem is not merely that we lack the right answers, but that we don't even have the right questions until God introduces us to his interpretation of reality.

Remember, Satan's first strategy was to persuade Eve that God was stingy and narrow-minded: "Has God really said that you cannot eat from *any* tree in the garden?" Of course, God had said no such thing, as Eve acknowledged in her reply. It was just the one tree in the middle of the garden: the Tree of the Knowledge of Good and Evil, which we might call the Tree of Autonomy (self-rule). "God knows that when you eat from that tree you will be like him, knowing good and evil," Satan continued. The assumption is that God is just keeping us down, holding us back from realizing our own inner potential and divinity.

We have to realize that for all of us, by nature, this is where we start in our interpretation of reality. We are the center of the universe, legislating for ourselves good and evil, truth and error, life and death. However, from this perspective everything is upside down. It is not because God is a control freak, but because he is in fact God and we are not that we must surrender our claim to interpret anything properly as autonomous individuals. We interpret sin as normal, pride as a virtue, and selfishness as inevitable for getting what we want out of life. It is a measure of God's lavish generosity that he does not let this charade continue. It is because of his grace that God will not allow us to determine the questions any more than the answers. For our own good, we should not want God to be relevant for our life, but to establish his own sovereign relevance and break up whatever ground underneath our feet that we thought was *the real world* and *daily living*.

When God breaks in upon us through his Word, we are confronted with a series of contradictions. We learn that we do not even know the meaning of our daily lives or modern culture, or human identity and flourishing until God interprets us, our lives together, and our history in the light of his actions. We do not know what we really need until God's confrontation provokes a crisis that faces us with deeper problems than bad hair days.

What Would Mary Do?

The angel Gabriel did not come to Mary in order to ask how God could be a bigger part of her life, but to announce that he had a big part for her in his play. Nowhere does the text say that she is worthy, but the angel announces that God has shown her his gracious favor

(Luke 1:28). God is the active party; Mary is the recipient. Not only will the one she bears be the Savior of the *world*; Mary will be the mother of *her own* Redeemer. There was no "starter kit" for this sort of thing, no set of conditions that Mary is to fulfill in order to qualify for this role. "Don't worry, Mary, *he* is the Savior; you are among those whom he will save. God is doing this, not you. Just believe my words." Mary's response is wonderful: "Behold, I am the servant of the Lord; let it be done to me according to your word" (Luke 1:38).

I am all in favor of making Mary a model for the rest of us—if we actually respond the way she did. She realized that she was not in a position to deliver Israel. She was not the Lord of the covenant, but a servant. She does not say, "All this I will do," but "let it be done to me according to your word." She acknowledges that in this act of believing the angel's report, she is a passive recipient of a donation. The angel's word—which is nothing less than the first announcement of the gospel in Luke—is in the driver's seat. Talk about being rescripted! Here is a nobody, a Jewish girl (probably a teenager), from the backwoods of what was once the Holy Land but is now a troublesome outpost of the Roman Empire. Now she is the mother of God, because the one who will gestate in her womb is no less than God the Son.

Rushing to Elizabeth's house, Mary would normally be greeted by her much older distant relative in familiar terms. But not today. On this visit, Elizabeth "exclaimed with a loud cry, 'Blessed are you among women, and blessed is the fruit of your womb! And why is this granted to me that the mother of my Lord should come to me?' " (Luke 1:42–43). A strange announcement by the angel; now a strange greeting from Elizabeth, whose child, John, leaped in her womb to join in the celebration (v. 44). Mary is not greeted as a meritorious saint. Elizabeth does not celebrate her virtues that qualified her for this role. She simply says, "Blessed is she who believed that there would be a fulfillment of what was spoken to her from the Lord" (v. 45). *Blessed*, not *worthy*. Finally, in her song—the Magnificat—Mary points away from herself to God as her Savior and Israel's deliverer (vv. 46–55). Her heart "rejoices in God my Savior, for he has looked on the humble estate of his servant." Of course, her estate will change now. "For behold, from now on all generations will call me blessed." But why? Because of the things that she has done? No, for she tells us, echoing various Psalms (and the Song of Hannah), "for he who is mighty has done great things for me, and holy is his name." She credits this blessing to God's *mercy* and goes on to celebrate God's act of raising up the poor and humble and bringing to nothing the high and mighty of the world. "He has helped his servant Israel, in remembrance of his mercy, as he spoke to our fathers, to Abraham and to his offspring forever" (v. 55). Mary knows that this is a fulfillment of the covenant that God swore to Abraham, not a renewal of the covenant that Israel swore at Sinai. And she knows her new part in the play.

The Magnificat is one of five songs that cluster around the nativity narrative. Good News makes people sing. It made Mary sing all the way to the cross, even in hope-laced lament, letting go of her own son in order to take her place with the rest of those who will believe the Good News that will be proclaimed as a result of his death and resurrection.

If we bring the Scriptures into the conversation at the point of its application, it will be like the punch line without the joke. The gospel is not the Bible's answer to all of our felt needs that we think we already have; it is the news that can only be reported by a herald. "Popular education, the cultivation of morality and patriotism, the nurture of the emotions—none of these really needs us theologians," Karl Barth reminds us. "Others can do these and similar things much better than we can. The world knows this and acts accordingly. We are examined and rejected, and rightly so, before we become apprentices in such dilettante occupations." The church only has a usefulness, along with our speaking, "when it stands under a norm."[4]

The Cross Isn't an Accessory

After calling his disciples, Jesus prepared them for the journey ahead of them, beyond his own crossbearing and resurrection (Matthew 10). They too will bear their cross, suffering not for sin but for their testimony to the sin-bearer. Persecution will come: even parents and siblings will hand over their family members to the authorities (vv. 16–24). During this journey with his disciples in the flesh, Jesus will secretly disclose to them his identity, but then after fulfilling it, "what you hear whispered," he instructs, "proclaim on the housetops," with the fear of God prevailing over the fear of human adversaries (vv. 26–33). "Do not think that I have come to bring peace to the earth. I have not come to bring peace, but a sword. For I have come to set a man against his father, and a daughter against her mother, and a daughter-in-law against her mother-in-law. And a person's enemies will be those of his own household." It will be time to take up one's own cross. "Whoever finds his life will lose it, and whoever loses his life for my sake will find it" (vv. 34–39). Later in the journey, when Jesus prepares them for his own crucifixion (Matt. 16:25), he repeats this enigmatic line, adding, "For what will it profit a man if he gains the whole world and forfeits his soul?" Immediately after his ascension, the dominos started to fall. Some caved in, renouncing Christ, while others persevered. Peter, who denied Christ three times, ended up being crucified upside down, because he did not consider himself worthy to be executed in the same manner as his Savior. So what does this mean: "Whoever finds his life will lose it, and whoever loses his life for my sake will find it"? The context, of course, is the imminent persecution of the disciples and indeed the wider church. Those who cling to their life as it is will never receive eternal life. The securities of this fleeting lifespan pale in comparison with the riches of the inheritance that the saints have in Christ. (This is the point that the apostle Paul makes in Romans 8:17–25.)

Such passages speak directly to suffering brothers and sisters in China, India, Nigeria, and Saudi Arabia, but what about the rest of us? We like to imagine sometimes that we too share in Christ's sufferings, but we do not suffer in the same way or to the same degree as the martyrs and the persecuted. The suffering that Jesus had in mind is not the general troubles that believers face in common with unbelievers, such as physical or financial hardships. It was suffering for their witness to Christ that Jesus had in mind.

Yet precisely because we do not find ourselves threatened with death for the sake of the gospel, those of us in liberal democracies may be the ones who find it most difficult to accept Jesus's exhortation. Like a cross that is worn around one's neck, Christ can become an accessory. Rather than being commanded at gunpoint to deny Christ, we are led by the devil into the wilderness of consumerism, shopping for identities. Far from being harried and harassed, we are shown the kingdoms of this world that can be ours if we will only turn away from Golgotha. We don't have to become atheists. We do not even have to renounce Jesus Christ. In fact, we can sell everything from rock concerts to coffee mugs with Jesus as the trademark. All that is necessary is for us to cling to ourselves—the securities, aspirations, felt needs, and relationships that define us and that we have chosen for ourselves—rather than to God's saving love in Christ and the identity for which he has chosen us.

To put it simply, Jesus's warning about finding our life by losing it versus losing our life to find it presses us to ask ourselves this question: *Do I define the Jesus story or does it define me?* Is Jesus's significance objective and universal, which I am simply to acknowledge and embrace, or do I determine his significance in my own life? Paul tells believers, "For you have died, and your life is hidden with Christ in God" (Col. 3:4).

This is more radical than anything that we could conceive. According to the gospel, "I" don't really *exist* anymore. Our self-identity is not a stable "thing," but is defined by the story that we tell—or hear—about ourselves. Of course, the gospel does not obliterate my identity; it comes to save nature, not to destroy it. However, my nature "in Adam" is corrupt, in bondage to sin and death. Even in my moral striving, I am decadent. Even in my craving for spiritual experience, I am an idolater. Another makeover or transformation will not really change my *identity*. I must be crucified and buried with Christ—and raised with him in newness of life.

We can retain our autonomy (self-rule) by simply *adding* Jesus to our life, as an accessory. Roman religion was always making room for another god in the imperial cult; it was the claim that Christ alone is Lord that brought the early Christians to the coliseum. In fact, they were accused of atheism because they did not believe in enough gods! Furthermore, many of the titles for Christ in the New Testament (including "Lord" and "Savior") had been attributed to Caesar. Becoming a Christian meant (and still means) *renouncing* the lords and the stories that they tell in order to be united to Christ.

The salvation that God promises in Christ requires my death. Here I am, cheerfully going about my daily affairs, picking and choosing the roles I would like to play from the advertisements, movies, and "put-together" people I admire around me. I may even find a role for Jesus, although who am I to say that others are wrong for finding someone or something else more helpful for achieving their goals in life? Then along comes the law, nailing me, telling me who I really am, telling me how this character I have written for myself is doomed. I begin to question the believability of my screenplay. And then God hands me a new script: the Good News that I am no longer a child of Adam, stranger and alien to God's promises, but a child of God in Jesus Christ, stranger and alien to the world's spin. I no longer can see God as existing to make me happy, to satisfy my felt needs, even to give me a sense of well-being and add a few suggestions to improve my life. He comes to kill me and to make me alive. Repentance means I give up my script; I stop pretending that I can write the story of my life. Through faith in Christ, I become a character in God's story, part of the new creation.

Mourning and Dancing

Even more than the announcement of victory in Europe, the declaration of Christ's victory over sin, death, hell, and the devil draws us away from whatever headlines, scripts, plots, props, sets, and costumes that we were following according to our own life movie. God's story is no longer a subplot of ours, but is the headline that captures our attention. Perfect strangers are aroused by their shared hearing of Good News to embrace each other in a communion that is deeper than any natural community, even one's own family.

The ministry of John the Baptist is compared and contrasted with that of Jesus at various points in the Gospels. Later in his ministry Jesus said, "I tell you, among those born of women no one is greater than John; yet the least in the kingdom of God is greater than he" (Luke 7:28)—because of the superior phase of redemptive history Jesus was inaugurating. Those who refused to be baptized by John "rejected God's purpose for themselves" (Luke 7:31). Jesus then compares the present generation to children playing the funeral game and the wedding game, "and calling to one another, 'We played the flute for you, and you did not dance; we wailed, and you did not weep.'" On one hand, John played the funeral dirge, but most of the people and religious leaders did not feel the sting of their guilt. Instead, they claimed that he had a demon. On the other hand, Jesus brings the Good News to sinners and he is rejected as "a glutton and a drunkard, a friend of tax collectors and sinners!" (vv. 31–35). As the last old covenant prophet, John and his ministry of impending judgment on Israel had to give way to the arrival of the Lamb of God. "Now after John was arrested, Jesus came to Galilee, proclaiming the Good News of God, and saying, 'The time is fulfilled, and the kingdom of God has come near; repent, and believe in the Good News'" (Mark 1:14).

As in Jesus's day, the children of this age know neither how to mourn nor dance properly. G. K. Chesterton observed that Christianity's outer ring is dark enough, with its grave view of original sin, judgment, and hell, but in its inner ring "you will find the old human life dancing like children, and drinking wine like men; for Christianity is the only frame for pagan freedom." "But in the modern philosophy the case is opposite; it is its outer ring that is obviously artistic and emancipated; its despair is within."[5]

For the unbelieving world a kind of superficial happiness and general well-being full of entertainments but lacking any real plot hides the fear of death. It's like the scene in Monty Python's satirical *Holy Grail* where victims of the Black Death are being carted away to the morgue, some prematurely, protesting, "I'm getting better!" Apart from God's grace, we cannot come to terms sufficiently with our mortal wound or enter into the genuine revelry and mirth of God's kingdom. Denying our sin (not just *sins*, but our sinful condition), we're too silly for a funeral; finding the gospel foolish, we are too timid for a real celebration. "Repent, and believe the Good News": this command forms the two aspects of conversion: repentance toward sin and faith toward God. After the funeral there is dancing. In repentance, we say no to the idols, powers, rulers, and lies of this present evil age and in faith we say yes to Christ, "in whom all of God's promises are 'Yes!' and 'Amen!'" (2 Cor. 1:20).

Repentance

Repentance (*metanoia*) means "change of mind." It is treated in Scripture as first of all the knowledge of sin produced by the law (Rom. 3:20). Jesus promised to send the Spirit as an attorney sent to convict us inwardly of God's righteousness and our unrighteousness (John 14–16). This knowledge, however, is not merely intellectual but emotional—it involves the whole person.

We see the features of repentance finely exhibited in David's prayer of confession:

> Have mercy on me, O God, according to your steadfast love; according to your abundant mercy blot out my transgressions. Wash me thoroughly from my iniquity, and cleanse me from my sin. For I know my transgressions, and my sin is ever before me. Against you, you alone, have I sinned, and done what is evil in your sight, so that you are justified when you pass judgment. Indeed, I was born guilty, a sinner when my mother conceived me. You desire truth in the inward being; therefore teach me wisdom in my secret heart. Purge me with hyssop, and I shall be clean; wash me, and I shall be whiter than snow. Let me hear joy

and gladness; let the bones that you have crushed rejoice. Hide your face from my sins, and blot out all my iniquities. (Ps. 51:1–9)

First, we recognize that David is not simply *ashamed* of his behavior but *guilty*. Second, although he has sinned cruelly against Bathsheba and plotted the death of her husband, he recognizes that his sin is first and foremost *against* God. Repentance is not only remorse for having wronged our neighbor but is a recognition that God is the most offended party. Third, David does not try to atone for his sins or pacify God's just anger by his remorse. David confesses that before God's throne he is condemned and he does not try to justify himself. Fourth, David acknowledges not only his sinful *actions* but his sinful *condition* from the hour of conception. Repentance pertains not simply to certain sins; pagans can be remorseful concerning their immoderate behavior. Rather, it is the revulsion of the whole soul toward its alliance with sin and death.

Although such godly sorrow leads David to despair of his own righteousness, it does not lead him to the final despair that often leads the ungodly to either self-destruction or a searing of their conscience. As Paul observes, "For godly grief produces a repentance that leads to salvation and brings no regret, but worldly grief produces death" (2 Cor. 7:10). After all, "God's kindness is meant to lead you to repentance" (Rom. 2:4). While the law produces a *legal repentance* (fear of judgment), the gospel engenders an *evangelical repentance* that bears the fruit of real change. David turns outside of himself to his merciful God. Here we see the closest possible link between repentance and faith. By itself repentance is merely the experience of damnation—until one looks by faith to Jesus Christ.

Often repentance is more broadly defined to include actual change in character and behavior, but Scripture describes this as "the fruit of repentance" (Matt. 3:8) or "deeds consistent with repentance" (Acts 26:20; cf. Matt. 7:16; Luke 3:9; 8:15; John 12:24; Rom. 7:4; Gal. 5:22; Col. 1:10). In this sense, of course, repentance is always partial, weak, and incomplete in this life. Nor is it a onetime act. As the first of Luther's *Ninety-five Theses* states, "Our Lord and Master Jesus Christ, in saying 'Repent ye,' etc., intended that the whole life of believers should be penitence."[6] The Spirit brings us to repentance by convicting us of sin by the law, the gospel leads us to faith in Christ, and this faith produces within us a hatred of our sin and a craving for righteousness. Since our tendency even as believers is still to turn back toward ourselves and trust in our repentance, we must be driven again to despair of our righteousness as well as our sins by the law and cling to Christ. Therefore, this is not a once and for all transition from legal repentance to faith in Christ to evangelical repentance, but a perpetual cycle that defines the Christian life.

In Roman Catholic theology and practice, this call to repentance is replaced with a system of penance. As the Renaissance scholar Erasmus discovered, the Latin Vulgate had erroneously translated the Greek imperative "Repent!" (*metanoēsate*) as "Do penance!" (*poenitentium agite*). Rome defines such penance as involving four elements: contrition, confession, satisfaction, and absolution.[7] Since few are able to rise to the level of true contrition (genuine sorrow for sin), attrition (fear of punishment) is deemed suitable for this first stage. For forgiveness, each sin must be recalled and orally confessed to a priest, who then determines a suitable action or series of actions to perform in order to make satisfaction for the sin. Only then can the penitent receive the absolution.[8]

However, there are Protestant ways of smuggling penance back into the gospel. Many of us recall "rededication" rituals, especially in our youth. I remember joining friends in writing my sins on cards and then throwing them into the bonfire at the closing night of summer camp. Weeping in a catharsis mixed with shame and joy, I thought that I had finally proved to God that this time I really had surrendered all and would "lay all on the altar."

In this theology, repentance is understood not only as a change of heart or mind but as a new obedience and is typically regarded as a condition rather than result of forgiveness. Even in broader evangelical circles, some Christians struggle to the point of despair over whether the quality and degree of their repentance is adequate to be forgiven, as if repentance were the ground of forgiveness and the former could be measured by the intensity of emotion and resolve.

However, according to Scripture it is not our tears but Christ's blood that satisfies God's judgment and establishes peace with God (Rom. 5:1, 8–11). God heals the bones that he crushes and raises up those whom he has cast down. "But he gives all the more grace; therefore it says, 'God opposes the proud, but gives grace to the humble'" (James 4:6). The law begins repentance, by convicting us of sin, but only the gospel can lead us to boldly claim God's promise with David: "Let me hear joy and gladness; let the bones that you have crushed rejoice. Hide your face from my sins, and blot out all my iniquities" (Ps. 51:8).

Whenever repentance is marginalized in conversion, it is usually because of an inadequate sense of God's holiness and the just demands of his righteous law. The consequence is that conversion is represented merely as moral improvement: the *addition* of certain distinctives of Christian piety. Biblical repentance, however, involves a fundamental *renunciation* of the world, the flesh, and the devil: including every pious experience or deed in which we have trusted. The whole self must be turned away both from self-trust and the autonomy that demands final say as to what one will believe, whom one will trust, and how one will live. The effects of this change of mind remain an unfinished task throughout our earthly pilgrimage.

Faith

Arrested, arraigned, and indicted, in repentance we turn away *from* ourselves—our untruths, sins, and our fraudulent claim to righteousness—and in faith we look *to* Christ for salvation and for every spiritual gift. To put it differently, in repentance we confess (with David) that God is justified in his verdict against us and in faith we receive God's justification. The righteousness of God brings us to our knees in guilt, while the gift of righteousness from God raises our eyes to Christ as our only hope. Dead to sin and alive to Christ once and for all in regeneration (Rom. 6:1–11), we are called to die daily to our old self and live daily by "the free gift of God," which "is eternal life in Christ Jesus our Lord" (vv. 12–23).

In the Hebrew Scriptures, to believe (*he'emin*) is *to consider established*. Literally, it is to say *'aman* (amen) to God's saving work. Other words (*chasah*, "to take refuge"; *batach*, "to trust or lean upon") also convey the idea of faith as involving trust as well as knowledge and assent. In the New Testament, the noun *pistis* (and its cognate verb *pisteuein*) is understood as confidence in the testimony of another—most frequently, as reliant trust in Jesus Christ. Often, it is *believing into* Christ, actually rolling ourselves over onto Christ for salvation. It is also described as looking to Christ, feeding on Christ, and receiving Christ. These instances (besides many others) underscore the role of faith *in the act of justification* as a passive receiving and resting in Christ. However, the faith of the justified is also active in good works (James 2:26).

The command to believe does not turn faith into a work. On the contrary, it is a command to cease our labors and enter God's rest (Heb.

4:1–9). Just as "God's grace has appeared" in the gospel itself (Titus 2:11), so Paul also speaks of faith as arriving: "Now before faith came, we were imprisoned and guarded under the law until faith would be revealed." Because "Christ came," "faith has come . . ." (Gal. 3:23–25).

While upholding the continuity of faith in Christ from Abraham (indeed, from Adam and Eve after the fall) to the present, the New Testament also announces that something new has dawned. The law itself could not create faith, hope, or love but because of sin could only place the world in prison awaiting the redeemer (Gal. 3:22–23) or under a guardian awaiting its maturity in order to receive the inheritance (v. 24). In the Old Testament, as in the New, it was only the promise of the Messiah that kept faith alive.

Throughout the book of Acts, Christ is proclaimed and the appropriate response is repentance and faith. In Hebrews, the great fathers and mothers of Israel are commended for their faith in the promise even though they did not yet see its fulfillment (Heb. 11:1–12:2). Moses and his liberated followers, according to Paul, "drank from the spiritual rock that followed them, and the Rock was Christ" (1 Cor. 10:4). In fact, the wilderness generation is said to have "put Christ to the test" when they rebelled (v. 9).

Faith is therefore not a generic optimism: a positive outlook on life. It is not even a general trust in God and his promises to care for us. Saving faith is not merely "believing God for big things." Saving faith is very specific: *clinging to God's saving mercy in Jesus Christ as he is given to us in the gospel*. Faith produces the fruit of love and good works, but in the act of justification it simply hears and receives. There is no virtue in faith itself that justifies. Even the weakest faith clings to a strong Savior.

It is frequently noted that there are three aspects to this saving faith: knowledge, assent, and trust. Faith involves *knowledge*. Our personal act of faith shares in "the faith once and for all delivered to the saints" (Jude 3), which is a body of doctrine. This common faith clarifies the content of faith's object: Christ's person and work. We can no more set knowledge (doctrine) over against a personal relationship (experience) in this instance than we can in our relationships with other people. We cannot place our trust in someone apart from knowing certain things about that person's character, will, and works. My wife would be unimpressed if I defended my ignorance about her with the excuse that I wanted to experience "a person, not a proposition," and the same is true of faith in God.

Faith also involves *assent*. We are accountable for this knowledge. Do we believe that God has given his Son for sinners and raised him on the third day for their justification? Yet genuine faith not only knows and assents to the truth, but *trusts* in Christ as one's only hope. Faith is not only the belief *that* Christ is God incarnate, crucified, and raised on the third day, but is, in Calvin's words, "a firm and sure knowledge of *the divine favor toward us*, founded on the truth of a free promise in Christ, and revealed to our minds, and sealed in our hearts by the Holy Spirit."[9] Faith is simply "confidence in the divine favor and salvation."[10] Faith not only believes that Christ suffered and died and was raised to life for sinners. "You believe that there is one God," James writes. "You do well. Even the demons believe—and tremble!" (James 2:19). But the demons do not trust in God as he delivers himself to sinners in Christ through the gospel. According to the polls, many Americans believe that some faith in God is necessary for salvation. However, according to most people, it need not be knowledge of and assent to God as he is revealed in his incarnate Son through the gospel. And it certainly does not require personal trust. However, faith is defined in Scripture as knowledge, assent, and personal trust in the Savior.

In the words of the Heidelberg Catechism, "True faith is not only a sure knowledge whereby I hold for truth all that God has revealed to us by his Word, but also a firm confidence which the Holy Spirit works in my heart by the gospel that *not only to others but to me also*, remission of sins, everlasting righteousness and salvation are freely given by God, merely of grace, only for the sake of Christ's merits."[11]

Faith is not a feeling, even though it is often accompanied by profound experience. It does not well up within us. Rather, it is provoked in us—created in us—by the external announcement of the gospel. When the Spirit opens our hearts to the gospel's beauty, we simply find ourselves believing the report.

Anxiously anticipating the quite premature delivery of our triplets, I will never forget the moment that the doctor looked at me and announced, "They're all alive!" It was not a foregone conclusion (at least for one of them) and until that report, my wife and I were in suspense. All of the wishful thinking—even from certified medical professionals—could not alleviate that suspense, turning possibility into actuality. I could *believe* all I wanted in a successful delivery, but I had no promise to rely on, either from God or the doctors, and the intensity of my believing it had nothing to do with the state of affairs. My confidence depended entirely on the words that the doctor uttered. Similarly, the gospel is *news* because it reports a completed event. Faith does not make something true, but embraces the truth.

The more we hear and understand concerning the gospel, the more our faith grows and strengthens. Nevertheless, the weakest faith clings to a sufficient Savior. Faith itself does not save us from judgment any more than the quality of one's confidence in the lifeguard is responsible for being rescued from drowning. It is the rescuer, not the one rescued, who saves. In fact, it is in the very act of rescuing that a victim finds himself or herself clinging to the rescuer in confidence. I have yet to see a headline like, "Drowning Victim Rescued by Superior Clinging." It is always the lifeguard who is credited with the rescue. It is *on account of Christ* that we are justified, through faith, and not on account of our faith itself.

Get on Your Feet: From Sitting to Dancing in the Street with Strangers

For those who believe, the verdict of the last judgment has already been rendered. In this light, one would think that the gospel would be the major headline, today or any other day. The day each of us came to faith (if we can recall a definite point) may not be all that newsworthy for everyone else as it is for us. It is not surprising that my personal religious experience does not grab the headlines. I would not even be surprised if the press ignored major "religion" stories. However, given the fact that most Americans at least say that they believe in hell and the reality of the last judgment, surely the announcement that we can know *now* the verdict of that day would be the most important discovery. Of course, we want to know how wars will turn out, how people will recover from natural disasters, and so on. But surely the arraignment of humanity before God is the most universally decisive event awaiting us all. What if we could peer into the future to know what will happen on that day and what God's verdict will be? This verdict has already been announced to all who receive and embrace it through faith alone. This verdict is *heard* and *believed*, even though its effects are not always *seen* and *measured*.

In the old days, boys would stand on the sidewalk selling their newspapers, yelling, "Hear ye, hear ye!" That is what we are called to do, whether in the public assembly as ministers of the gospel, or in our informal witness to our neighbors and co-workers. We are not telling them to transform their lives or to adopt a self-help program. We are not even holding up our own experience as the big news that should move them to accept Christ. They should not believe what we are reporting simply because they see that it puts a smile on our face or a spring in our step. We are just announcing the headline: "There is therefore now no condemnation for those who are in Christ Jesus" (Rom. 8:1). The news speaks for itself!

Jesus announced, "Whoever believes in him is not condemned, but whoever does not believe is condemned already, because he has not believed in the name of the only Son of God" (John 3:17–18). It is this headline that keeps our faith alive even when we are dying inside, when we do not have a smile on our face or a spring in our step. So why doesn't everybody flock to this Good News? Jesus explains, "And this is the judgment: the light has come into the world, and people loved the darkness rather than the light because their deeds were evil. For everyone who does wicked things hates the light and does not come to the light, lest his deeds should be exposed" (vv. 19–20). As he said earlier in this same conversation, no one gets this gospel—even a religious leader like Nicodemus—until they are born again from above.

To receive the Light, we must have our darkness exposed; to be clothed in Christ's righteousness, we must acknowledge our righteousness as filthy rags; to live in Christ, we must die to our former identity. Only the Spirit can raise those who are "dead in trespasses and sins" (Eph. 2:1), so that we can accept the news: both the bad and the good of it. We must repent of the yellow journalism that we used to believe and accept the story that God reports. Even now, around the world, many are still being transferred from Adam's ruins to Christ's estate. Therefore, Paul concludes his argument in Romans 10, "As it is written, 'How beautiful are the feet of those who preach the Good News!' . . . So faith comes from hearing, and hearing through the word of Christ" (vv. 15, 17).

We Don't Make the News, We Just Report It

We have seen that God's Word calls us outside of ourselves, to an extroverted existence: looking up to God in faith and out to the world in love and service. We are not the news; God is. And once the Good News pulls us outside of our narrow inner world of "spin," we become reporters ourselves.

Especially in TV news, the reporter increasingly becomes the news. There is now a celebrity "news show" for every ideological perspective, from one extreme to the other. News is packaged as entertainment, the success of each program made dependent on the cleverness with which the ideologue can persuade the audience of one position and mock those of his or her rivals. Eventually, we come to learn more about the host than the issues and the size of the audience depends on the charisma of the deliverer more than on the trustworthiness of the content that is delivered. Parallels with the church today become obvious. As a result, particular churches take on the personality of the pastor, including his politics, socioeconomic location, ethnic distinctives, and consumer tastes. It is not the news, but the reporter, who shapes the identity of Christ's body.

This can happen on a broader scale, where the church more generally makes itself the news. The early church was powerless to make itself the headline. In fact, harassed and persecuted out of the synagogues and other public buildings, believers were often forced to meet together in private homes. Nevertheless, the Good News concerning Christ spread like fire throughout the known world. As the saying goes, "The blood of the martyrs is the seed of the church." Christ's fame spread throughout Caesar's empire.

With its growth, however, the church began to make itself the big story. Success had its own set of problems. As the church received toleration and then was even made the official religion of the empire under Constantine, many of its leaders became worldly rulers, mirroring the mighty lords of the secular kingdom. Christ's conquest over sin, death, hell, Satan, and the principalities and powers of this age was not the news itself as much as it was the basis for the church's conquest over the kingdoms of this age through its alliance with secular political power. The church became a culture—a civilization—rather than "a kingdom of priests" announcing a new regime with a heavenly King who dispensed his heavenly gifts through Word and sacrament.

Today, the church in America has become so identified with its secular culture that it is difficult to tell them apart. Wanting to retain our last vestiges of power, popularity, and privilege, our churches and Christian movements often seek to grab the headlines. We try to build a kingdom through press releases, crowded stadiums, programs, and "relevant" communication. Like news celebrities, we pander to particular constituencies in order to gain a larger share of the market, instead of simply keeping to our script, proclaiming Christ and him crucified to the nations.

The gospel changes lives precisely because it is not about us—even our changed lives—but about Christ. The life of every Christian is filled with enough inconsistencies to disprove the Christian faith every day if it were based on our changed lives. The history of the church is littered not only with heresies and schisms but with crusades, inquisitions, and the justification of atrocities in the name of Christ. Yet in all of this we can point away from ourselves, individually and collectively, to "the Lamb of God, who takes away the sin of the world" (John 1:29). In fact, it is only by repenting of our spiritual pride and casting ourselves ever anew on God's mercy in his Son that we can become servants rather than masters of our neighbors.

It is not our relevance and impact but Christ's that creates its own saving publicity. Not even the apostles made themselves the headliners: "I decided to know nothing among you," Paul declared, "except Jesus Christ and him crucified" (1 Cor. 2:2). "But far be it from me to boast except in the cross of our Lord Jesus Christ . . ." (Gal. 6:14). "For we are not, like so many, peddlers of God's word, but as men of sincerity, as commissioned by God, in the sight of God we speak in Christ" (2 Cor. 2:17). The apostles are not *lords*, but *ambassadors* (2 Cor. 5:20). Ambassadors do not create their own job descriptions, policies, or agendas, but announce, explain, defend, and apply the agenda of their head of state. The church today must get out of the business of writing up its own press releases and rediscover the power of God in the gospel. We are not the Good News, but its recipients and heralds; not the newsmakers, just the reporters.

The News That Turns Us Inside Out

The proclamation of the Word turns us inside out. As the Westminster Larger Catechism puts it, the reading "but especially the preaching" of God's Word is appointed as God's "means of grace" precisely because of its way of "driving us outside of ourselves" to cling to Christ.[12] By summoning us outside of ourselves to receive his judgment and justification, God introduces us to the great outdoors, above the dungeon we have dug for ourselves and in which we have lived as if it were the real world. We do not gather around the celebrity but beneath the balcony from which God summons us to call on his name.

Do we believe that it is God's own act of arraigning us before his judgment seat, rendering the verdict of the last day here and now? Or does the translucent podium reveal that the preacher is more visible than the Word is audible? And does the bar stool indicate that speakers think that their communication will be more relevant and effective if they share their own thoughts, reflections, experiences, and wisdom than if they assumed that they were a more anonymous herald? Do they see themselves as ambassadors sent and commissioned by the great King or as founders of their own ministry?

Recently, I saw a televised memorial service marking the anniversary of the September 11, 2001, terrorist attacks. Aside from the usual confusion of Christ with national identity, the event was impressive. Uniformed soldiers, presidents, and joint chiefs of staff, stepped up to the microphone and the crowd fell silent, each hearer distracted from his or her ordinary activities. Although we know that instead of bringing us breaking news, each speech will probably do no more than offer remarks on the significance of that event, we listen intently. Along with those gathered there, we in the television audience secretly, even unknowingly, hope that they will not express their personal opinions, feelings, and ideologies, but say something that gives some hint of the significance of this event beyond its tragic consequences. More aware of their public office than of their own public persona and charisma, they seemed to be more deeply impressed with the weight of their commission than with themselves.

How much more do we come with high expectations when God gathers us for his event, where he actually creates a new people on the basis of a new covenant? We hear the preacher's voice, hoping that in and through it we will also hear another voice, another speech, that comes from God's Word in the power of the Spirit. We know that the preacher could not know these things simply because of superior wisdom or contact with the culture. We hope that something will be said. *Said*. Something that we did not already know, something that we could not have known until he said it. We expect news. We wait expectantly. Will the minister spread a feast in the desert in Christ's name? Just the Word—news from the battlefield that might justify our hope—is all that we ask. Do they look us in the eye and tell us that God has conquered Satan, death, and hell? Are they really sure that he has? And even if they are, do they believe that it is the most important news that they could bring that day? Is it the front-page story or is it regularly moved to the back pages, assumed rather than announced?

Even if the world finds this Word offensive, at least it is the voice of God that they hear, waking the dead and uniting them to his Son. Whatever it is that makes this Word strange, it is at least worth hearing. It is not capable of being assimilated to our familiar routine, experiences, and moral striving. In *The Problem of Pain*, C. S. Lewis wrote,

> The characteristic of lost souls is "their rejection of everything that is not simply themselves." Our imaginary egoist has tried to turn everything he meets into a province or appendage of the self. The taste for the other, that is, the very capacity for enjoying good, is quenched in him except in so far as his body still draws him into some rudimentary contact with an outer world. Death removes this last contact. He has his wish—to lie wholly in the self and to make the best of what he finds there. And what he finds there is Hell.[13]

It is the work of the Spirit through the gospel to find "lost souls" and to unite them to Christ and therefore to a communion of saints.

In that wonderful yet often painful process of becoming part of Christ's body, we still want to make the news ourselves but instead find ourselves being incorporated into the news of Christ's doing, dying, rising, and ruling. As we suffer the *death* of our cherished inmost self—that little devil—we become alive really for the first time.

6

THE PROMISE-DRIVEN LIFE

Laid out on the couch with the flu one Saturday, I flipped on the TV for an extraordinarily long time. The whole day was exercise equipment, how to become real estate rich with no money down, and Suze Orman gave me her steps to financial security. As much as we all make sport of this sort of thing, it attracts us. As we have seen, there is a good reason for this: we are wired for law. Not just because we are Americans, but because we are human beings, we are a "can-do" people. Everyone knows right from wrong. Rules, steps, formulas, advice, exhortations, suggestions for managing our life better: these are not wrong in themselves. We just need to know the difference. First, we need to know the difference between God's commands and human wisdom. The latter may be helpful, but it is not the standard by which we are judged. Second, we need to know the more basic difference between commands and promises; law and gospel.

Even the ordinary wisdom of the world can be useful. The problem comes when we forget that we are fallen children of Adam and that we cannot fix our deepest moral crisis. For that, we need Good

News, not good advice. We need God's unfailing promises, not more purposes and programs. Suzie Ormand's financial advice and Jake's home gym can help me improve my life, but nothing they say can transfer me from death to life. If I am sufficiently motivated, a good diet and exercise plan can help a lot. No one has ever consulted me about financial planning, but even I can recognize that if I follow half of what Suzie says, I could be a much better steward. (I bought the video. Don't ever leave your credit card within reach if you spend a Saturday watching TV. I nearly bought three separate gyms and a few things for my wife.) These folks do not even have to be Christians to provide good, common sense instruction in daily affairs.

We all need goals. More importantly, we need to know the purpose for which we exist. But the bad news is that we—all of us—have fallen short of it. So knowing why we are here and what we are supposed to do does not change the fact that we are failures in the big picture. In fact, the "finish line" only measures how far we are from it. From the last several chapters we have seen that justification (God's verdict of righteousness) is the *origin* of the Christian life, not the *goal*. We live from the already completed fact of our being chosen, redeemed, called, and justified in Christ to our present sanctification and future glorification in him. When it comes to our standing before God, we need a *report*, not a new *resource*.

Knowing our purpose in life is a form of law. Everyone is born into this world as God's image bearer, with a consciousness of being created for God's glory. However inchoate and suppressed, it is an inescapable fact of our existence. When we hear that our chief end is "to glorify God and to enjoy him forever," our conscience is pricked. We have fallen short of God's glory and our chief end seems more characteristically defined by enjoying ourselves, perhaps with God's help.

We need to know our purpose in life, but we should be under no illusion that we are pulling it off. At this point, the only message that qualifies as Good News is that Christ has fulfilled it as our representative and has made us sharers in both his justification and resurrection life, so that one day we will also share in his glory. Whenever we move from God's purpose for our lives to advice for how to fulfill it, we unwittingly go around Christ's cross to seize our own glory here and now. This is the danger inherent in taking the gospel for granted. As pastors and parishioners, it is easy to conclude that we need the gospel to be saved, but now we need to know how to live. Of course, we do need to grow in our understanding of God's purposes and moral commands as well as in our own obedience to them. Yet we are on the wrong track if we think that the gospel was only necessary for "getting saved" and not for staying saved—even for growing in holiness. It is always "in view of God's mercies" that we can offer ourselves as "a living sacrifice" (Rom. 12:1–2). Our sanctification no less than our justification depends on Christ's absolution, so that we live out of gratitude rather than guilt and out of faith rather than self-trust. No longer trying to make God indebted to us, we receive his gift and share it with others. The gospel makes us extroverts: looking outside of ourselves to Christ in faith and to our neighbor in love.

What are you driven by? What really gets you up out of bed in the morning? When everything around you seems to fall apart and life doesn't seem to work, what anchors you? Is it things that you *see* (circumstances as they appear to you) or is it something you *hear* (God's promise) that determines things for you? Is it something inside of you or something external to you, a word that comes from outside completely challenging your experience of things? Are you driven by power, wealth, ambition, self-esteem, the acceptance of others? Or perhaps by nobler things, like making the world a better place, loving God and your neighbor, a sense of purpose and meaning?

As evidenced by Rick Warren's phenomenal bestseller, *The Purpose-Driven Life*, the passion for meaning and purpose has not been extinguished by the daily grind or by the unrelenting buzz of our consumer culture. *While affirming the importance of having clear goals and a worthy focus in life, I am urging us to put purposes in their place, as servants of promise.* No longer under the law's condemnation, the justified are free now to respond to God's commands out of thanksgiving for the God whose character it displays and out of love for our neighbors. The gospel saves us, giving us a reason to walk through the wilderness to the promised land, and the law guides us, giving us directions for that journey. *Christians are driven by God's promises, and directed by God's purposes.* Two passages—Genesis 15 and Romans 4—bring this point home powerfully.

Wrestling with the Promise (Genesis 15)

Even after his military victory and the remarkable event of being offered bread and wine with a blessing from Melchizedek, Abram's greatest problem is that he has no heir, no one to carry on the calling that God has given him. His world, as he sees it anyway, is bleak. "After these things the word of the LORD came to Abram in a vision, 'Do not be afraid, Abram, I am your shield; your reward shall be very great'" (Gen. 15:1). Abram and Sarai had been called out of the barrenness of moon worship in the city of Ur by God's powerful word which created faith in the promise (12:1). There is the reward of the land of Canaan, but ultimately the whole earth ("father of many nations"), of which the land of Canaan will serve as a type. The New Testament even tells us that Abraham himself was looking *through* the earthly promise to its heavenly reality (Heb. 11:10, 13–16). The earthly land of promise would be a small-scale copy of what God would one day bring to the whole earth from heaven forever.

The message that God delivers is sheer promise. This covenant is not like the one with Adam or, later at Sinai, with Israel, which was conditioned on their personal fulfillment of the law. It was a gift to be received, not a task to be undertaken. God simply declares, "I am your shield. Your reward shall be very great." This is what ancient Near Eastern lawyers would have called a "royal grant." Similar to a peerage, royal grants were an outright gift of title and land from a monarch to a subject in view of extraordinary service.

However, what good is an inheritance without heirs? Abram wonders, "O Lord God, what will you give me, for I continue childless, and the heir of my house is Eliezar of Damascus?. . . . You have given me no son, and so a slave born in my house is to be my heir" (Gen. 15:2–3). The empirical facts of the case—what Abram *sees*—appear to be overwhelming evidence against the testimony of the promise. Nevertheless, God counters again with the promise, offering the innumerable stars as a sign of the teeming offspring who will come from his loins. "And [Abram] believed the LORD; and the LORD reckoned it to him as righteousness" (vv. 5–6). Abram's response is not one of blind optimism or positive thinking. Abram finds himself believing the promise that he has heard.

Faith does not create; it receives. It does not *make* the invisible visible or the future present or hope reality. It *receives* that which is *already* given. Grace precedes faith. It is not finally accepting the goodness of the world, or my own goodness, but receiving God's goodness toward me in spite of the way things really are with me and with the world.

Further, this passage tells us that Abram believed God and was then and there *declared* righteous. Abram is not exactly the perfect picture of moral integrity. He routinely argues with God, questions

God's promise, and in his own effort to secure his own future, has a child by his servant Hagar even though God had declared that the promise would come through Sarai. Trying to save his own neck, at one point Abram even lies to a king, telling him that Sarai is his sister rather than his wife! This is hardly the moral character we would hold up to our children for imitation. Yet God preaches the gospel—the utterly one-sided Good News of what *he* has done and will do—and Abram suddenly finds himself believing.

Trusting God's promise, Abram is "justified" then and there. The Hebrew word for justification (*chashav*) is right out of the legal terminology of the courtroom. If the accused is "righteous" (i.e., in the right before the law), then he or she is acquitted—more than that, actually judged to be a fulfiller of all righteousness and therefore the rightful heir of his kingdom. It is clear enough from the story (before *and* after this event) that Abram is not personally righteous, yet he is declared righteous.

This doctrine of justification is at the core of the divine-human paradox: How can I have the assurance that I am accepted before God as righteous when I continue in sin? How can I trust God for ultimate relief when, right now, my life is full of hopelessness? It all seems like pie in the sky. I *see* my life. I *know* my circumstances and the possibilities for my future. Nevertheless, by pronouncing Abraham just, Abraham is just. The promise makes it so, and it is received through faith. If we can get this right in our understanding of justification— our standing before God—it will radically alter every other aspect of life. So decisive is this event in the patriarch's life that he is literally renamed. No longer Abram ("father"), he is now Abraham ("father of many") and Sarai is Sarah—even while Sarah herself is still barren. We already begin to see that the promise itself—the word spoken by God as "Good News" or "gospel"—gets the ball rolling and keeps it rolling. It not only speaks of a new world, but already creates it.

Although he believes the promise, Abram seeks greater confirmation. "How will I know that these things will happen?" he asks. At this point, one might wonder why God did not move on to another set of candidates for "parents of the promise." Isn't that the way we often behave toward people who doubt our word or our abilities to perform what we have promised: "Don't let the same dog bite you twice?" But God couldn't, because this covenant was sworn by God himself, without any conditions assumed by the human partner. This salvation is going to come through Abraham and Sarah, not through anyone else. It is the seed from Sarah who will save the world. God doesn't make general

promises with lots of fine print and caveats. They are specific and this
promise rests entirely on God's will and effort. As the New Testament
reminds us, "If we are faithless, [God] remains faithful, since he cannot deny himself" (2 Tim. 2:13). The promise was grounded in the
fact that God chose Abram, not that Abram chose God. God cannot
change his electing purpose and in any case he knew all along that he
was electing scoundrels. That is why it is called *grace*.

So again God condescends to Abram's weakness by giving him a
vision, recorded in the latter half of this chapter (Genesis 15). What a
strange vision it was! As Abram falls asleep, God passes through the
severed halves of animals (vv. 12–21). This can only be understood in
the light of the treaty-making ceremonies of the ancient Near East.
When a greater king (like an emperor) wanted to take a lesser king
and his people under his wing, he would write up a charter or treaty.
First, the treaty would give a little history justifying the annexation
of this smaller kingdom: "I have delivered you from the Egyptians.
Therefore, you will acknowledge only me as your great king." This
would be followed by clear stipulations: "Do this," "Don't do that."
Then there were the sanctions: "If you fail to keep these decrees and
statutes, I will. . . ." Finally, the treaty would be sealed by a ceremony
in which the lesser king would walk behind the greater king, passing
between the severed halves of animals, taking upon his own head the
same fate should he fail to keep this covenant. In other words, the
responsibility was entirely on the side of the lesser king.

What is remarkable about this vision, however, is that it is God—the
great King—who takes this ceremonial walk down the aisle *alone*, with
Abram in a deep sleep. The fulfillment of God's promise of salvation for
Abram and Sarai, and all of those who will be blessed through their seed
(Christ), will not depend on them, but on *God*, who assumes the curses
of his own covenant should the promise fail to be realized in history. It
is not because of Abram's faithfulness that he has received this royal
grant for himself and his heirs, but because of God's faithfulness to his
electing purposes in eternity which were made and realized in Christ.

As Paul would later attest in Galatians 3:19–20, specifically referring
to this covenant with Abraham, no covenant could be more firmly
anchored in God and his promise rather than in the faithfulness of
the human partner than one that God swears by himself. The covenant that Israel made with God at Mount Sinai was dependent on
their oath ("All this we will do"). Yet the covenant that God made
with Abraham is different:

> Now to Abraham and his Seed were the promises made. He does not say, "And to seeds," as of many, but as of one, "And to your Seed," who is Christ. And this I say, that the law, which was four hundred and thirty years later, cannot annul the covenant that was confirmed before by God in Christ, that it should make the promise of no effect. For if the inheritance is by law, it is no longer of promise; but God gave it to Abraham by promise. (Gal. 3:16–18 NKJV)

In Galatians 4, Paul uses an allegory of two mountains (Sinai and Zion), which Paul correlates with Hagar and Sarah. So far, this would not be terribly jarring. Judaism recognizes a distinction between Sinai (dependent on human faithfulness) and Zion (God's eternal promise) in the Old Testament, and his readers would have as well. Furthermore, they knew that the slave Hagar was the mother of Ishmael and Sarah was the mother of promise. But the next move is odd: Paul says that the earthly Jerusalem is really the child of the slave, in bondage to Mount Sinai, while the heavenly Jerusalem is filled with liberated hosts—Jews and Gentiles—who have entered God's holy sanctuary in freedom and joy by grace alone in Christ alone. In other words, when history is interpreted on this side of Christ's appearing, even those who are descended physically from Sarah are actually the spiritual heirs of Hagar and they are prisoners arraigned at the foot of Mount Sinai. They are bearing their own personal responsibility for the curses that this covenant pronounced on all who fail to do everything contained in the law.

So in Genesis 15, God preserves Abraham's life by assuming the curses of the covenant in the case of breach, walking alone through the severed halves. And in Genesis 22, when Abraham follows God's command to sacrifice Isaac, God provides a substitute at just the right moment, before the knife is plunged into the son of promise. Circumcision was a partial "cutting off" of the foreskin, which pointed to the seed who would be entirely "cut off" for the sin of his people: "the Lamb of God who takes away the sin of the world" (John 1:29). Of course, Abraham did not realize everything that was going on at the time—the plot was still unfolding. It is always easier to understand the earlier scenes and subplots once you've read the whole story. Yet all along—even in Abraham's day—the plot centered on Christ and his saving work (Gal. 3:15).

Out of his confession of faith, Abraham now could continue his pilgrimage not on the basis of his physical vigor or Sarah's fertility (in other words, what he can see and attain by his own efforts), but on the sole basis of the word of promise that he heard. We will either rely on the visible realities we *see* or the invisible realities we *hear* preached to us, but we cannot rely on both. Unbelief is unavoidable: either we will doubt the credibility of the divine word in the face of life's realities or we will doubt the credibility of this world's so-called "givens" in the face of the divine promise. We have to become better *un*believers in what we see and experience within ourselves if we are to become better *believers* in the divine promise.

Faith ignores statistics, "the way things are," and the possibilities or impossibilities that we have to work with. Faith ignores these not because it is a blind optimism, but because it knows and believes God and his promise. In faith, we are willing to let go of our dependence on what we see and experience here and now in order to embrace the announcement that a new world has been created by God's declarative word. God's promise creates a new world out of darkness and void, fertile pastures of fruit bearing trees out of the infertile soil of unbelief and ungodliness. This covenant is not a call to *attain* a future that Abram can see and control, but to *receive* a future that God has spoken into being. Sarai's infertile womb is the canvas upon which God will paint a new creation.

And they both are renamed. The promise gives them a new identity. Of course, all of this is counterintuitive. We get what's coming to us, right? Good guys finish first. God helps those who help themselves. No, says the gospel, God justifies the wicked and creates new life out of barrenness, hope out of despair, life out of death. That is how the apostle Paul explains this story of Abraham in Romans 4.

The Fulfillment of the Promise (Romans 4:13–25)

These passages from Genesis 15–17 form the backdrop for much of Paul's teaching. Israel had confused the promise covenant made with Abraham and the law covenant that Israel made with Yahweh at Sinai. Nobody can be justified by means of a law covenant, Paul insists, but only on the basis of a promise covenant. So Paul brings Abraham to the witness stand. He is "an example for us," Paul says, but not for the reasons we may have learned in Sunday school. The rabbis of Paul's day (like Paul himself before his conversion) thought that Abraham had *merited* his justification before God by his obedience (the "merit of the fathers," it was called). Yet, as we have seen, the story in Genesis just does not give that much credence. If Abraham were to be judged on the basis of his own righteousness, he might be able to boast before other sinners, but not before a holy God, Paul says (vv. 1–2).

Then how is Abraham an example to us? Paul tells us that he serves as the paradigm case of the earth-shattering truth that God justifies (declares righteous) those who are in themselves "wicked"—not on the basis of works, but through faith in the promise. If Abraham could not be justified by his own righteousness, how can the rest of us who claim Abraham as our forefather? *Abraham is an example to us of the fact that God justifies the wicked.*

Paul is contrasting law logic with promise logic in Romans 4. He uses the same phrase—"through the righteousness of faith" (v. 13)—that he will use in chapter 10, contrasting the law logic of *our ascent* ("go get it") with the promise logic of *God's descent* ("God gave it to you"). So when it comes to how we are justified—that is, set right before God and made heirs of all the gifts that he has for us—*law* and *promise* represent antithetical means of inheritance. We know the difference between a contract ("I'll do this if you do that") and a bequest ("I hereby leave my estate to . . ."). That's the difference here between employees and heirs (Rom. 4:4). Christ's perfect fulfillment of his Father's revealed will is the basis and his death is the legal event that distributes the royal estate to all of his beneficiaries.

The contrast is either/or again in verse 14: "For if those who are of the law are heirs, faith is made void and the promise made of no effect. . . ." It's not just that faith is also necessary, but that faith and works are absolutely antithetical as means of attaining this justification. The last part of the sentence (v. 15) reads, "Because the law brings about wrath; for where there is no law there is no transgression." It is the law that exposes our sin and makes it utterly sinful, counting our wrongs not as "mistakes," "self-expression," "foibles," or even "not being all that we could be," but as a wicked and willful transgression of God's explicit command. The law speaks and the old self dies.

The law cannot create faith because it tells us what is *to be done.* It can only announce to those who transgress it what they have *not* done; consequently, it brings despair in its wake. The promise, by contrast, tells us what *has been done* by someone else. That is why it brings life. Once the law's just sentence has been satisfied in Christ, it is no longer our executioner, but instead plots the course for our gospel-driven life. Outside of Christ, our hearing of the law merely reminded us constantly how far we fall short of God's glory. But now the law has no power other than to guide those whom it has justified in Christ along their pilgrimage in spite of every setback and failure.

Then in verse 16 Paul says, "Therefore it is of *faith* that it might be according to *grace*, so that the promise might be sure to *all* the seed, not only to those who are of the law, but also to those who are of the faith of Abraham, who is the father of us all . . ." (emphasis added). See the logic of the promise? Paul will add one more pearl to the string later, but the point thus far is clear enough: Only if we receive the inheritance by faith is it all of grace, and therefore able to reach the ends of the earth.

It is important to recognize that *God's promises are not simply a pledge of a future reality, but bring about that reality in the present.* We see this clearly in the way Paul talks about the law *doing* certain things and the promise *doing* certain things. In verse 14 of our passage he says, "For if those who are of the law are heirs, faith is made void and the promise made of no *effect*, because *the law brings about wrath*; for where there is no law there is no transgression." The promise (or gospel) preached *creates* faith, just as the law actually brought about our condemnation. The law not only warns us of God's coming wrath; it "brings about wrath," just as the judge's act of sentencing a criminal actually effects the criminal's condemnation.

Throughout Scripture we are taught that God's word is effectual: it brings about whatever God speaks, whether in creation, providence, or redemption. God spoke the world into being by his creative word and upholds it by that word each moment. After the human fall into sin, he issued his life-giving promise and, despite continuing sin and rebellion, overcame unbelief by his powerful word. "So shall my word be that goes forth from my mouth; it will not return to me empty, but it will accomplish what I please" (Isa. 55:11). God's speech is "active and living," Scripture says (Heb. 4:12). His law not only stands over us as a list of rules we have failed to keep, but crawls inside our conscience, like an IRS audit, "and is a discerner of the thoughts and intents of the heart. And there is no creature hidden from his sight, but all things are naked and open to the eyes of him to whom we must give an account" (v. 13). This is why the writer to the Hebrews says that we need to flee to our great High Priest as our only hope (vv. 14–16). The law is successful in condemning, driving us to despair of ourselves, to seek salvation outside ourselves. The gospel is successful in giving us faith to receive Christ and all his benefits.

Back to Romans 4, then. The gospel doesn't just *speak about* a world that might come to be if we all just got our act together; it *speaks a new world into existence*, where no capacity existed, and that is exactly the language that Paul uses in verses 17–22. God creates death and life by *speaking*. This is why Paul returns again to the example of Abraham and Sarah as the construction site of a new creation, produced by the promise. Here is the logic: "For this reason it depends on *faith*, in order that the promise may rest on *grace* and be guaranteed to *all* of his descendants," both Jew and Gentile (v. 16, emphasis added). He adds, "as it is written, '*I have made you* the father of many nations'—in the presence of the God in whom he believed, *who gives life to the dead and calls into existence the things that do not exist*" (v. 17, emphasis added).

We must not miss the emphasis here on God's action, as Paul compares the miracle of salvation to creation itself. Just as God spoke the world into existence without any contribution from the creation itself, he speaks a new world of salvation into being apart from our decision or effort. And just as Abraham is declared righteous by this proclamation then and there, Paul observes, he was declared then and there "father of many nations" despite all appearances to the contrary. "Hoping against hope, he believed that he would become 'the father of many nations,' according to what was *said*, 'So numerous *shall* your descendants be' " (v. 18). God's *saying* makes it so. Salvation comes, then, not by doing certain things but by hearing certain things and embracing them by faith, which is itself created by the Spirit through the preaching of the promise. Not all parts of the Word give life, as Paul says later (Rom. 7:10): "And the commandment, which was to bring life, I found to bring death." If Paul were not a *transgressor*, the law would pronounce him just, but as it is, it can only bring death. The *promise*, by contrast, brings life—out of nothing.

This is the scandal of justification: How can God declare us righteous if we are not inherently righteous? Isn't this a legal fiction? Doesn't it make God a liar? But that's like thinking that God cannot say, "Let there be light" unless there is already a sun to give it. God himself *creates* the conditions necessary for the existence of his work. When he says, "Let there be light!" the sun exists. When he says, "Let this ungodly person be righteous," "this barren woman be pregnant," "this faithless person embrace my Word," it is so. When we really understand justification, we really understand how God works with us in every aspect of our lives before him. *Christ* lived the purpose-driven life so that we would inherit his righteousness through faith and be promise-driven people in a purpose-driven world. He did gain the everlasting inheritance by obedience to everything God commanded, driven by the purpose of fulfilling the law for us, in perfect love of God and neighbor, and he bore its judgments against us. His resurrection guarantees that the law of sin and death does not have the last word over us. He fulfilled the original purpose and commission for human existence, glorifying and enjoying his Father to the fullest. And he did this as our covenantal head, our representative, not simply as a moral example. Just as we were "in Adam" at the fall, we were legally included "in Christ" as he fulfilled all righteousness, bore our sins, and rose from the dead in victory.

Relinquishing hope in the ordinary powers of human nature, Abraham was given genuine hope in God for the first time. The future was now *God's* future, not his own. He didn't have to work it all out, plot and plan, scheme to bring about the inheritance (as he had done before). Thus, because of the power of the *promise*, not his own goals or resolve, Abraham could turn his eyes away from "his own body, already dead (since he was about a hundred years old), and the deadness of Sarah's womb" (v. 19). "He did not waver," again, not because of any inherent virtue of his faith, but because he "was *strengthened* in faith, giving glory to God, and being fully convinced that what He had promised He was also able to perform" (v. 21, emphasis added). In other words, it was because of the *object* of faith, not the *act* of faith itself that Abraham could stand firm.

This is such a practical point for us because even if we accept that we are saved by grace and not by our own works, our bent toward "law logic" (ascending and attaining) encourages us to turn faith itself into the "one thing" we do to achieve God's blessings. If we could just believe enough, we could please God, or maybe claim healing or financial prosperity, fix our family, or really do something great for the kingdom of God. Yet faith itself is part of that total package of salvation that comes entirely from God as pure gift (Eph. 2:8–9). Again, faith does not create the promised blessing; the promise creates faith.

As anticipated above, Paul adds here another glistening pearl to the chain of the promise logic: If the inheritance comes by faith in the promise and not in the works of the law, then faith gives all "glory to God" (v. 20). Faith gives no glory to self, even to our act of faith. It is directed entirely to God and his promise. Faith is strong only to the extent that the promise is strong. Abraham knew that God could perform what he had promised. "And therefore 'it was accounted to him for righteousness'" (v. 22). *Salvation—or what Paul here calls the inheritance—comes by faith alone, in Christ alone, through God's Word alone, so that it may be by grace alone, to the end that all the glory will go to God alone.*

Between the Devil and the Deep Blue Sea: What Really Drives You?

Like a sailboat equipped with the most sophisticated guidance technology, our Christian life may be decked out with the latest principles for victorious living, with spiritual coaches telling us what will make life really "work" for us and for our families. Often new Christians especially sail out of the harbor under full sail, eager to follow the guidance system, making use of the gadgets, enthusiastically listening to every fellow boater who has some advice to offer. Yet, as many long-time believers know, eventually the winds die down and we find ourselves dead in the water. Then when storm clouds gather on the horizon, we discover that all of the guidance technology and good advice in the world cannot fill our sails so that we can return safely to the harbor. The equipment can plot our course, tell us that a storm is coming, and indicate our present location, but it cannot move us one inch toward the safety of the harbor. In other words, if we are looking for motivation in the Christian life, it cannot come from motivational principles; only the gospel fills our sails.

Satan doesn't mind the gadgets. In fact, he has patented a lot of the spiritual technology for keeping us from looking to Christ in the beginning, middle, and end of our lives. Anything that keeps us looking within—even if he can use the name of Jesus and Bible verses to support it—will serve his purposes for shifting our faith from Christ to ourselves. Many Christians think that they need Good News—the gospel promise—in order to become Christians, but then, precisely because faith is always active, looking for something to do for God's glory and the neighbor's good, the temptation is to think that we grow out of this basic need for the gospel. We become impressed with the fruit more than the vine. Obviously, this soon leads us to wonder why there isn't more fruit, better fruit. If this self-examination doesn't lead us to crawl out of ourselves and flee to Christ, it will end in despair (if we are honest) or conceit (if we are not). Like Abraham, even after he believed and was justified, we find ourselves still questioning the promise as we look within ourselves and around at the circumstances that seem to count against God's promise. We fall back on ourselves, trying to strategize our own way to the inheritance. God did not take the gospel for granted, but kept preaching it into the hearts of Abraham and Sarah.

Yet we easily think that we needed the gospel to power us out of the harbor into the wide blue sea. What we really need now is direction, counsel, suggestions, and wisdom for living. However, apart from the gospel the law does not offer mere advice; it says, "Do or die." Because the logic of works righteousness is our native religion as sinners, we will always fall into our old patterns of self-justification. Or we will throw off this burden, declaring independence from God and accountability to his law. Earlier I compared the ascetic pietism that formed Nietzsche's portrait of Christianity and the nihilistic philosophy that he advocated to the religious leaders of Jesus's day who could neither dance nor mourn. Only the gospel finally delivers us from the swinging of the pendulum between legalism and antinomianism (lawlessness). Only when we are delivered from the condemnation of the law through the gospel are we truly free *and* truly ruled for the first time in our life.

While God's wise directions are necessary, apart from the ever-present word of *promise* that despite our failures at sea, God is at the helm piloting us to safety, we will eventually give up on sailing altogether. Purposes, laws, principles, suggestions, and good advice can set our course, but only the gospel promise can fill our sails and restore to us the joy of our salvation.

A few years ago, a woman visited our church. Struggling in her marriage, she said that her church was not really helping her through the crisis. "The pastor is preaching a ten-week series on 'How to Have a Better Marriage,'" she reported. Now one might think that a series on improving one's marriage would be practical, relevant, and useful to someone like this. "But what I really need is forgiveness," she confessed. She realized that the faith that she needed to pursue reconciliation with her husband could only be fanned into a flame by the gospel. She kept coming back. Forgiven much, she loved much—at least more than she had—and her husband was amazed that instead of nagging him about his failures, she was extending forgiveness and love to him. Eventually, he broke down and acknowledged his own sin and received the same forgiveness that had softened her heart. It is not that she did not receive exhortations, especially in private counseling, but that she had a new desire to follow them because she had again taken her place simply as a receiver—a beneficiary—of grace.

Not all cases have such a happy ending, of course. In those cases, God's promise-making and promise-keeping faithfulness is really put to the test. How sufficient is Christ and his saving work? How good is the Good News? Is God's promise reliable even when everything I see and feel leads me to believe that I have gone too far?

Our answer comes in the concluding verses of this remarkable passage:

Now the words, "it was reckoned to him," were written not only for his sake alone, but for ours also. It will be reckoned to us who believe in him who raised Jesus our Lord from the dead, who was handed over to death for our trespasses and was raised for our justification. Therefore, since we *are* justified by faith, we *have* peace with God through our Lord Jesus Christ, through whom we *have obtained* access to this grace in which we stand; and we boast in our hope of sharing the glory of God. (Rom. 4:23–5:2 NRSV)

This promise is not something that we can attain; it is the gift that keeps on giving, the present that we open again and again. We need the gospel throughout our whole life.

Faith is *defiance.* The law breaks off our attachments to our own righteousness, possibilities, hopes and aspirations, fears, and accomplishments by telling us that the game is over. We are not who we thought we were and there is no way forward for us. We are dead in our tracks, which is where the gospel always finds us.

Faith tells the world, "I know this is how it is with me and that from the look of things, there is no hope. Your exhortations will not work anymore, if they ever did, but there is someone else who did everything that needs to be done for me." Abraham's faith defied every possibility that he *saw,* in favor of the "impossible" word that he *heard.* This is why "faith comes by hearing . . . that is, the word of faith which we preach" (Rom. 10:17). To trust in God is to distrust every other promise maker. The world makes a lot of promises: "try this product and you'll be. . . ." Seeking to be relevant, the church too can become a shopping mall of false promises that yields despair or self-righteousness, rather than faith and the fruit of the Spirit. What we need most, not just at the beginning, but in the middle and at the end of the Christian journey, is *Good News.*

Following Jesus

Sharing his priorities for the next thirty years, best-selling author Richard Foster disclosed his "spiritual formation agenda" in a recent *Christianity Today* article. Foster observes that there is a lot of interest these days in "social-service projects." "Everyone thinks of changing the world, but where, oh where, are those who think of changing themselves?" He also complains that an overemphasis on grace in some circles "will not allow for spiritual growth."

Having been saved by grace, these people have become paralyzed by it. To attempt any progress in the spiritual life smacks of "works righteousness" to them. Their liturgies tell them they sin in word, thought, and deed daily, so they conclude that this is their fate until they die. Heaven is their only release from this world of sin and rebellion. Hence, these well-meaning folks will sit in their pews year after year without realizing any movement forward in their life with God. . . . People may genuinely want to be good, but seldom are they prepared to do what it takes to produce the inward life of goodness that can form the soul.[1]

Foster also blames much of the distraction from spiritual growth on "a Christian entertainment industry that is masquerading as worship" and "an overall consumer mentality that simply dominates the American religious scene."

A member of the Society of Friends (Quakers), Foster does not include in his agenda for spiritual transformation the public ministry of Word and sacrament. He calls us to "do all we can to develop the *ecclesiola in ecclesia*—'the little church within the church,'" referring to the examples of Lutheran pietism's *collegia pietatis*, John Wesley's "holy clubs," and the "inner mission" of the Norwegian pietists. As Foster observes, these Protestant movements have their roots in the heritage of Catholic spirituality, identified especially with Francis of Assisi, Theresa of Avila, John of the Cross, and Thomas à Kempis.

Born in 1380, Thomas à Kempis was formative in the development of a movement known as the Brethren of the Common Life, in whose grammar schools Erasmus and Luther, among many others, were reared. His classic, *The Imitation of Christ*, has sold (and continues to sell) more copies than any other book besides the Bible. It was one of my mother's favorites and was assigned in my introductory Bible class at a Christian college. There are valuable insights in this book, especially its simple but sometimes profound wisdom concerning the practice of a devout Christian life.

Nevertheless, poring over this work again recently, I was reminded of what is missing from this celebrated classic: most glaringly, *Christ in his saving office*. It is not an understanding of doctrine "that makes a man holy and just," he writes in his opening paragraph, "but a virtuous life makes him pleasing to God." "I would rather feel contrition than know how to define it." His twenty-fourth chapter, on how to appear before God's judgment, excludes any mention of Christ or his gracious mediation; the fires of purgatory are meant to be felt in this life, drawing us to contempt of this world and the body, in order to ascend God's holy hill through inner purification.

My purpose is not to critique this classic devotional, or to tackle the question of spiritual discipline. Rather, it is to interact with the paradigm of sanctification (the Christian life) as chiefly the imitation of Christ.

I find much of what Foster says above about contemporary spirituality persuasive. I find him spot-on in his worry that the holiness of God has been eclipsed by the ephemeral exuberance of entertainment passing for worship and consumerism packaged as mission and discipleship. *Antinomianism* (literally, antilawism) teaches that because we are saved by grace, apart from works of the law, we have no obligation to follow the precepts of God's moral law in the new covenant.

I do not think that the evangelical movement today has thought enough about its doctrine to be self-consciously antinomian. Rather, I think that we have become distracted from God's Word—both his commands and his promises. Usually, antinomianism and legalism are regarded as opposites, but they are actually coconspirators against the gospel-driven life. Jesus upbraided the religious leaders of his day for setting aside God's law to obey human commands. It is so easy for us to exchange both God's means of grace *and* God's moral commands for our own principles of spiritual growth. In the process, we simultaneously turn gospel into law and it is not even God's law, but our own, that we use as the measuring stick for our progress.

I think that Foster is right that there is also a kind of "cheap grace" that fulfills the fond dreams of the antinomian who comforts himself with the syllogism: "God likes to forgive, I like to sin: what a great relationship!" Even if we eschew antinomianism, there is a kind of laziness that does not revel equally in the "already" of new life in Christ and the "not yet" of its consummation. There are too many passages in Scripture that call us to go on to maturity, to leave our old life behind, and to strain toward the prize. Many of those passages are found in the same chapters as our favorite verses on the Good News of salvation by grace alone through faith alone in Christ alone. For example, after announcing that we are saved by grace alone—and that even faith is a gift—Paul adds, "For we are his workmanship, created in Christ Jesus for good works, which God prepared beforehand, that we should walk in them" (Eph. 1:8–10).

But I'm not sure how directing people to *greater* concentration on themselves is going to overcome the narcissistic captivity of our times. As Thomas Finger has documented in *A Contemporary Anabaptist Theology*, the Anabaptists—whose leaders were trained by the Brethren of the Common Life—were no more interested in the justification of the ungodly than Rome.[2] The whole emphasis was on discipleship, defined as the imitation of Christ.

The *Spiritual Exercises* of Ignatius of Loyola are of a similar orientation. Ignatius founded the Jesuit order for the express purpose of opposing the Reformation. Though not without occasional praise, Luther saw his experience with the Brethren of the Common Life as encouraging a theology of glory: ascending to God through works and mysticism. Calvin looked upon his schooling at the ascetic Collège de Montaigu as "servile labor" under the burden of severe regulations and no gospel, while Ignatius recalled fondly his time there as a student.

Evangelicals have always been technique-oriented. Give us a formula or a daily plan and we will follow it. Sometimes when we are overwhelmed by the graciousness of God in the gospel, we merely exchange a simplistic *acceptance* of formulaic sanctification for an equally simplistic *denial* of daily disciplines, such as private prayer and Bible reading. Reformed spirituality is centered on the public means of grace (preaching and sacrament) together with the corporate assembly in the prayers and singing of the people of God. It also has a high view of family worship, with daily Bible reading, catechism, and prayer. How is a busy family going to squeeze into that daily schedule time for personal Bible reading and prayer? Isn't it enough that we go to church and spend time with the Lord as families?

It is striking to me that Luther, Calvin, and other reformers—many of whom (like Luther himself) were former monks—did not throw the baby out with the bathwater. Sharply critical of using monastic rituals to ascend a ladder to God, they nevertheless held private as well as public prayer in the highest possible estimation. Luther thought that the busier he was in a given day, the more he needed to prepare for it through earnest prayer and reading of Scripture. The Puritans not only wrote sermons and doctrinal treatises, but devotional guides, meditations, and books of prayer. We do not rise up to God and offer our piety to the king of heaven; God comes down to us. But when he does descend to us in forgiveness and grace, should we not avail ourselves of every opportunity to receive his gifts? God has promised to meet us in his Word—yes, especially as it is proclaimed in public assembly, but also as we mine its riches throughout the week. And we not only invoke our Rescuer's name on the Lord's Day, but every morning and evening.

The issue is not whether we engage in personal disciplines or habits of meditative prayer and reading of Scripture, but whether we do so in a gospel-driven manner. Is it a technique for personal transformation or is it a saving and sanctifying encounter with the Triune God who has met us in his incarnate Son? Are we working *toward* our justification or *from* it? Are we being drawn to look outside of ourselves, to Christ, or are we feeding our natural tendency to focus on ourselves and our inner life? Obviously, if the significance of Jesus Christ lies principally in his offering a moral example, faith in Christ is not absolutely necessary. Moral lessons about the importance of love, sacrifice for others, surrender to God's will, and so forth, can be drawn from myriad examples in the history of religions. We do not need an incarnate, righteousness fulfilling, curse-bearing, resurrected Savior if salvation comes by imitation.

More than Imitation

Already in Augustine, Bernard of Clairvaux, and a few other medieval writers, there was an emphasis on *union with Christ*. In this marriage, Christ receives our debts and despoiled treasury and we inherit his righteousness and life. Long before Luther, Bernard referred to this "great exchange." Augustinians recognized that defining salvation or the Christian life as the imitation of Christ (*imitatio Christi*) presupposes a woefully inadequate doctrine of sin and therefore of God's saving grace in Christ.

What this Augustinian tradition still lacked, however, was the Reformation's clarity concerning the nature of grace. Where they saw it chiefly as a medicinal substance infused into believers to make them progressively holy, the reformers recognized that grace is first and foremost God's favor toward sinners on account of Christ. This "justice" or "righteousness" by which we stand accepted in God's presence is imputed, not infused; declared immediately, not progressively realized. At the same time, they just as strongly affirmed that God's Word does what it says. Everyone whom God declares to be righteous is also progressively sanctified.

While remaining sinful, believers now struggle against indwelling sin. But why struggle? If the full remission of sins and favor with God is the believer's possession through faith alone, and God's grace is greater than our sin, why shouldn't we go on sinning? That is the question that Paul knew his teaching on justification (treated above) would provoke. His answer, in Romans 6, is that the same Good News that announces our justification also announces our death, burial, and resurrection with Christ. Paul does not threaten with the fears of purgatorial fires or worse, but simply declares to those who believe in Christ that he is not only the source of their justification but of their deliverance from sin's all-controlling dominion. They still sin, but never in the same way that they did before. Now they love what they hated and hate what they loved. I am among a dwindling number of exegetes who still believes that Romans 7 focuses on this paradox: only believers struggle with sin, because sin is both an enduring reality (with many setbacks) and yet the believer's enemy.

Nowhere in this lodestar passage for the Christian life does Paul direct our attention to the imitation of Christ. He has already painted too dark (realistic) a picture of human depravity to imagine that the devil, the world, and our sinful hearts could meet their match in our deeper commitment to follow Christ's example. Yet he does not ignore the issue of conformity to Christ. Rather, he teaches something far greater than an example to imitate. He calls us not simply to imitate Christ but to be crucified, buried, and raised with him. Since we *are* in Christ, we must act accordingly: daily putting to death the deeds of unrighteousness, and bearing the fruit of our union with him. But before he speaks an imperative, he announces the indicative of the gospel: Christ's saving work has accomplished far more than we imagined.

The Spirit's work of uniting us to Christ makes us not mere imitators but living members of his body. We are incorporated—baptized—into Christ's death, burial, and resurrection. Paul does not say, "Be like Jesus." He says, "You *are* like Jesus. He is the head, and you are part of his body; he is the first fruits and you are the rest of the harvest. As goes the head, so go the members. You are now swept by your forerunner into the new creation. So how can you continue living as if none of this ever happened?"

It is easy for us to rely on the gospel for forgiveness and justification but then to look elsewhere for our renewal and sanctification. However, Paul says that it's all there: "in Christ." Only after saying this does Paul then issue the imperative to live a life that is consistent with this truth.

Jesus said the same thing in John 15. We have no life in ourselves, he tells them. There are no resources for following Jesus, imitating him, becoming his disciple. We are dead branches, cut off, without hope in this world. However his disciples are not only forgiven; joined to him as the life-giving vine they become living branches, bearing fruit that will remain. Only then does Jesus issue his imperatives to love and serve each other as he has loved and served us.

There is a world of difference between having a role model whose example we fall short of ever reproducing and having yourself "killed" and re-created as branches of the Tree of Life. Doing what Jesus did is different from bearing the fruit of Christ's righteous life. In fact, the most important things that Jesus did cannot be duplicated. Because he fulfilled the law in our place, bore our curse, and was raised in glory to take his throne at the Father's right hand, we can have a relationship with him—and with the Father—that is far more intimate than the relationship of a devotee to a guru, a student to a teacher, or a follower to a master.

Following Christ is not the means of, much less an alternative to, but is the consequence of our union with Christ. Like Christ's own death, burial, and resurrection, baptism is not a repeatable event. So our Christian life is focused on objective, perfectly completed events in the past, of which the Spirit has made us beneficiaries through the gospel here and now. "Therefore, since we *have been* justified by faith, we *have* peace with God through our Lord Jesus Christ" (Rom. 5:1, emphasis added)—whether we have that peaceful, easy feeling or not. We fail every day to imitate Christ, but this does not keep us from believing the objective promise of God's Word that the Spirit is gradually conforming us to Christ's likeness.

Instead of making us lax, this should fuel our pursuit of godliness. It is not sticks and carrots that drive us on like slaves, but the gospel that fills us with the joy of children and coheirs with Christ. Instead of trying to figure out whether it is well with our soul because of our subjective experience or measurable progress, we press on even with weak faith and often compromised repentance, knowing that God has done, is doing, and will do what he has promised.

Even after the announcement of D-Day, as Allied troops landed at Normandy and won the decisive conflict, the war did not end until V-Day: the announcement of victory in Europe. Every day in the Christian life is simultaneously victorious—because of Christ's decisive conquest—and a struggle with new skirmishes and conflicts as the enemy refuses to acknowledge the truth of its defeat. This is what Romans 6–8 is all about.

Even when Scripture calls us to follow Christ's example, the relationship between master and pupil is asymmetrical. Jesus refers to his impending sacrifice for sinners as the model for his followers in Matthew 20:28, for example. However, it is obvious from the context that Jesus's act of self-sacrifice is unique and unrepeatable. We are not called to die for our neighbors' sins or to bear the wrath of God in their place. When Paul calls us in Philippians 2 to "have the same mind" as Christ in his self-humiliation, he obviously is not calling us to set aside the heavenly glory and power belonging to the second person of the Trinity and to descend to earth—even hell itself—in human flesh. We are not incarnations of God. Nevertheless, we are beneficiaries of his incarnation, united in body and soul to his glorified flesh. Therefore, we are called to imitate his humility.

As George Lindbeck observed, imitation has its place, but not under the category of "gospel." The call to follow Christ and his example is an imperative—the third use of the law directed to Christians rather than to unbelievers.[3] The "imitation of Christ" paradigm of spirituality makes Christ's self-sacrifice and humility an analogy for our discipleship. The "union with Christ" paradigm makes our love and service an analogy of Christ's inimitable accomplishment. *Being in Christ is the perpetual source of our becoming like Christ, not vice versa.*

Calvin offers helpful insights on this point in his comments on Jesus's prayer in John 17. Believers are "sanctified by the truth," which is God's Word (v. 17), "for the word here denotes the doctrine of the Gospel": here Calvin challenges the "fanatics," who imagine a sanctification that comes from an "inner word" apart from the external Word.[4] "And for their sakes I sanctify myself," Jesus prays (v. 19).

> By these words he explains more clearly from what source that sanctification flows, which is completed in us by the doctrine of the Gospel. It is because he consecrated himself to the Father that his holiness might come to us; for as the blessing on the firstfruits is spread over the whole harvest, so the Spirit of God cleanses us by the holiness of Christ, and makes us partakers of it. Nor is this done by imputation only, for in *that* respect he is said to have been made to us *righteousness*; but he is likewise said to have been made to us *sanctification* (1 Cor. 1:30) because he has, so to speak, presented us to his Father in his own person, that we may be renewed to true holiness by his Spirit. Besides, though this sanctification belongs to the whole life of Christ, yet the highest illustration of it was given in the sacrifice of his death; for then he showed himself to be the true High Priest, by consecrating the temple, the altar, all the vessels, and the people, by the power of his Spirit.[5]

The goal is "that they may be one" (v. 21).[6] Calvin is as much on home ground in discussing the richness of the organic, horticultural metaphors as the legal. While they are distinct, the organic and the legal are two sides of the same covenantal coin.

Paradoxically, it is this very liberation that issues in constant inner struggle, since we belong definitively to the new creation—"the age to come"—with Christ as our first fruits and the Spirit as the pledge. Yet we still live in "this present evil age" and continue to pretend that we are not those whom God has willed us to be in Christ. Pagan ethics knows only of a battle between the higher and lower self, trying to get the mind to keep the passions in check so that we will live a balanced life between pain and pleasure. Such ethics knows nothing of God's decisive victory. It therefore knows nothing of the battle between the Spirit and the flesh, which means the triumph of the age to come—justification and new life—over this present age of sin and death. Christians are not those who have finally discovered a balanced lifestyle to keep them from extremes, but are those who have died and have been raised with Christ. Natural ethics and the enabling power of the Spirit in common grace may check immoderate habits, but the Spirit creates a new world through the gospel.

Just as Paul's treatment of justification led logically to the question, "Should we continue in sin in order that grace may abound?" (Rom. 6:1), the Reformation unleashed radical elements that went well beyond the views of the Reformers. Lutheran theologian Gerhard Forde reminds us, "Luther had hardly begun to proclaim the freedom of the Christian before he had to fight against abuse of the term. He did not do this in such a way as to speak about the good works that must be added to faith. Instead, he did so by calling people back to that faith that occurs 'where the Holy Spirit gives people faith in Christ and thus sanctifies them.'"[7] Luther's response at this juncture was precisely Paul's: Though justified through faith alone, this faith "is never alone, but is always accompanied by love and hope," according to the *Formula of Concord*.[8]

Apart from the imputation of righteousness, sanctification is simply another religious self-improvement program determined by the powers of this age (the flesh) rather than of the age to come (the Spirit).

This gospel not only announces our justification, but our participation in the power of Christ's crucifixion and resurrection. Therefore, we cannot look to Christ at the beginning, for our justification, and then look away from Christ to our own progress and countless manuals that offer formulas for spiritual and moral ascent when it comes to the Christian life (sanctification). Again Forde is insightful:

In our modern age, influenced by Pietism and the Enlightenment, our thinking is shaped by what is subjective, by the life of faith, by our inner disposition and motivation, by our inward impulses and the way they are shaped. When we think and live along these lines, sanctification is a matter of personal and individual development and orientation. It is true that we also find this approach in Luther. No one emphasized more sharply than he did our personal responsibility. . . . But this approach is secondary. "The Word of God always comes first. After it follows faith; after faith, love; then love does every good work, for . . . it is the fulfilling of the law."[9]

Even in sanctification, "the focus is not upon the saints but upon sanctification, upon the Word of God in all its sacramental forms, and also upon secular institutions that correspond to the second table of the law. . . . Only God is holy, and what he says and speaks and does is holy. This is how God's holiness works, which he does not keep to himself, but communicates by sharing it."[10]

What this means is that we who once were curved in on ourselves, seeing the world but not really seeing it rightly, must be called out of ourselves to be judged as ungodly and then dressed in Christ's righteousness. This is necessary not only for our justification but for our sanctification as well. Not even the best example will save us. We need to be justified *and* sanctified on the basis of Christ's work for us. In sanctification, our growth in personal holiness—which is usually observable to others more than to us—is the effect not of our imitation of Christ, but of our union with Christ.

Our identity is no longer something that we fabricate in our bondage that we mistake for freedom. "To become new men means losing what we now call 'ourselves,'" C. S. Lewis observes. "Out of our selves, into Christ, we must go."[11] "Your real, new self (which is Christ's and also yours, and yours just because it is His) will not come as long as you are looking for it," he adds. "It will come when you are looking for Him." To be in Christ is to be "very much more themselves than they were before."[12] "He invented—as an author invents characters in a novel—all the different people that you and I were intended to be. In that sense our real selves are all waiting for us in Him. It is no good trying to 'be myself' without Him."[13] "To enter heaven," he says, "is to become more human than you ever succeeded in being on earth."[14]

Far from creating a morbid subjectivity and individualism, as is often charged, this view frees us from being curved in on ourselves, fretting over our own souls. Sanctification is a life not of acquiring but of receiving from the excess of divine joy that then continues to overflow in excess to our neighbor and from our neighbor to us.

"Christ for Us" and "Christ in Us"

According to an assertion of the great Roman Catholic historian of philosophy, Etiènne Gilson, "For the first time, with the Reformation, there appeared this conception of a grace that saves a man without changing him, of a justice that redeems corrupted nature without restoring it, of a Christ who pardons the sinner for self-inflicted wounds but does not heal them."[15] A surprising number of Protestants—including evangelicals—seem to share Gilson's misunderstanding.

While Rome simply assimilated justification to sanctification, the Reformation position affirmed both as distinct yet inseparable gifts. G. C. Berkouwer replies to those who deny Luther's interest in God's gracious renovation of believers: "To anyone who has had a whiff of Luther's writings this conception is incredible. Even a scanty initiation is enough to be convinced that justification for Luther meant much more than an external event with no importance for the inner man."[16] Like the relation of the doctrine of substitution in relation to other aspects of the atonement, forensic justification not only allows room for other benefits of Christ; it is their source and security.

The reformers saw "Christ for us" and "Christ in us"—the alien righteousness imputed and the sanctifying righteousness imparted—as not only compatible but as necessarily and inextricably related. Those who are justified through faith are new creatures and begin then and there to love God and their neighbor, yielding the fruit of good works. Reformed churches agree with the Lutheran confession that if sin has free sway over one's life, "the Holy Spirit and faith are not present."[17] However, it is not simply that justification and sanctification always go together in the application of redemption, as if they were parallel tracks; justification is the only reason that there can be any sanctification of sinful believers. And both are granted in our union with Christ. The real question, then, is whether justification is the *source* of new obedience or its *result*. In fact, presenting our bodies as a living sacrifice, according to Paul, is "our reasonable [*logikēn*] worship" in the light of "God's mercies" that have been explored to that point (Rom. 12:1). It is the Good News that yields good works. Salvation is not the prize for our obedience but the source. In the light of God's mercies in Christ, offering ourselves as living sacrifices actually makes sense.

I have mentioned before that Scripture integrates drama, doctrine, doxology, and discipleship in ways that we easily overlook. Christian faith and practice arise first of all out of a dramatic narrative: the unfolding plot of redemption from Genesis to Revelation. This story gives rise to doctrines: specific conclusions that God himself reveals as to the meaning and implications of this divine drama. The doctrines provoke us to faith, wonder, and praise. Our sails filled with the gust of grace, we sail out of the harbor into the wide open spaces of the world, loving and serving our neighbors in thanksgiving and joy. Without the biblical drama, the doctrine is abstract; without the doctrine, the doxology is much ado about nothing; without the doxology (shaped by the drama and the doctrine), discipleship is just another makeover: a few more fig leaves to conceal our nakedness.

Conclusion

I agree with Richard Foster's concern to step away from our daily routines and to be silent before the Lord, to receive his commands and promises, and to pour out our cries, praises, and intercessions to the Father, in the Son, by the Spirit. Many of us coming out of pietistic evangelicalism may easily over-react, neglecting—even ridiculing— habits of daily Bible reading and prayer that nourish our souls. I think Foster is right that the problem for evangelicalism today is not that it is too monastic, but that it is too worldly. However, Christ has not left us as orphans, to fend for ourselves by finding spiritual directors and our own means of grace. He promises to work in us by his Spirit through preaching and sacrament. Christ is not dead. Nor must he be pulled down from his throne in order to be present in our lives. Paul says that he is present objectively through his Word and Spirit.

When it comes to his methods, Foster's advice is consistent with his message. Where Scripture teaches that Christ's objective work outside of us in public history is the gospel—"the power of God for salvation," Foster writes,

> The most important, most real, most lasting work, is accomplished in the depths of our heart. This work is solitary and interior. It cannot be seen by anyone, not even ourselves. It is a work known only to God. It is

the work of heart purity, of soul conversion, of inward transformation, of life formation. . . . Much intense formation work is necessary before we can stand the fires of heaven. Much training is necessary before we are the kind of persons who can safely and easily reign with God.[18]

This trajectory of the spiritual disciplines leads us to a host of means of grace besides Word and sacrament, and these other means are actually methods of our ascent rather than God's descent to us in grace. Instead of drawing us outside of ourselves, this trajectory takes us deeper into ourselves, clinging to what is happening within us rather than what happened for us, outside of us, two thousand years ago. The most important, most real, most lasting work is *not* accomplished in the depths of our heart but in the depth of history, under Pontius Pilate. It is precisely because of that accomplishment that we have every reason to meditate on the riches of our inheritance each day. And because of Christ's work outside of us, in history, we are not only justified but are being transformed from the inside out.

We do not need more spiritual directors, but more pastors who feed us, elders who guide us, and deacons who care for the flock's physical needs. Realizing more and more what it means to be living branches, we need more and more to put to death the actual deeds of unrighteousness and live more and more to the Father, in the Son, by the Spirit.

Baptized into Christ, fed richly by his Word and at his Table, let us not leave the festive day forgetful of God's service to us but be led back each day into his Word and into the world with joyful hearts to be conformed to Christ's image as we work, play, raise children, steward earthly resources, enjoy dinner with friends and breaks with co-workers. Live from Christ's work for you, with Christ's work in you, toward Christ's return to deliver you from this present evil age. Don't feed off of your New Year's resolutions; rather, feed off of your union with Christ. You are part of the harvest of which the glorified Christ is already the firstfruits! Then resolve again, every day, to return to Christ, to recall your baptism, and to repent of all that weighs you down and distracts you from running the race with your eyes fixed on him.

LOOKING AROUND, LOOKING AHEAD

A CROSS-CULTURAL
COMMUNITY

7

NEWS OF
WAR AND PEACE

GOD'S POLITICS FOR A NEW CREATION

On a cold November day in 1095, Pope Urban II roused the great crowd assembled before him to take up the cause of holy war against Islam. Instead of fighting each other, the people were told to unite against the common enemy and retake the Holy Land. "If you must have blood," he exhorted, "bathe in the blood of infidels."[1] Substituting itself for its ascended Lord, the church assimilated a civilization to that ecclesial body. The church father Eusebius declared that it was from Christ and by Christ that "our divinely favored emperor [Constantine], receiving, as it were, a transcript of the divine sovereignty, directs, in imitation of God himself, the administration of this world's affairs." Included in this, says Eusebius, is that the emperor "subdues and chastens the open adversaries of the truth in accordance with the usages of war."[2]

From the time of Constantine, the symbol of Christ's cross was emblazoned on the shields of imperial soldiers who cried out, *Christus est Dominus* ("Christ is Lord") as they plunged their swords into infidels. Though less violent, many Christians in America still demand visible symbols of Christianity in the culture. We expect presidential speeches to be peppered with references to God and our leaders to give some indication of their personal relationship with Christ. We want the nativity scene in the city park, even if it means that it has to sit beside other religious symbols. Sometimes, we even sing about the triumph of the Union in the Civil War by invoking the language of Christ's last judgment (as in "The Battle Hymn of the Republic") or the imagery of the new heavens and earth in the book of Revelation for "America, The Beautiful."

Where did Jesus go after he accomplished our redemption? And how did the church—and allegedly Christian empires—come to think that they could keep his seat warm until he returned in power and glory to reign on the earth? We've seen how the disciples themselves missed the point of Jesus's journey from Galilee to Jerusalem. He had prepared them in the upper room for his departure, as he explained how his ascension to the Father meant that the Spirit would descend to dispense the gifts of his victory. Even after the resurrection, when he explained how all the Scriptures pointed to his saving work, they were not ready for his ascension. Just before this momentous event, they still asked, "Lord, *now* are you going to restore the kingdom to Israel?" (Acts 1:6, emphasis added). They were still thinking about a kingdom of earthly power here and now, not a kingdom of grace. They were ready for the ax to fall, for the sheep to be separated from the goats, and for fire to consume the enemies of God. Instead, they are told to go throughout the world preaching the forgiveness of sins in Jesus Christ until he returns at the end of the age. As they stood gazing at the ascending Lord, the disciples were told by two angels, "Men of Galilee, why do you stand looking into heaven? This Jesus, who was taken up from you into heaven will come in the same way as you saw him go into heaven" (v. 11).

Refusing to be located in the time between the times, the church often substitutes itself for its absent Lord and then announces prematurely that the kingdoms of this world have become the kingdom of our God and of his Christ. Focusing on the challenges of secularism and Islam, evangelicals and Roman Catholics increasingly congeal around the salvaging of "Judeo-Christian" culture. In a *Time* article on the relation of Pope Benedict and Islam, conservative Catholic scholar Michael Novak explained concerning the pontiff: "His role is to represent Western civilization."[3]

American Protestantism has excelled at confusing the gospel with the American way. I was reminded of this recently when a pastor told me that he had tried to remove the American flag from the front of the church. Removing the pulpit, table, and font to make room for the praise team's stage was relatively light work, but the flag was apparently immovable. Just compare the pomp and circumstance with which Memorial Day and Independence Day are celebrated in churches across America with the relative obscurity of Ascension Day. Nobody expects the *New York Times* to celebrate Christ's victory over sin and death each week, but why should the *church* give the impression that there is something more important and more impressive to focus on than this report?

Obviously, a press release announcing the cure for AIDS would grab the front-page headline for weeks on end. We would all dance in the streets. Right now, there are Christians working alongside non-Christians in labs and on the field to try to achieve that success. However, only the church sends out the press release each week that the whole kingdom of Satan has been toppled forever; that we are now in the hand-to-hand combat phase of ferreting out guerrilla strongholds that have not yet yielded to the truth of their defeat, and awaiting the return of the King for the last battle. The end of all disease, poverty, oppression, violence, disaster, idolatry, and sin is at hand. Which is more powerful: the announcement of God's work or calls for us to usher in the kingdom? Once we realize that the gospel is the power of God for salvation, our action becomes a "reasonable service." However, if our service is front and center, the church may easily (wittingly or unwittingly) proclaim itself as the Messiah.

Satan thought that he had finally outwitted God. Knowing that God is just as well as loving, Satan knew that he could not simply let bygones be bygones; that God's image bearer lay in chains, and that the wages of sin is death. However, he was outwitted by God at the cross. Right where Satan and the powerful of this age could only see God's weakness, God revealed his most explosive power in the whole history of holy war. Right where he claimed victory, he had in fact lost everything.

We still have trouble knowing what time it is or what kind of kingdom Christ has inaugurated. If we are still thinking in terms of a fully-consummated kingdom of glory and power present now in the world in and as the church or in Christian movements, then the gospel will be considered foolish and the divinely prescribed methods of delivery (preaching and sacrament) will be judged too weak to really grab the world's attention. The challenge for us, as for the first disciples, is to believe in a kingdom that we hear, but do not see. Preaching the gospel, baptizing, teaching, administering the Supper, visiting the sick, caring for orphans and widows: *Of course*, we do these things. The "of course," however, betrays the fact that we often give lip service to these divinely mandated methods of the Great Commission, but our real interest lies elsewhere, in methods and programs that will *really* accomplish something important.

It is natural to think that the demagogues who roam the earth in search of victims are the ultimate enemies, but the biblical drama indicates that these are puppets of the powers and principalities of darkness in heavenly places. Terrorism, global warming, and AIDS are problems that we need to address as responsible human beings together with non-Christians in our common life together. Non-Christians are created in God's image, too, and still carry around in their conscience a sense of justice, civic friendship, and beauty. God preserved and protected Cain, the idolater and murderer, because he wanted the secular city to continue.

However, the Great Commission is not the Great Cultural Mandate, and the kingdom of Christ cannot be identified with any of the kingdoms of this age. The troubles of the secular city, in which the church shares and to which it sometimes contributes, are important matters to be addressed by believer and unbeliever alike, but they are symptoms of a more serious crisis: the reign of death and hell. If we could resolve our top ten crises in the world today, we would still have the devil on our back, sin mastering our heart, and everlasting death as the penalty for our mutiny.

As a minister, I am called regularly by God to make a political speech. A deeply partisan political speech. However, it is not to rally the troops in defense of Christendom against the infidels of various sorts. It divides not between Republicans and Democrats, liberals and conservatives, but between Christ and Antichrist. As heralds and ambassadors of the age to come, we are given the commission to go into all the world with the announcement that Jesus Christ is Lord and King, the only Sovereign who holds the keys of death and hell; who opens and no one can shut, who shuts and no one can open. It is he alone who will rid the world of evil by his wisdom and might, subduing chaos and leading his own into the place that even now he is preparing for them.

In this covenantal gathering, the cross is raised, not as a cultural symbol but as the proclamation of Christ crucified for sinners. Our role is not to represent Western civilization, democracy, or the free world, but the city of God, the New Jerusalem that is coming down out of heaven, as a bride prepared for her husband. It is this city alone that promises— and gives—true liberty to its sons and daughters beyond the ultimate triumph of death and hell. We witness to the ascended King who will return again to judge the living and the dead and reign forever.

No longer looking within for hope, the gospel draws our attention outside of ourselves to God's gracious action. In his earthly ministry, Jesus was always in a certain sense alone even with his disciples at his side. He knew what he came to do, and it was something that only he could accomplish. And now, at the ascension, he does not abandon his disciples but enters paradise as our living head to rule and to reign on our behalf. We look *out* to Christ, *up* to Christ where we are now seated with him in heavenly places, and then we look *around* to the coheirs that his heavenly reign has given to us as our new family and to the world to which he has called us as his witnesses and servants.

From Royal March to Enthronement (Psalm 68)

Unlike the first Adam, who led creation on a detour in the thanksgiving parade from its appointed path, this servant of the Lord finally fulfilled our human destiny. Psalm 68 records a royal march of Israel, foreshadowing the faithful Servant, Jesus Christ. The Psalm begins with the battle cry, "Let God arise, let his enemies be scattered!" (vv. 1–3).

God called Abram out of Ur and unilaterally pledged to give his descendants the land now occupied by various idolatrous peoples. Yet this was only the beginning: ultimately, through his offspring, the nations of the whole earth will be blessed (Genesis 15). Out of Sarah's barren womb, God created a new people by his word and Spirit, this time not commanding them to be fruitful and to multiply and to subdue the earth, but promising them that he will make them fruitful and multiply their descendants and subdue their enemies before them.

God fulfilled that promise, first on a typological level—by delivering Israel from Egyptian bondage. This liberation was just the beginning of the trek that would change the world. It was a march of Yahweh from Egyptian bondage to the giving of the Law at Mount Sinai to the arrival at Mount Zion: all of this typological of his march through history from creation and fall to redemption and consummation. However, Sinai is just a waystation en route to Zion. Israel's covenant with God is but a type, a parenthesis in redemptive history, pointing to the Jerusalem that is above and the King who reigns from heaven. In the words of Jewish scholar Jon Levenson, Psalm 68 "records a march of YHWH from Sinai, a military campaign in which the God of Israel and his retinue . . . set out across the desert."[4]

As important as Sinai is in the march, it lies midway between Egypt and the earthly Zion: Canaan. The focus shifts from Sinai to Zion, for example, in Psalm 97 (cf. Ps. 68:8–9; Deut. 33:2; Ps. 50:2–3). "The transfer of the motif from Sinai to Zion was complete and irreversible, so that YHWH came to be designated no longer as 'the One of Sinai,' but as 'he who dwells on Mount Zion' (Isa. 8:18). . . . The transfer of the divine home from Sinai to Zion meant that God was no longer seen as dwelling in an extraterritorial no man's land, but within the borders of the Israelite community."[5] And in the Zion traditions, Levenson comments, "there will emerge something almost unthinkable in the case of Sinai," an unconditional divine oath that God himself, above all the vicissitudes of human disobedience, will somehow arise and scatter his enemies and save his people. So Zion takes on a cosmic, universal role that Sinai never did. "Not only Jerusalem and the land of Israel, but even the people of Israel can be designated as Zion," as in Isaiah 51:16 and Zechariah 2:11.[6]

Leading captives from captivity, ascending, giving gifts to and receiving gifts from even his enemies, crushing the head of the serpent, and dwelling forever in Zion (Ps. 68:19–23), this is the King who "daily loads us with benefits, the God of our salvation," from whom alone we receive "escape from death." Although Levenson interprets Psalm 68 as a march from Sinai to Zion, echoing the trial of Adam from commission to consummation—and even points out the failure common to both—he concludes that Zion is finally absorbed into Sinai within Judaism. The ascent of Mount Zion, he suggests, is an allegory for "the ethical ascent of man."[7] Levenson even recognizes that this is where Christianity and Judaism part ways: Where the destruction of the temple in AD 70 transfers Jewish atonement from the earthly Zion to the inner hearts of the faithful, the New Testament announces that Christ is the true temple and those who believe in him are his living stones.[8]

Similar to Psalm 68, Psalm 24 was another "song of ascent," sung antiphonally by the Israelites as they made their annual pilgrimage up the hill of Zion to the temple. "Who may ascend the hill of the LORD and who may stand in his holy place?" The answer: only the person "with clean hands and a pure heart" (vv. 3–6). Verses 7–10 demonstrate that the only one who qualifies is none other than "the King of glory," who, after victory on the battlefield, commands the ancient gates of the sanctuary to open in order to receive him in triumph.

From his victory on the Mountain of Golgotha to his ascension to the true heavenly Zion and enthronement as the King of Kings and Lord of Lords, Yahweh leads captivity captive. This is already anticipated at various points in Jesus's ministry. The return of the seventy in Luke 10 anticipates the victory march. Jesus pronounces the "woes"—the covenant curses—upon the enemies of his kingdom, including Israel's religious leaders, while the seventy return with joy, breathlessly reporting to their Lord, "Even the demons are subject to us in your name." And Jesus said to them, "I saw Satan fall like lightning from heaven. Behold, I give you the authority to trample on serpents and scorpions, and over all the power of the enemy, and nothing shall by any means hurt you. Nevertheless, do not rejoice in this, that the spirits are subject to you, but rather rejoice because your names are written in heaven" (Luke 10:18–20).

As the captain of salvation, Jesus Christ in his earthly ministry marched from Sinai to Zion, leading captivity captive. Resisting the way of glory falsely promised by Satan in the temptation, Jesus went the way of the cross, marching all the way to the gates of hell to crush the serpent's head and to throw open the prison doors. Psalm 68 ends with the arrival of the military procession in the sanctuary of the great king who has ascended in triumph.

In his upper room discourse (John 14–16), Jesus prepared the disciples for his departure. He would be crucified, buried, and then rise again on the third day. Then he would ascend, both to send the Spirit from his throne and to prepare a place for us. In the meantime, on the basis of his victory ("All authority in heaven and on earth is given to me"), he commissions them to "go into all the world," proclaiming, teaching, and baptizing. In his covenant with Abram, God promised that in him and his heir (Jesus Christ) all of the nations of the earth will be blessed. This hope was kept alive by the prophets. Even in the process of pressing God's charges against Israel for violating the Sinai covenant, they prophesied the day when God himself would descend and build a highway from Jerusalem to Egypt, Assyria, and all nations (Isaiah 9). A remnant from all peoples would be gathered into the royal march of the great King, not to an earthly mountain and temple, but to the heavenly reality that the earthly Jerusalem only prefigured.

Holy War

So far we have seen how the gospel unfolds in Scripture as breaking news: both a courtroom drama and a war epic. In fact, the Greek word for "gospel" was used for the message of military victory brought by a herald from the battlefield to the capital. If the gospel is the big story of the Bible, the story behind the Bible's stories begins in Genesis 3:15, where God declares war on Satan and foretells the outcome: "I will put enmity between you and the woman, and between your offspring and her offspring; he shall bruise your head, and you shall bruise his heel." Taking up the gauntlet, Satan already seems to be in the lead when Cain kills Abel and is then banished from the covenant community. Nevertheless, God gives another heir to Eve, Seth, whose name means "Appointed." While Cain's line of descendants is distinguished by founders of culture in his great and violent city, the only thing mentioned about Seth's line is that "At that time people began to call upon the name of the LORD" (Gen. 4:26).

As both lines grew over many generations, Satan adopted a more subtle strategy than obvious murder: religious corruption of the godly line. The Sethites began to intermarry with the descendants of Cain and lose their covenantal identity:

> The LORD saw that the wickedness of man was great in the earth, and that every intention of the thoughts of his heart was only evil continually. And the LORD was sorry that he had made man on the earth, and it grieved him to his heart. So the LORD said, "I will blot out man whom I have created from the face of the land, man and animals and creeping things and birds of the heavens; for I am sorry that I have made them." But Noah found favor in the eyes of the LORD. (Gen. 6:5–8)

Through Noah and his family, a new covenant community was born—a remnant chosen by grace. Noah offered burnt offerings on an altar and God, pleased by the sacrificial aroma, promised not to bring such a wide-scale deluge even though "the intention of man's heart is evil from his youth." "While the earth remains, seed-time and harvest, cold and heat, summer and winter, day and night, shall not cease" (Gen. 8:20–22). Echoing the original creation, we read, "God blessed Noah and his sons and said to them, 'Be fruitful and multiply and fill the earth'" (Gen. 9:1).

The covenantal line continued through Shem and his descendants, while eventually the pagan nations came together to build their infamous Tower of Babel, in defiance of God and in celebration of their own presumed sovereignty. From Shem's descendants finally came Abram, though by then they too had become corrupt. With his wife Sarai, Abram was called by God out of a moon worshiping family to become the father of many nations through his greater seed, the Messiah. God unilaterally pledged his faithfulness to build a dynasty of faith from Abram and the patriarch believed the promise and was justified (Gen. 15:6).

As a result Abram and Sarai were now Abraham ("father of many") and Sarah ("mother of many"). Even though they both wrestled with their faith in the promise, trying at one point to secure their future hope by their own conniving instead of by faith in God's promise, God remained faithful. Putting Abraham's faith to the test, God demanded that he offer his only son Isaac on the altar for a sacrifice, but kept his hand from plunging the knife into his son. Instead, a ram was caught in a thicket and was offered as a sacrifice in Isaac's place, foreshadowing Abraham's greater son, Jesus Christ, who assumed his ancestor's place at the cross.

Just as God had told Abraham, Israel became a slave in Egypt and a cruel pharaoh arose who severely oppressed God's people, even to the point of slaughtering the male infants (Exodus 1), but the infant Moses escaped through the kindness of one of the pharaoh's daughters (Exodus 2). Eventually called by God to lead his people out of Egypt, Moses performed powerful signs—each of which represented the lordship of Israel's God over the Egyptian idols. Yet Pharaoh's heart was hardened. Finally, God claimed Egypt's firstborn sons in a plague (Exod. 12:29–32), commanded Israel to consecrate their firstborn sons to the Lord along with the Passover feast (Exod. 12:43–13:16), and then led his own children through the Red Sea on dry land and drowned Pharaoh's army (Exodus 14).

As God led his people on the march to Sinai and then on to Zion, he had to contend first of all with the unfaithfulness of Israel itself. Not even Moses was allowed to enter the Promised Land. However, in the land God resumed his war against the serpent, driving the enemies of God from his land under Joshua. These holy wars were simply part of that story behind the main story: the triumph of the offspring of Eve and Sarah over the coalition of powers and principalities arrayed against the Lord and his Anointed One. Now, as God's "firstborn," Israel is given the same commission, as a type of things to come.

Although David was devoted to the Lord, he was not messianic material. In fact, his adultery with Bathsheba, murder of her husband, and other acts of violence planted seeds of destruction within his own house. Nevertheless, God swore an unconditional oath that in spite of the reckless unfaithfulness of David's descendants he would keep a Davidic heir on the throne forever (2 Samuel 7). David promised to build God a house, but God replied that it is he who will make David a house (v. 11). "When your days are fulfilled and you lie down with your fathers, I will raise up your offspring after you, who shall come from your own body, and I will establish his kingdom. He shall build a house for my name, and I will establish the throne of his kingdom forever" (vv. 12–13). Solomon, David's son, only partially fulfilled this prophecy.

This dynasty leading to the greater Son of David continued to be threatened both from without and from within the nation itself. The war of the "offspring" continues, as wicked heirs of David lead the nation into idolatry and intermarriage, persecuting the prophets, and attempting to bring the royal line to extinction. If the serpent can intercept the sons of David, he can end the prospects of God's messianic kingdom.

In Isaiah 7–8, King Ahaz appealed to Tiglath-Pileser in a manner tantamount to acknowledging the Assyrian king as Israel's new suzerain (covenant lord): "I am your servant and your son. Come and save me . . ." (2 Kings 16:7). Here Ahaz chooses the politics of the nations over resting in Zion's King. Isaiah aptly named his own son "Shear-Yashub" ("A Remnant Will Return"). Once again God preserved an elect remnant that did not bow its knee to Baal. Throughout the history of Israel and Judah, even wicked kings rule simply because of God's promise to keep an heir of David on the throne until finally the greater Son of David would be installed as the world's everlasting king.

Mistakenly concluding that he had intercepted his messianic destroyer when Cain murdered Abel, Satan repeatedly sought the destruction of the Davidic line. For example, the wicked Queen Athaliah executed the royal house, but, unbeknownst to her, the infant Joash was hidden with his nurse in the temple to ride out Athaliah's cruel reign (2 Kings 11:1–3). When the priest Jehoiada discovered the boy, he commanded the captains to take the shields and spears of King David from the house of the LORD, "to guard the king [Joash] on every side." "Then [Jehoiada] brought out the king's son, put the crown on him, and gave him the covenant; they proclaimed him king, and anointed him; they clapped their hands and shouted, 'Long live the king!' " (vv. 9–12). The picture of Queen Athaliah entering the temple to learn the source of the commotion (vv. 13–14) parallels that fury of the outmaneuvered dragon in Revelation 12. The covenant restored, Judah undertook a thorough housecleaning, tearing down all of the sacred pillars and altars to Baal (vv. 17–20). Joash, who began his rule at seven years old, repaired the temple and began the operation of tearing down all of the idolatrous shrines, but even he eventually turned away from the Lord and was killed (2 Chron. 24:17–25).

The point of these stories is clearly not to provide moral examples. Nor are these texts of holy war meant as a pattern for us to execute God's judgment on idolaters and establish a theocracy. The covenant at Sinai established a purely typological kingdom that pointed to Christ's everlasting reign in glory. The Messiah has arrived in humility. He did not restore the typological theocracy established at Sinai, but the everlasting kingdom of his Father. Having ascended to his Father's right hand, he now reigns through his gospel. It is the era of forgiveness and grace, not of final judgment. Yet when he returns in glory, Israel's typological holy wars will pale in comparison. The vivid imagery of "the wrath of the Lamb" in the book of Revelation offers a glimpse into the climactic day of judgment that will arrive for the whole earth, when God finally and forever cleanses his garden from the serpent and its servants. Radical forgiveness now or radical judgment then: that is the message that we have to bring to the world today.

Christians interpret the "war songs" of the Psalms in light of the messianic king greater than David. Jesus Christ, then, is the King whom God has installed on his holy hill, requiring all rulers to pay him homage, even demanding that they "kiss his feet, or he will be angry, and you will perish in the way; for his wrath is quickly kindled. Happy are all who take refuge in him" (Ps. 2:11). In Psalm 144, attributed to David, we read, "Blessed be the LORD, my rock, who trains my hands for war, and my fingers for battle; my rock and my fortress, my stronghold and my deliverer, my shield, in whom I take refuge, who subdues the peoples under me" (vv. 1–2). "Salvation" in the Old Testament is understood in terms of a military victory. How we interpret these messianic references, however, makes all the difference, as we will see below.

The Messiah Arrives

Finally, the day arrived. Significantly, Matthew's Gospel begins, "The book of the genealogy of Jesus Christ, the son of David, the son of Abraham" (Matt. 1:1). The key figures in the genealogy remind us of their stories recorded in the Old Testament. Many of them were scoundrels. Some, like Rahab the prostitute who helped Israel's spies (Josh. 6:25), are honored in the list (v. 5). The lengthy (though abbreviated) genealogy ends, "and Jacob the father of Joseph the husband of Mary, of whom Jesus was born, who is called Christ" (v. 16). Underscoring the humility and gentleness of this phase of Christ's kingdom, the angels announce to common shepherds, "Fear not, for behold, I bring you Good News of great joy that will be for all the people. For unto you is born this day in the City of David a Savior, who is Christ the Lord" (Luke 2:10–11).

King Herod—the titular monarch that Rome allowed to rule Jerusalem as its puppet—received news from foreign dignitaries from the East that the king of the Jews had been born and they had arrived "to worship him" (Matt. 2:2). "When Herod the king heard this, he was troubled, and all of Jerusalem with him; and assembling all the chief priests and scribes of the people, he inquired of them where the Christ was to be born." Citing Micah 5:2 and other prophecies, the visitors replied, "In Bethlehem of Judea . . ." (v. 5). Echoing his strategy of slaughter from Cain to Pharaoh to Queen Athaliah, the serpent and his collaborator slaughtered the firstborn males in Bethlehem and its surrounding environs, but God had already commanded Joseph and Mary to flee for Egypt until Herod's death. "This was to fulfill what was spoken by the prophet: 'Out of Egypt I called my son'" (v. 15). So Jesus is the new Israel, sent into Egypt to save his brothers (like Joseph), returning to the promised land to take up his mission of finally crushing the serpent's head.

The War to End All Wars

The theme of holy war hardly disappears in the New Testament. Rather, it reaches its fulfillment—of which the Old Testament examples were merely previews. Jesus's march from Sinai to Zion—the Adamic trial from commission to consummation—began with the temptation in the wilderness. Adapting a page out of his old playbook with Adam, the serpent offers Jesus the world as if it were his to give. Rebuffed, Satan returns with more subtlety, trying to seduce Jesus into calling off his trial by turning stones into bread. This time, however, the serpent meets the Last Adam, who, instead of eating the fruit he finds pleasing to the eye and desirable to make one wise, quotes Scripture: "Man shall not live by bread alone, but by every word that comes from the mouth of God" (Matt. 4:4, from Deut. 8:3). When Satan challenges him to jump from the pinnacle of the temple, Jesus responds, unlike Adam and Israel, "Again, it is written, 'You shall not put the Lord your God to the test'" (v. 7).

But Jesus's march—in his first advent—is not a military campaign to destroy his enemies and drive them out of a geopolitical land. He will do this when he returns in a universal judgment that Israel's holy wars could only faintly anticipate. But for now, it is a kingdom of grace and weakness, not a kingdom of glory and power. It arises and expands on the Good News that it has heard, not on the visible reign of righteousness, peace, and justice that will one day settle forever across the earth.

In his Sermon on the Mount (paralleling Moses' delivery of the Law at Mount Sinai), Jesus issues his famous decrees: "You have heard it said, '. . . ,' but I say, ..." He is not here condemning the Law of Moses but announcing a regime change. There was a time when there was a holy land and holy wars, when pagan nations were to be driven from the land, but now is the era of forgiveness, Good News, and grace. When his disciples James and John wanted to go back to the Old Testament script—or prematurely invoke the last judgment itself—by calling down fire on the Samaritan village that rejected Jesus, the Lord "rebuked them and they went to another village" preaching the Good News (Luke 9:51–56). Yet there is warfare. Satan was cast out of heaven, where he accused the saints day and night (Luke 10:15–18; Rev. 12) and he is now bound so that he can no longer deceive the nations and keep the elect from believing the gospel (Mark 3:27). In this phase of the war, the focus (both of God and Satan) is on the testimony to Christ and the faith of his saints. All of Satan's batteries are aimed at the progress of the gospel.

After Jesus sent the seventy disciples out on a mission to heal and proclaim his name, they returned breathless: "Lord, even the demons are subject to us in your name!" "And he said to them, 'I saw Satan fall like lightning from heaven'" (Luke 10:15–18). Yet this same Jesus clearly—more emphatically than any biblical figure—warns of the day when he will come in the clouds to judge, separating the sheep from the goats for everlasting life and everlasting destruction together with the ancient serpent (Matthew 24).

The holy war theme is drawn upon by the New Testament, but within a distinct politics. The overtly military recognition of Yahweh, "Through you we push back our enemies" (Ps. 44:4), can now be heard in the light of Jesus's declaration that "the gates of Hades will not prevail against" the church to whom Christ has given the keys to bind and loose through the law and the gospel (Matt. 16:18–19).

One day the theater of this conflict will be geopolitical. There will be a violent clash between the king of heaven and the rebellious powers of the earth. In the Olivet discourse, Jesus explains that the Son of Man will come in glory and power at the end of the age. "You will see the son of man sitting at the right hand of Power and coming on the clouds of heaven" (Luke 22:69, with Matt. 26:64; Mark 14:62). There was a partial realization of this in the vision of Stephen at his martyrdom (Acts 7:56), which preconversion Paul approved (8:1), as also in the vision of Paul himself on his way to another campaign against the believers in Damascus (9:1–6). Yet we still await the second part of that manifestation, his "coming on the clouds of heaven," marking the transition from a kingdom of grace to the kingdom of glory.

In all of these episodes, it becomes clearer that the question of the kingdom does not turn on the "willing or running" of its would-be inaugurators. The story behind all of these stories is the cosmic battle launched in Eden, reaching its climax in the massacre of the male infants by Herod (Matt. 1:13–23). The "exile" in Egypt and repatriation to Nazareth announce that this singular child is recapitulating Israel's history and in so doing, the triumph of the "seed of the woman" over the serpent and his human agents. In fact, in Jesus's outlook, the opposition of his own people to the kingdom that belonged to them was really a playing out of this cosmic battle:

> You snakes, you brood of vipers! How can you escape being sentenced to hell? Therefore I send you prophets, sages, and scribes, some of whom you will kill and crucify, and some you will flog in your own synagogues and pursue from town to town, so that upon you may come all the righteous blood shed on earth, from the blood of righteous Abel to the blood of Zechariah son of Barachiah, whom you murdered between the sanctuary and the altar. (Matt. 23:33–35)

Abel by faith brought the sacrifice God had commanded, while Cain did not (Gen. 4:4–8, with Heb. 11:4). Even Peter's attempt to dissuade Jesus from the cross was treated by Jesus as the voice of Satan (Matt. 16:23).

For Jesus, then, the story behind the stories is not ethnic cleansing or even the restoration of an earthly theocracy. Good and evil cannot be easily classified in the static categories of ethnic, national, or political allegiance. "Outsiders" and "insiders" are redefined in exclusive reference to him. Exorcisms and healings in the New Testament, therefore, are not odd habits of an ancient people lacking the proper tools of psychological and medical analysis, but are redemptive historical signposts, harbingers of the new creation: Jesus's contest with the powers of the age. *Christus victor* meets *Agnus Dei*; the conquering King and the substitutionary Lamb are one and the same in this unique person and his kingdom. Jesus responds to the elation of the seventy at being able to subdue even the demons (in the language of treading on serpents, redolent of Gen. 3:15) with the even greater news that their names are written in heaven (Luke 10:15–18).

While the strong man may be bound, and consequently the extraordinary ministry of Jesus and his disciples succeeded by the ordinary ministry of Word and sacrament, our warfare continues "against the rulers, against the authorities, against the cosmic powers of this present darkness, against the forces of evil in the heavenly places" (Eph. 6:12). Discovered especially wherever the progress of the gospel most threatens the kingdom of Satan, such pernicious forces become as visible in the heresies and schisms of the church as in the arrogance and rebellion of the nations.

The cosmic struggle that dominates the story from Genesis 3 to the Apocalypse is that war between the serpent and his seed and the woman and hers. In fact, Revelation 12 can be seen as a snapshot of that redemptive historical battle, with the "woman clothed with the sun, with the moon under her feet, and on her head a crown of twelve stars" (v. 1). Crying out in the agony of childbirth, she is threatened, as "another portent appeared in heaven: a great red dragon, with seven heads and ten horns, and seven diadems on his heads."

> His tail swept down a third of the stars of heaven and threw them to the earth. Then the dragon stood before the woman who was about to bear a child, so that he might devour her child as soon as it was born. And she gave birth to a son, a male child, who is to rule all the nations with a rod of iron. But her child was snatched away and taken to God and to his throne; and the woman fled into the wilderness, where she

has a place prepared by God, so that there she can be nourished for one thousand two hundred sixty days. (vv. 4–6)

At this point, we read, "war broke out in heaven," with the devil and his angels defeated. "Then I heard a loud voice in heaven, proclaiming, 'Now have come the salvation and the power and the kingdom of our God and the authority of his Messiah, for the accuser of our comrades has been thrown down, who accuses them day and night before our God'" (vv. 7–10). The martyrs triumph by their testimony to the Lamb. "Rejoice then, you heavens and those who dwell in them! But woe to the earth and to the sea, for the devil has come down to you with great wrath, because he knows that his time is short!" (vv. 11–12). Verses 13–17 then capture something of this persecution of the enraged, if overthrown, enemy who "went off to make war on the rest of her children, those who keep the commandments of God and hold the testimony of Jesus." It is by its witness to Christ in the gospel that Satan's house is looted and its prisons are emptied. "The God of peace will soon crush Satan under your feet," Paul reminds us (Rom. 16:20).

Spiritual Warfare Today

The "spiritual warfare" that marks our age of redemptive history is easily distorted. Dualistic mysticism turns it into a war between a supposedly higher and lower self (spirit and body). Martin Luther spoke of the relief he had when he took his vows as a monk, and his disillusionment when he realized that even though he had left "the world" to focus exclusively on "spiritual things," he had not actually left his own sinful self behind. He was no different than before. He might be able to avoid the business of everyday life, but he could not conquer the source of his sins and anxieties.

Some mystics today think simply by turning within and drumming up an intense spiritual experience, they will at last attain union with God. Some spiritual warfare schemes sound more like science fiction than redemptive history, attempting to identify specific demons over particular regions and vices, breaking generational curses, and finding the devil under every rock. But this misunderstands the nature of spiritual warfare. It is not a battle between nature and grace, but between sin and grace, and it is not in our power to conquer.

As Ephesians 6—the key spiritual warfare passage—makes explicit, Satan focuses his efforts on extinguishing or corrupting our faith in Christ. That is why all of the weapons he lists for the believers' struggle have to do with the objective Word of the gospel rather than on our own cleverly-devised, if superstitious, technology. Satan's favorite holiday is not Halloween, but Christmas and Easter—in fact, every Lord's Day when Christ gathers his people to himself. He foments external persecution and internal corruption of God's Word and the believer's faith. The Antichrist himself will assume his throne not in a capital of secular power but in the *sanctuary* of God (2 Thess. 2:4). From Genesis to the Gospels, Satan's favorite haunt is not wild parties and séances, but God's courtroom, where he can accuse believers day and night. That is why it is so significant that Christ cast Satan out of heaven by his victorious life and entered the heavenly court in his victorious ascension. It means that in heaven—where our salvation is determined—there is no prosecutor, but only a defense attorney for the people of God.

Others conceive of spiritual warfare in geopolitical terms. Especially in various forms of liberation theology, it is not a war between the higher and lower self but between the poor and the rich, women and men, colonialists and subjugated peoples. There are also liberation theologies of the "right": conservative ideologies that create their own simplistic vision of good versus evil that deflects guilt from ourselves to someone or something else.

If the more mystical version resembles the heresy of Manicheanism, with a clear separation already between light and darkness, the righteous children of heaven and the demonic children of earth, this version of warfare comes close to Pelagianism. As we have seen, this heresy assumes that all people are basically capable of saving themselves and the world with the proper laws, exhortations, strategies, and methods. Yet Ephesians 6 counters this perspective as well: "For we do not wrestle against flesh and blood, but against the rulers, against the authorities, against the cosmic powers over this present darkness, against the spiritual forces of evil in the heavenly places" (vv. 10–12).

This is not to deny the reality of sinful structures of violence, oppression, and injustice evident in political and economic systems. However, these are mere symptoms of the world's bondage to sin and death. Believers are called to struggle alongside unbelievers in alleviating the symptoms of our race's common bondage. However, the church in its official capacity, as bearer of the Great Commission, is the only institution in the world that can address the problem at its heart. It speaks not merely of a better world, but of a new creation. Only the church can declare the message that it has heard: that through Christ and faith in his victory, death will not have the last word; that violence, oppression, and injustice will not be an unending struggle; that disease and hunger will not claim the bodies of millions forever. It is the victory of the seed of the woman over the seed of the serpent that Christ has achieved and the visible effects of that conquest will be fully realized when Christ returns in glory. Right now Christ is ruling from heaven, in common grace over the nations and in saving grace through the proclamation of the gospel (Col. 1:15–23).

Wherever human beings are seduced into deeper self-confidence and away from the proclamation of Christ and his kingdom, the battle lines are drawn. "For all the promises of God find their Yes in him. That is why it is through him that we utter our Amen to God for his glory" (2 Cor. 1:20). *All* of the weapons mentioned in Ephesians 6 that the Spirit has placed at our disposal in this warfare focus on the delivery of the gospel to the ends of the earth, to our neighbors in their unbelief, and to believers in their constant struggle to hold fast to their confession. A church that drops its armor and weapons— namely, the gospel as it comes to the world in Word and sacrament—is Satan's goal in this interim between Christ's two advents.

The Conquering King Ascends

Christ's ascension opened up a fissure in history, locating the church in the precarious collision of the two ages: this age of sin and death and the age to come. It is easy in the absence of Christ's visible reign in the flesh on the earth to substitute ourselves or the church. What we are doing right now on earth becomes the front-page news. However, we miss the whole point if we fail to see that it is still what Jesus is doing that is the big news. He ascended to heaven in order to rule and subdue history to his gracious and holy designs, dispatch his Spirit to sweep sinners into his victory parade, and to spread his kingdom of peace to the ends of the earth.

In Ephesians 4, we—new covenant believers—get swept up into this victory march. Just as the dragon's tail swept a third of the angels from heaven in his fall in Revelation 12, the Savior's ascension sweeps into his wake a remnant from every tribe and tongue on earth. However, this triumphant march is not like the holy wars of the Old Testament.

Christ does not call his people today to drive the serpent's emissaries out of a holy land by the sword. He came to crush the serpent's head himself. In this contest, Jesus must fight alone. No one but Jesus hung on that cross, bearing the weight of the world's sins. Nevertheless, his resurrection draws innumerable captives into his train. He reigns as victor for us in heaven, while we bring news of his victory to the earth. The world does not welcome this news any more after his resurrection than when he first arrived. The announcement of Good News provokes the rage of the dragon and although he knows that he has lost the war with the seed of the woman, he spends his last days in pursuit of his coheirs.

Verses 1–6 of Ephesians 4 record a march, as believers "walk in unity." As he writes this epistle, Paul himself is under house arrest in Rome, "the prisoner of the Lord." Even in prison he is not the captive of Satan or Caesar; he is the *Lord's* prisoner, under his reign. Despite their intentions, the devil and his ambassadors are actually serving the Lord's reign through Paul's ministry. He calls the Ephesians to "walk worthy of the calling you have received, with all lowliness and gentleness, with longsuffering, bearing with one another in love, endeavoring to keep the unity of the Spirit in the bond of peace" (vv. 1–2). This exhortation stands in sharp contrast to the old covenant command to eliminate the serpent and his seed from God's holy land by the sword. Yet it also stands in contrast to the complaining, backbiting, and attempted mutiny against Moses's leadership exhibited by the Israelites on their march through the desert.

Having been raised from spiritual death and seated with Christ (Eph. 2:1–5), saved by grace alone through faith alone (vv. 6–9), believers are predestined to walk in good works together toward their destination (v. 10).

In our own experience, we find that when one part of our body doesn't work, the rest of the body chips in to compensate. Even in stroke victims, when the injured part of the brain can no longer perform its function, another sector picks up the slack and rewires the neurons under its sphere. Paul is saying that, in contrast to the world's "every man for himself," survival of the fittest mentality, believers must be forgiving and patient with each other, ready to cover up faults rather than parade them. The chief concern is the health of the body, not the pride of any part. Yet this countersociety is only possible because the risen and ascended Christ is the head of this body, dispensing his gifts.

This unity is a gift already given, not a goal for us to attain. With the two hands of Word and Spirit, the King creates a body of which he is the head. That unity is already lodged in God's election, redemption, calling, and sealing elaborated in Ephesians 1. However, we must be "eager to maintain the unity of the Spirit in the bond of peace" (Eph. 4:2). The participle used here underscores the fact that this unity must be a priority for every believer and the church corporately. It is a struggle, always an urgent task. It is never finished, because there are always threats to it.

Yet the preservation of this unity depends ultimately on its source. In other words, we cannot drum up this unity by our own resources. It cannot be enforced. The imperative to preserve this unity depends always on the indicative fact that we are united by Christ and his gospel. "There is one body and one Spirit—just as you were called to the one hope that belongs to your call—one Lord, one faith, one baptism, one God and Father of all, who is over all and through all and in all" (Eph. 4:4–5).

Notice what is not included here: one universal pastor or form of church government, one movement, one program, or one experience. Longing for a more visible security than the gospel that we hear proclaimed, we are easily misled into thinking that if we could only unite behind a pope or a charismatic leader or a revival, we could really know who is in and who is out. At last there would be true unity. Doctrine just gets in the way. Let's just love Jesus and transform the world.

However, we are directed here to find our unity precisely in the doctrine: "one Lord, one faith, one baptism." If you want to find the "one body" and "one Spirit," you must look for the place where Christ is proclaimed in Word and sacrament. If the proclamation of the gospel *creates* this united body of liberated prisoners in the first place, then its faithful proclamation *in* the church is essential for preserving the bond of unity already secured by Christ's saving work. No wonder, then, the ministry of the Word is so crucial in Paul's delineation of the gifts here. The King not only *saves*; he *preserves* the body that he has saved through his current gift-giving reign.

We *are* one in Christ (chapters 1–3); therefore, let us *walk together* according to this high calling. Our conquering King will not keep the spoils of victory all to himself. As he lived for us, died for us, and rose for us, he rules for us in heaven, until all of his enemies and ours are defeated.

Taking His Throne, Dispensing the Spoils of Victory

Both in the upper room discourse and in Luke 24, Jesus explains that when he ascends and is enthroned in heaven, he will divide the spoils of his victory. He will send the Spirit and make his followers witnesses. Now Ephesians 4:7 announces Christ's distribution of the spoils and verse 8 explicitly cites Psalm 68: the song of the royal march from Sinai to Zion. In the incarnation, the Son of God "descended into the depths of the earth," and now he ascends "above the heavens"—far above all power, rule, and authority. He now has "the name above every name" and "all authority in heaven and on earth." As the victorious conqueror, he now divides the spoils and showers his people—even enemies—with gifts. In his descent (birth), he received gifts from Gentile rulers; now in his ascension, he loads down his liberated captives with the spoils of victory.

As Paul interprets this Psalm, all believers share "the inheritance of the saints": the gift of grace and "the calling to which you have been called" (Eph. 4:1). Every believer shares equally in the *gift* (singular) of Christ. However, the *gifts* (plural) being distributed here by Christ in his ascension refer specifically to offices in the church. None of the gifts are for private use (as we often assume in our individualistic spirituality today): each of us has a gift that the whole body needs. Verses 7, 8, and 11 repeat the emphasis on Christ's act of giving: "has been given," "Christ's giving," "he gave gifts," and "it was he who gave." The church is always on the receiving end in its relationship to Christ; never the redeemer, but always the redeemed; never the head, but always the body; never the ruler, but always the ruled. When we ask, "Where is Jesus, what is he doing, and why hasn't he returned?" we have our answer here.

In Christ's ascension, "he led a host of prisoners captive" (v. 8a). Once again, this is common to all believers. "He gave gifts to people" (8b). Here Paul changes the Old Testament reference: instead of *receiving* gifts, God is *giving* them. Interestingly, the Jewish Targum interpreted Psalm 68 as referring to the ascension of Moses, who now gives the Law as a gift to the world.[9] But Paul interprets Psalm 68 in the light of Christ's ascension having actually occurred. It is not the ascension of Moses, but of Christ, that Paul proclaims. Even if Moses had ascended to heaven (as later Jewish tradition held), Christ has ascended "far above all the heavens" (v. 10) and his gift here is not Torah but grace (v. 7).

By Paul's time, the Feast of Pentecost was increasingly associated with the giving of the Law at Sinai and Psalm 68 was the key hymn for this celebration.[10] Paul sees this Psalm as ideal for Ascension Day and Pentecost Sunday, to be sure, but for a different ascension and a different Pentecost than Judaism recognized. Christ's descent into the "lower regions, to the earth" (Eph. 4:9–10) probably refers to his incarnation rather than to a visit in conquest to Hades, but either way the contrast is striking: from the lowest humiliation to the highest exaltation. He certainly descended into hell by bearing the curse for us. He descended lower and ascended higher than anyone before or after him. He ascends Mount Zion, with captives in his train, to be installed as King of kings and Lord of lords. His filling of the whole cosmos (v. 10b) refers not to his physical presence but to the extent of his dominion.

All saints share equally in this liberation and the inheritance that Christ has won for us. However, he showers his redeemed hosts with the gift of ministers whom he commissions for dispensing his spoils: "And he himself gave some to be apostles, some prophets, some evangelists, and some pastors and teachers . . ." (v. 11). These are the gifts that Paul mentions here as being poured out on his people. They are servants, waiting on Christ's guests at his lavish feast. These offices were not set up by human authority, but are gifts that "he himself gave" for distributing his inheritance. He gave prophets and apostles and now, even after these extraordinary offices have run their course, having laid the foundation, he continues to give pastors, teachers, and evangelists who equip the saints by their service.

Some of our modern translations interpret the original in verse 11 as pastors and teachers being given "for the equipping of the saints for the work of ministry," but there are good reasons to prefer the older translation of the King James Version, which reads, "for the perfection [completion] of the saints through the work of [their] ministry."[11] In other words, it is "the work of the ministry," entrusted now to pastors, teachers, and evangelists, that brings completion to Christ's body.

So far in this book we have seen that the *content* of the gospel is God's free gift of salvation in Jesus Christ and the *method of delivery* is the proclamation of this gospel. In this way, both the message and the method are God's work, his gift. Now we begin to see more clearly how the *community* that results from the work of the Father in the Son and by the Spirit is also defined by the gospel. *The church does not build the kingdom, but receives it and therefore worships God with gratitude and awe* (Heb. 12:28). Far from establishing a clericalism that excludes laypeople from Christ's gifts, the ministry of Word and sacrament that Paul highlights in Ephesians 4 is the means through which Christ distributes them for the completion and maturity of the whole body in the gospel.

That this work of ministry is given in an official and distinct sense to pastors and teachers is further demonstrated by the fact that Paul contrasts its effect (namely, maturity) with "being tossed to and fro with every wind of doctrine" and "the whole body" can be served. Other gifts are given for the good of the body, and Paul highlights those elsewhere (Romans 12 and 1 Corinthians 12). However, his focus here is the gift of the gospel ministry that keeps us from being "children, tossed to and fro by the waves of doctrine, by human cunning, by craftiness in deceitful schemes" (Eph. 4:14).[12] The ministers are not equipping the *saints* for *the work of ministry*; they are Christ's gift for *ministering to* the saints so that they will become mature and complete in Christ. They are *served* by Christ himself through the ministry of pastors and teachers. While we need every member and every gift to be fully operative, the central concern of the body of Christ is the faithful maintenance of the ministry of Word and sacrament. Through this ministry, we are all recipients of the unity of the faith, the knowledge of the Son of God, and maturity in Christ. So that which we all possess jointly already in Christ (one God and Father, one Spirit, one Lord, one faith, one baptism) is preserved by Christ from generation to generation.

It is entirely possible to believe that the gospel is a message of God's free grace in Christ, but then to devise methods that are inconsistent with it. The gift is free, but there are all sorts of things that you must do to receive it. Even if we restrict ourselves to the means of grace (preaching and sacrament) that Christ appointed as consistent with the gospel of grace, we can turn the community into a kingdom of activists rather than of receivers. There is indeed much for believers to do in the fellowship of saints and in the world, but they can only love and serve their neighbors if they have already been richly served by Christ's ministry.

The Pastoral Epistles clearly outline the nature, qualifications, and functions of the offices of pastors, elders, and deacons in the church. One need not hold political office in order to love and serve one's neighbors. It is not just police officers but parents, employers, and apartment councils that settle disputes and breaches of responsibilities. We would consider it a dereliction of duty if one simply watched his neighbor's house burn down while waiting for the fire department when he could easily have extinguished a trash fire with a garden hose before it got out of hand. Similarly, the whole body of Christ works together, teaching, admonishing, exhorting, serving, and giving. Yet this no more eliminates the need for offices in the church than our common civic responsibility eliminates the need for public officials, police officers, and firefighters.

The first few verses of Ephesians 4 support the priesthood of all believers, but the rest of the passage teaches that Christ has instituted specific offices in his church for the public ministry. *All believers are priests, but not all are ministers.* In Romans 12 and 1 Corinthians 12 Paul lists a variety of gifts that the Spirit has poured out on the whole body, but it is the ministry of the Word that feeds every part. The sheep are not "self-feeders" and the church does not simply provide resources for Christian activity. Rather, through the ministry of Word and sacrament and the spiritual and physical care of elders and deacons, every part of the body is served and is enabled to serve the body as well as its neighbors in the world. He has gifted ministers to do the work of the ministry so that "we all" can become mature in Christ.

Precisely because this ministry of the Word is preserved in the church, the whole body is made a cloud of witnesses to Christ's triumph, grounded in the gospel that they are privileged to share with their neighbors. We often hear that "doctrine divides; service unites," or that what we need now are "deeds, not creeds." Yet Paul assures us that a church that is built up in the faith, instead of being tossed back and forth on every wave of doctrinal fashion, will not only be mature, but will be prepared to confront the powers of this age and witness to the common inheritance that we all share together in Christ.

Joining the Thanksgiving Parade

On this basis, we are called to "no longer walk as the Gentiles do, in the futility of their minds" (Eph. 4:17). Ignorant of Christ's victory, they give themselves over to every evil practice (vv. 18–21), but believers have "put off [their] old self" and have "put on the new self, created after the likeness of God in true righteousness and holiness" (v. 24). "Look carefully then how you walk, not as unwise, but as wise, making the best use of the time, because the days are evil." Instead of losing ourselves in self-indulgence, believers are called to come together in worship, "addressing one another in psalms and hymns and spiritual songs, singing and making melody to the Lord with all your heart, giving thanks always and for everything to God the Father in the name of our Lord Jesus Christ, submitting to one another out of reverence for Christ" (vv. 15–21). Once again we see the pattern that we observed in Romans, as Paul moves from the dramatic narrative to doctrine to doxology to discipleship. Through the ministry of the Word, especially through preaching and sacrament, the Spirit sweeps all believers into the train of Christ's victory and generates the wider gift-exchange in the body that leads to witness and service in the world.

The sacrifices of the Old Testament were of two types: *guilt offerings* and *thank offerings*. As the writer to the Hebrews points out, drawing on Psalm 40, God's ultimate delight is not in guilt offerings, which reminded both him and the worshipers of their sin:

> Consequently, when Christ came into the world, he said, "Sacrifices and offerings you have not desired, but a body you have prepared for me; in burnt offerings and sin offerings you have taken no pleasure." Then I said, "See, God, I have come to do your will, O God (in the scroll of the book it is written of me)." (Heb. 10:5–7 NRSV)

The writer points out that in saying this, Christ "abolishes the first"—that is, the guilt offering under the shadows of the law—"in order to establish the second"—that is, a fragrant life of thankful obedience. "And it is by God's will that we have been sanctified through the offering of the body of Jesus Christ once for all" (vv. 8–10).

We recall Paul's statement in Romans 1:22 that with the fall human beings were no longer thankful to God. Humanity no longer fulfilled the purpose of its existence: "to glorify God and to enjoy him forever." But Christ has replaced Adam as the leader of the thanksgiving parade. He did not fulfill God's will out of drudgery. Psalm 40:6–7, which Hebrews 10 places on the lips of Jesus, is followed by the further statement in verse 8: "I *delight* to do your will, O my God; your law is within my heart" (emphasis added). In fact, Jesus told his disciples, "My food is to do the will of him who sent me and to accomplish his work" (John 4:34). With each new morning, Jesus awoke in eager anticipation of fulfilling his Father's commission.

Finally there is one who has offered up not only a single guilt offering but a whole life of thankful obedience, "a fragrant offering and sacrifice to God" (Eph. 5:2). This means that there are no more debts for those who are in Christ. The line in the otherwise fine hymn, "O to grace how great a debtor . . . !" has it wrong. We *were* debtors to the law, but are debtors no more. With no more guilt offerings, the only thing left for us is to offer our bodies as living rather than dead sacrifices of praise and thanksgiving (Rom. 12:1).

Because our representative head has already offered both the satisfying thank offering and guilt offering, taking his throne in consummated glory, we as his beneficiaries follow in his thanksgiving parade. Paul writes, "But thanks be to God, who in Christ always leads us in triumphal procession, and through us spread in every place the fragrance that comes from knowing him" (2 Cor. 2:14 NRSV). There is nothing that we can offer to God as an offering for our sins. So now, as "a holy priesthood," we offer up our lives as "spiritual sacrifices acceptable to God through Jesus Christ" (1 Pet. 2:5).

Thus, there is a new political order at work in this present evil age. It has not yet replaced the existing order, but its presence in embryo is a sign of the cosmic reign that will one day be fully revealed. The royal march of Psalm 68 still echoes in Ephesians 6, where Paul appeals to believers to put on "the whole armor of God" as they make their pilgrimage to the city of God in Christ's train. Paul makes it clear that in this phase of holy war, our weapon is the gospel rather than the temporal sword:

> Stand therefore, and fasten *the belt of truth* around your waist, and put on *the breastplate of righteousness.* As shoes for your feet put on whatever will make you ready to proclaim the *gospel of peace.* With all of these, take the *shield of faith*, with which you will be able to quench all the flaming arrows of the evil one. Take the *helmet of salvation*, and the *sword of the Spirit*, which is the word of God. (Eph. 6:12–17 NRSV, emphasis added)

So now we have Christ's answer to his disciples when they asked at his ascension, "*Now* are you going to restore the kingdom to Israel?" Right at the moment they ask this, Jesus leaves. But where does he go? He goes to heaven to claim the prize of his victory—not only for himself, but for us. And he sends his Spirit to lead the ground campaign of grace.

In this present phase, we are neither merely waiting for Christ to establish his kingdom, nor building his kingdom of power and glory through our own impressive campaigns. Rather, we are *recipients* and *heralds* of his victory and his heavenly reign at the Father's right hand. Christ's earthly ministry seemed weak in the eyes of the world: he was a good man, a victim of imperial violence, but with some good examples and ideas about how we should love each other. But the Creator, Redeemer, and King of the earth? Surely not this Jesus, cut down in the prime of his life. Similarly, every earthly kingdom surpasses the temporal power, pomp, and glory of the heavenly kingdom. Nevertheless, just as Daniel prophesied, this kingdom of David's greater son endures from generation to generation and brings the everlasting treasures of the heavenly Zion to a world in captivity. The Roman Empire was shaken, and fell. So too has Christendom. There is only one kingdom that cannot be shaken. "Therefore, since we are receiving a kingdom that cannot be shaken, let us have grace, by which we may serve God acceptably with reverence and awe" (Heb. 12:28 NRSV).

The Sports Page

The New Testament compares the Christian life to running a race: a marathon rather than a sprint. In fact, it is a relay race, where we run our race and then pass the baton. In fact, the writer to the Hebrews speaks of our running the race with "a cloud of witnesses" cheering us on from the stands, as we unload every sin that weighs us down. This race will not be won by us; it has already been won by our forerunner, Christ. Because of this fact, "let us run with endurance the race that is set before us, looking to Jesus, the founder and perfecter of our faith, who for the joy that was set before him endured the cross, despising the shame, and is seated at the right hand of the throne of God" (Heb. 12:1–2).

An endurance race is not a sprint and this is not an individual marathon but a team relay. Precisely because our leader has already won it for us, we can endure. Battered by persecution, Paul passed the baton to young Timothy, saying that "the time of my departure has come." "I have fought the good fight, I have finished the race, I have kept the faith," Paul says. Here is the apostle to the Gentiles, the greatest missionary in the history of the church, and yet he does not speak about his unique achievements. He does not even speak of fighting well, but of fighting the good *fight*, and not of breaking records but simply of *finishing* the race. Instead of a gold medal, the original Olympics awarded a wreath that winners wore as a crown. With that analogy in mind, Paul could conclude, "Henceforth there is laid up for me the crown of righteousness, which the Lord, the righteous judge, will award to me on that Day, *and not only to me but also to all who have loved his appearing*" (2 Tim. 4:6–8, emphasis added). The crown of righteousness has already been won by Christ and Paul already knows that it will be awarded to him publicly on the stage of world history, because in faith he has already received the verdict of the last day. And in spite of his remarkable place in the history of the church, he recognizes that it is a team sport. He will receive the crown together with all the saints who have run the race.

Don't Just Sit There, Go!

There is a time to *sit* and there is a time to *stand* and there is a time to *go*; a time to be a passive recipient of grace and a time to be an active witness and servant. Dancing with strangers in the streets at the news of Christ's victory, we become a community. And from that community we are sent into the world with the Good News in our hearts and on our lips, animating our hands to love and serve our neighbors. The disciples were eyewitnesses of the risen Christ, but in the forty days between his resurrection and ascension he taught them about himself from all the Scriptures. It was from this intense period of instruction that the disciples became the apostles whose message is distilled for us in the New Testament.

Christ's ascension and reign at the Father's right hand gives the church its *authorization* to go, confident as his ambassadors that "whoever receives the one I send receives me, and whoever receives me receives the one who sent me" (John 13:20). It is the authorization to tread on serpents—not the medieval crusader's cry, "Christ is Lord," while cleaving the skull of an infidel, but the proclamation of "that Word above all earthly powers"—which pulls down strongholds and extends Christ's realm through the gospel.

Christ's present reign at the Father's right hand is not an unproductive hiatus in his ministry on our behalf. Rather, it is securing in heaven the realities that the Spirit is bringing to us and within us, individually and corporately, on earth. God's grace is not an infused substance or a created thing, but God himself—in Christ—favorably turned toward us, bringing salvation. Paul says that "the grace of God has *appeared*" (Titus 2:11). "But when the goodness and loving kindness of God our Savior appeared, he saved us, not because of works done by us in righteousness, but according to his own mercy, by the washing of regeneration and renewal of the Holy Spirit, whom he poured out on us richly through Jesus Christ our Savior, so that being justified by his grace we might become heirs according to the hope of eternal life" (Titus 3:4–7). Similarly, the writer to the Hebrews tells us that Jesus Christ "has appeared once for all at the end of the ages to put away sin by the sacrifice of himself" (Heb. 9:26). Yet we still "long for his appearing" at the last day (1 Tim. 6:14–15; Titus 2:13; 1 John 2:28; 3:2).

But as Christ's reign is a productive interim in heaven, the delay in his return is a productive period for gathering guests for his feast. It is the "today" of salvation, before the door closes. In his earthly ministry, Jesus met each day to fulfill all righteousness on our behalf, but in the present era we live to announce the arrival of his gift of righteousness that allows us to stand in his presence at his return in judgment. In his speech to the Athenian philosophers, Paul announced, "The times of ignorance God overlooked, but now he commands all people everywhere to repent, because he has fixed a day on which he will judge the world in righteousness by a man whom he has appointed, and of this he has given assurance to all by raising him from the dead" (Acts 17:31). It is not that the gospel and the call to repentance are absent from prior revelation, but that there is now a sense of urgency, as "the end of the ages" has come. The appearing of Christ brings the last judgment into our history and the descent of the Spirit arraigns us in God's courtroom, judging and justifying sinners, so that they receive that final verdict in the present. The verdict of judgment day is already being announced: condemnation for all who do not believe in Jesus Christ, and justification for all who embrace him (John 3:15–17).

This is the political headline, not just of this week or even this year, but of this age until the last day. Whatever ignorance and idolatry God tolerated in the past, the appearing of Christ has brought a decisively new era of judgment and salvation. There is the stench of decay and death, as reality in bondage to corruption cries out for liberation. Yet there is also the music of a banquet hall that even now restores a certain luster to every leaf and deeper, richer colors to every landscape. We are all placed in the valley of decision, choosing whether we will continue to surrender our lives to the age that is fading away or to be caught up in the Spirit whose penetrating energies make us citizens of the age to come.

The fear of hell is the reasonable response of sinners to this revelation and its reality is part of the urgency of the church's mission and message. Sent from the front by the conquering King to report the outcome of the war to the kingdoms of this age, the church in its official capacity has a narrow occupation with extraordinary effects: "Therefore, we are ambassadors for Christ, God making his appeal through us. We implore you on behalf of Christ, be reconciled to God.

For our sake he made him to be sin who knew no sin, so that in him we might become the righteousness of God" (2 Cor. 5:20–21).

The church is an embassy—the colony of heaven—to which the victims of Satan's tyrannical reign flee to escape this present evil age. There is no other name of any other king upon whom we may call to deliver us from our most dangerous foes but this one who has descended and ascended and will come again for his own.

Before it is called to *do* anything, the church is called to *receive* something—and not only once, but again and again: namely, the announcement that even in its weakness, suffering, half-heartedness, and a legacy of faith stained by unfaithfulness, Christ is King. Only because all authority *has* been entrusted to him is the church authorized to go into all the world with the Good News that Jesus Christ is Lord and the confidence that the gates of hell will not prevail against it. After sitting to hear the news, we are raised to our feet in joyful praise:

> What then shall we say to these things? If God is for us, who can be against us? He who did not spare his own Son but gave him up for us all, how will he not also with him graciously give us all things? Who shall bring any charge against God's elect? It is God who justifies. Who is to condemn? Christ Jesus is the one who died—more than that, who was raised—who is at the right hand of God, who indeed is interceding for us. Who shall separate us from the love of Christ? Shall tribulation, or distress, or persecution, or famine, or nakedness, or danger, or sword? . . . No, in all these things we are more than conquerors through him who loved us. For I am sure that neither death nor life, nor angels nor rulers; nor things present nor things to come, nor powers, nor height nor depth, nor anything else in all creation, will be able to separate us from the love of God in Christ Jesus our Lord. (Rom. 8:31–39)

8

HOW THE GOOD NEWS CREATES A CROSS-CULTURAL COMMUNITY

I have referred to the 1945 *Life* cover photo of strangers dancing in the streets together in joyful embraces at the news of victory in Europe. Recipients of a report of the victory achieved by others—their fellow citizens—across the sea, they would never be the same again. If the news is big enough, it can change lives forever. Coming from heaven, the gospel has an even greater power to turn strangers into a family. Revelation 5:9 records the scene from a heavenly perspective, heralding Christ who "purchased with his blood people from every tribe, kindred, tongue, people and nation," making them into "a kingdom of priests to our God." "And they will reign forever." There is no story, no movement, no demographic niche that you could be a part of that compares with this one.

Whenever the Scriptures speak of the Good News, it is not only a matter of individual salvation but of God's pledge to save the whole world through Abraham's seed (Genesis 15). The gospel is not *about* us and what we have done; rather it is the Good News *for* us. The church is not simply the effect of the gospel, but is itself part of the Good News that is promised. That's why for Paul in his epistles keeping up divisions between Jew and Gentile is tantamount to denying the gospel. Salvation and the church are not actually different topics. The precepts unique to the old covenant law separated Gentiles from Jews, but the previous covenant with Abraham was that all nations would be blessed through the future heir of Abraham and Sarah. Through the people of Israel—more specifically, through the true and faithful Israelite, Jesus Christ—God has created a worldwide family that is justified by grace alone, in Christ alone, through faith alone.

When God raises our eyes from ourselves to his Son through the gospel, we begin to see ourselves surrounded by a community of people who are no longer simply neighbors but brothers and sisters. My closest friends are a lot like me—and no wonder, since I chose them and they chose me. We chose each other because we shared similar backgrounds, experiences, and tastes. Even if we come from different racial backgrounds and family histories, we generally share similar tastes in music, hangouts, political views, and other cultural preferences. My parents' favorite music and restaurants do not really do it for me. I would rather hang out at places that people in my generation prefer, listen to my own favorite groups, and develop friendships with people from my own generational and cultural profile. All of this has its place.

However, the church is different. Christ and his gospel is the tie that binds. I did not choose these people to be my brothers and sisters; God did. Like me, they are elected, redeemed, called, and justified by God in Christ. Paul tells a divided, arrogant, and immature church to consider who they were when they were called to Christ:

> Not many of you were wise according to worldly standards, not many were powerful, not many were of noble birth. But God chose what is foolish in the world to shame the wise; God chose what is weak in the world to shame the strong; God chose what is low and despised in the world, even things that are not, to bring to nothing things that are, so

that no human being might boast in the presence of God. And because of him you are in Christ Jesus, who became to us wisdom from God, righteousness and sanctification and redemption, so that, as it is written, 'Let the one who boasts, boast in the Lord.'" (1 Cor. 1:26–31)

It is not my church to shape into my image, according to my own cultural preferences, ethnic background, politics, or socioeconomic location. It is Christ's community—and *he* is the location that we all share together. He is the demographic niche and the political rallying point of this kingdom. I still belong to other groups based on my cultural affinities, but my *family* is not something I choose; it is something I am chosen for.

This is not a community or kingdom that I would—much less *could*—build; it is a feast that I am called to join. It is not generated by our clever ideas or communication, but by God's declarative Word: "Be silent before the Lord God! For the day of the LORD is near; the LORD has prepared a sacrifice and consecrated his guests" (Zeph. 1:7). The words and sacraments of the world create affinity groups for those with similar tastes based on generational, socioeconomic, political, racial, and consumer demographics. However, when the Spirit comes through his Word and sacraments, "the powers of the age to come" break into this present evil age (Heb. 6:4–5). The church becomes a *cross*-cultural community in the truest sense, defined by Christ's work rather than our own.

A Cross-Culture

What is your church like? More importantly, what came into your mind first when you read that question? Here is one possible answer: We have great music, programs for every age group and interest, lots of ministry opportunities, clean nurseries, and an awesome youth group. I feel at home there: it's a great place to make friends and establish community (i.e., there are a lot of people there like me). Here is another possible answer, though probably less popular: The Word is faithfully preached, the sacraments are faithfully administered according to Christ's institution, and the elders and deacons look after the spiritual and temporal welfare of the people.

Increasingly, our worldly associations and identities are allowed to determine the composition of our churches. Not that long ago, evangelical missiologists were defending the separation of races based on the principle that people like to be with people who are like them. South African theologians have pointed out that the invocation of this principle in mission work laid the groundwork for apartheid. The new word was "contextualization." Oddly, "incarnational ministry" came to mean dividing the body of Christ in a way that simply mirrored the world's competing interests.

Now that racial segregation is less explicitly deployed as a church growth strategy, we carve up Christ's body into socioeconomic and generational segments. The youth group is of relatively recent vintage: an invention of the 1960s and '70s. And now it has taken on a life of its own. Often young people grow up in the church without ever really being in the church and worshiping together with saints who have walked with the Lord for many years. Then we wonder why they are not integrated into the church when they leave for college and prefer to join a college ministry but not the local church. A younger believer recently asked me what faithfulness looks like in older years. Not having believing parents, and ready to start a family, he was looking for the kind of mature fellowship that characterized the community in Acts and he could not find it in his church.

Some churches use demographic marketing to appeal to different musical styles, with country western, rock, and jazz services. I read recently of a growing movement of "cowboy churches," where preachers deliver brief talks from their horses to other riders in their saddle and depart to the song, "Happy Trails." There are churches where Democrats feel at home, and others that seem like the Republican Party at prayer. For all of its criticism of the consumerism that pervades the philosophy of their parents' seeker churches, even the emergent church movement seems no less defined by its own kind of generational narcissism. Across the spectrum, our churches are giving the impression that we believe more in the powers of this present age than in the powers of the age to come. Appealing to (and feeding) this narcissism, the culture bombards us constantly with the uniqueness of our generation, the revolutionary changes that will come to the world because of it, and the imperative of decision makers to cater to our every whim. And the church follows along.

However, we have seen that both the gospel and its appointed means of delivery are odd, surprising, disorienting, and beyond our control. The gospel creates its own odd community. We cannot manufacture grace; we cannot package Christ. Unlike our golden calves, it is a gift that we cannot give ourselves. God elects us for this kingdom, purchases it, and remains the sovereign chooser of the methods he will use to build it. Only when that gospel is liberated from our domestication and the means of grace are no longer a distraction from "the real work of ministry," will our churches be set free from their captivity to lords that cannot liberate. Paul spoke of our being imprisoned not only by the law's condemnation but by "the elementary principles of the world." However, he tells the Galatians, "As many of you as were baptized into Christ have put on Christ." Since we are justified by faith, "There is neither Jew nor Greek, there is neither slave nor free, there is no male and female, for you are all one in Christ Jesus. And if you are Christ's, then you are Abraham's offspring, heirs according to promise" (Gal. 3:27–29). Christ did not come to break down the wall of hostility between Jew and Gentile and to unite them into one people through his own body only to allow this body to be divided into other worldly demographics.

Wouldn't it throw the whole industry of church marketing for a loop if our churches were truly defined by the cross? How could ministry be revolutionized for every generation if "one Lord, one faith, and one baptism" were the common factor that united the young to the old, the old to the young, whites and blacks, Asians and Latinos, opera subscribers and rappers? Reducing everything to the ephemeral, perpetually reinventing tastes and styles in order to capture new markets that the market itself creates, is the way marketing works. Obsolescence is not a consequence of the culture of marketing; it's the point. And church leaders fall in line. Invoking a by now faded ad from an Oldsmobile commercial, the president of a large confessional denomination recently said, "This is not your father's denomination." So much for God's promise to be the God of the fathers and their children after them. For a faith that is passed along "from generation to generation," capitulation to the culture of marketing is not a means of grace—the new creation breaking into the old—but a means of surrender to this passing age.

To escape this captivity, we must recover our focus on the drama, doctrine, doxology, and discipleship that center on Christ. For the drama, we need to find our story in God's rather than the other way around. Then we need to stop thinking that doctrine is an impediment to God's politics in the world and realize that it is only by renewing our minds by that Word that we can begin to flush out the corrupt assumptions that we have taken for granted. For a while now, we have encouraged a human-centered orientation that makes us the stars of the show. If salvation lies ultimately in our hands and we are born again because of a decision that we made, then it follows that the church is just another voluntary association that we have chosen. Just as we have chosen Christ because we have calculated a positive return on investment, we choose our churches the same way. At no time since the Reformation have we needed a clearer preaching and teaching of God's sovereign grace in election, redemption, calling, justification, sanctification, and glorification.

But doctrine is not enough. We need to be brought to the place where we are actually recipients of the gift disclosed in the drama and the doctrine. Like a newsweekly, the Good News has to be delivered— every week—and not only in the sermon but in the liturgy, the prayers, the songs, and the Supper.

The pastor at our church is affable enough, but he is not the drama. From his sermons you would never know much about him: his hobbies, sports, interests, how he voted in the last election, or that he loves U2 and Matchbox 20, Tolkien, and the movie *Tombstone*. Some sermons are good, some are great, and all are Christ-centered, drawing us into the unfolding drama of redemption. He not only teaches us what election, redemption, justification, and sanctification mean; he proclaims God's electing and saving grace to us. He is immersed daily in the study of the Word and in prayer. We not only need instruction; we need proclamation. And not only proclamation, but the divinely ordained means of ratifying and certifying that this gift belongs to us: namely, baptism and the Lord's Supper. Every week, Communion is celebrated as God's ratification of his proclaimed gospel. Through these means, the Spirit creates and strengthens our faith, which yields praise, and from this genuine discipleship emerges. This discipleship is not an individualistic self-help program, however. It too is a communal enterprise, drawing constantly on the means of grace, and submitting ourselves to the care and discipline of the elders.

Our church was planted several years ago, by a mostly Dutch immigrant church in a predominantly Dutch immigrant denomination. Ordained in this body, I am part of a growing number of "outsiders" who have been welcomed into this fellowship of saints with a rich heritage. Increasingly, our churches—especially new church plants—reflect a broad ethnic, generational, and socioeconomic profile. Among the many encouraging things that older members in our churches hear as non-Dutch believers join is the surprise especially of younger people who have had visits from the pastor and elders. This has been going on for generations—centuries, in fact—and those who have been raised in it sometimes take it for granted. Newcomers report with excitement,

"They just *called* me on the phone. And then they came over—*to my apartment*—and we had a couple of cups of coffee as they asked me how things were going, read some Scripture, and prayed with me." Some are surprised because they are new Christians. Others are surprised because they were raised in churches where this just never happened—many had never met their pastor and did not know their elders' names.

Let's face it. A lot of us belong to the generations that raised themselves. Much of our life was spent with other kids—even in the youth group. Our grandparents were in a nursing home and our extended relatives lived far away. The last thing we need is a church that keeps us sealed up in our own compartment with others of similar experiences in life. We need to be integrated into *the body of Christ*. Younger believers don't need another speaker to come in and tell them about dating, self-esteem, and relationships. They need to *have* relationships with saints who have put on a few miles in the Christian life and have faced challenges to their faith and practice that younger believers have not. And the lessons learned from these relationships need to be passed on to the rest of us in unplanned, unchoreographed, and unplugged conversations.

The power of the Spirit working through the means of grace suddenly hits us as we watch a couple who recently lost their son in a car accident receive Communion with tears rolling down their faces. When I walk into our church, I see a glimpse of the marriage supper of the Lamb, with brothers and sisters who are Latino, African American, Asian, and Caucasian. Next to crying infants and a new believer, there is a couple in their nineties who have known the Lord their whole lives. There is simply nothing as extraordinary as this ordinary gathering of Christ's people. It is an unspeakable—indeed, mystical—joy.

The Society Page

We can imagine that many in Times Square just minutes before that *Life* photograph was taken were preoccupied with their own personal stories. One person might have been thinking about stopping off to pick up some vegetables for dinner, another about the burden of getting back to the office to finish a task, still another about preparations for her wedding next Tuesday. Yet when the big announcement of victory in Europe was heard, everything stopped. Thoughts turned outward, to the news that concerned everyone, and individuals with their own relatively narrow plans, hopes, dreams, and felt needs became a community of Americans.

Jesus had something similar in mind when he spoke of a great feast that a king had prepared (Luke 14:15–24). Offering regrets, the invited guests gave what they thought were good excuses: they were too busy with their worldly cares to make it to the celebration. So the king sent his messengers into the slums and alleys to find guests for the big event. Matthew recounts a similar parable, where Jesus compared the kingdom of heaven to a king who arranged a wedding celebration for his son. The special guests treated the invitation lightly. It is significant that the main antagonists in Jesus's parable are the religious leaders, who not only decline the invitation because of more ostensibly pressing and relevant concerns, but kill the servants (the prophets) out of religious zeal. Yet the servants were sent to the back alleys and returned with success: "And the wedding hall was filled with guests." However, one man was there without a wedding garment and was bound and cast "into outer darkness," where there is "weeping and wailing and gnashing of teeth" (Matt. 22:1–13). Only those who are clothed in Christ's righteousness—however despised they may be in the eyes of the religious leaders—will be seated at the wedding feast in Christ's kingdom. "For many are called, but few are chosen" (v. 14).

God has his own kingdom and his own politics for building and expanding it. It is not our kingdom, but his, and we are not only invited to the feast as guests but as the bride of his Son. Satan does not care if our churches are full, as long as people are not being clothed with Christ. Our own ideas, agendas, and efforts may create special interest groups, but only the gospel can create an international, intercultural community of the baptized who reach out to the world both in witness and in service through their daily callings.

In the HBO series "Band of Brothers," a group of soldiers from widely varying backgrounds become an inseparable family that to this day meets at annual reunions. It was not their hometown, ethnicity, socioeconomic status, education, or musical preferences that bound them together, but their common stories, experiences, and interdependence during a horrible war. World War II was the overarching narrative that wove their lives together. How much more is the victory of Christ worthy of being the tie that binds people from every nation, generation, gender, and social location to the festival of everlasting Sabbath? While other organizations, parties, and nations can be formed through our activism, the church is a community created by God alone and his politics consists of Word and sacrament. Luke reports, "And they devoted themselves to the apostles' teaching and fellowship, to the breaking of bread and the prayers" (Acts 2:42). It was from these concrete practices that a new society was created by God and spread rapidly to the ends of the earth.

The Ministry of the Word

Throughout the book of Acts, the growth of the church is synonymous with *the spread of the Word*. Similarly, in one of his sermons, Martin Luther explained why he refused the path of some radical Anabaptist groups that attempted to foment political revolution and bring in Christ's kingdom through force:

> In short, I will preach it [the Word of God], teach it, write it, but I will constrain no man by force, for faith must come freely without compulsion. Take myself as an example. I opposed indulgences and all the papists, but never with force. I simply taught, preached, and wrote God's Word; otherwise I did nothing. And while I slept or drank Wittenberg beer with my friends Philip and Amsdorf, the Word so greatly weakened the papacy that no prince or emperor ever inflicted such losses upon it. I did nothing; the Word did everything. Had I desired to foment trouble, I could have brought great bloodshed upon Germany; indeed, I could have started such a game that even the emperor would not have been safe. But what would it have been? Mere fool's play. I did nothing; I let the Word do its work.[1]

The prophets and the apostles did not think of their words as dead ink on a page. "For the word of God is living and active . . ." (Heb. 4:12). The Father preached the world into existence out of nothing, through the mediation of his Son and the perfecting agency of his Spirit. Furthermore, he upholds all things in every moment by his word. Greater even than these works, though, is God's word in saving sinners. In speaking, God not only describes various states of affairs but creates and changes them. This Word not only tells us about an event long ago; its proclamation is the event in which God, here and now, rewrites our script.

Recall the logic of Paul's argument in Romans 10. Zealous works righteousness seeks to make God present by pulling him down or diving into the depths as if to bring Christ up from the dead. Yet Christ is alive, at the right hand of the Father, and is as near to us as the preaching of the gospel. We do not even have to go get this message; we do not have to make it relevant, exciting, or living and active. Simply by virtue of what it is (the preaching of Christ) and the one who brings it (the Spirit), this Word is effective. Furthermore, God brings it to us through a herald, while we sit. He appoints and sends ambassadors to declare this news. They do not send themselves, but are sent. Unlike the false prophets in Jeremiah 23, they have stood in God's council.

The Ministry of the Sacraments

Some readers may wince at the very word "sacrament" as a remnant of medieval ritualism. However, baptism and the Lord's Supper are instituted by Christ as the means of grace alongside his Word. Given the fact that the *Great Commission* is to go to the ends of the earth with the gospel, "baptizing and teaching," it is strange that many today associate Word and sacrament ministry with dead orthodoxy or at least distinguish it from being "missional." The *promises* of the new covenant are ratified by the *signs and seals* that he has appointed. These are the weapons of Christ's kingdom, deployed by his ambassadors. Once again, our natural response is, "Surely *that* can't be it. Just *look*—the people are passively sitting there. That's not going to change the world." But before we go flying off to heaven to bring God down to us or into the depths as if to bring Christ up from the dead, Paul reminds us, the risen Christ—together with all of his power and all of his gifts—is as close to you already as "the word of faith that we proclaim" (Rom. 10:8).

I have already pointed out the difference between a law covenant and the covenant of grace in terms of a contract and a last will and testament. This is why we sit to hear it read instead of stand to swear, "All this we will do." Baptism and Communion ratify this gracious covenant. Like the blood splashed on the doorposts of the Israelites in Egypt (rather than the blood splashed on them by Moses at Mount Sinai), the sacraments place God's saving and royal seal on his beneficiaries. The Tree of Life, the rainbow, circumcision, and Passover: these are the signs and seals of the old covenant that directed faith toward Christ. Now that he has come, his new covenant is ratified by the two sacraments that Christ ordained in his earthly ministry. The new covenant is a pledge of God's gracious goodwill toward us in Jesus Christ and baptism and Communion certify his oath.

Therefore, baptism must be seen chiefly as God's ratification of his promise—like the rainbow that confirmed his covenant with Noah. It is not chiefly our act of commitment or our remembering, but God's remembering his own oath (Gen. 9:15). I know that as surely as I see the water applied, God pledges his whole kingdom to me and my children as his heirs. God's promise comes before my obedience; in fact, it is always God's pledge that creates my response of faith and love. Abraham believed and was justified—and only then was circumcised as a "sign" and "seal of the righteousness that he had by faith" (Rom. 4:11). However, he was commanded to circumcise his sons as a sign and seal of this same covenant of grace. Circumcision called forth a response of personal faith and repentance, but it was first of all God's claim on believers and their children, his pledge of grace which included that very faith and repentance.

In contrast to the countless personal and church growth programs on the market today, baptism and the Lord's Supper (like the preaching of the Word) draw us outside of ourselves to cling to God's promise in Christ, in dependence on the Spirit. We are mere recipients of baptism; God is the active party. Only by being made receivers first are we made active in the works of faith. Therefore, baptism is not first and foremost our act of commitment, but our being made beneficiaries of God's commitment. As such, it is not simply an act that was performed in the past, but a fact of divine promise that we return to daily both for our assurance of God's favor and for the strength to fight against the world, the flesh, and the devil whose tyranny was objectively toppled by Christ's victory. It is his victory, in which he has caused us to share, that baptism signifies and seals to our conscience.

Understanding baptism as God's work for us that elicits our response (instead of vice versa) makes all the difference. All Christians believe that baptism marks the beginning of the Christian life. If that initiatory act is conceived primarily as the public ratification of a law covenant, "All this we will do," then it is not a ratification of the covenant of grace in which God says, "All this I have done and now pledge to you." Baptism as chiefly a means of our commitment fits with an imitation of Christ model of discipleship. Baptism as chiefly a means of grace fits with a union with Christ model. If we are constantly returning to our decision, our conversion experience, and our commitment to ground our growth in holiness each day, then we will always be looking for new words and sacraments to keep us going. Of course, baptism calls forth our commitment to die daily to self and live to God in Christ, but it can only do that because it comes to us from God alone, in Christ alone, by grace alone. *As God's sovereign pledge, baptism is the inexhaustible spring to which we return every day, not to compare our life with Christ's but to find our life in Christ.*

As baptism is the bath at the beginning of the Christian journey, the Supper is the meal that constantly refreshes us with heavenly food along the way through our daunting pilgrimage. Word, baptism, and the Supper: these are the Spirit's weapons in the kingdom that Christ is building. Throughout our warfare in this life, the Spirit brings us back to our location "in Christ," signified and sealed in our baptism and our shared meal. Through these means of grace, the Spirit not only gathers us together in Christ but continues to build us up into Christ as our living head. In this way, the church is no longer merely one voluntary association alongside others, but the only truly *cross-cultural* communion of saints in the world.

God's Agenda for a New World Order: Different Politics for Different Kingdoms

The world has its politics and, as citizens of both kingdoms, we participate alongside unbelievers in discerning the best way to regulate the common good. We vote, work, celebrate birthdays, serve, and volunteer throughout our common life with our neighbors in the world. We are shaped—even subconsciously—by all sorts of dogmas and rituals of our secular culture. However, in the kingdom of Christ we are the ones who are elected by God, recipients of his grace, and are thereby made not only coheirs but fellow guests and exchange his good gifts between each other in the communion of saints.

God's politics does not call us to despise the politics of this passing age, but it does cause us to recognize that only his action can create a kingdom not only of common citizens negotiating their rights in the public square, but a kingdom of priests who share Christ as the most precious inheritance in common. When, in the pursuit of relevance, the politics of this present age (including niche demographic marketing) determines the identity of our churches, Christ's politics are thwarted, his Spirit is quenched, and his kingdom becomes assimilated to the kingdoms of this age.

The Lord's Supper is not just another opportunity for us to do something, even if it is as simple as remembering. It is certainly not an act of the community in constituting its own identity. Rather, each time we gather at the Table in faith, Christ gives himself to us as our food and drink. He becomes our identity and fulfills his own agenda in our midst. It is a state dinner in which the Great King ratifies his treaty: the last will and testament that makes us heirs of his estate. Why should the Supper be celebrated so infrequently and, in many cases, at an evening service for fear of offending, perplexing, convicting, or perhaps intriguing unbelievers who witness the saints at their family dinner? "For as often as you eat this bread and drink the cup," Paul instructed, "you proclaim the Lord's death until he comes" (1 Cor. 11:26). Where did we get the idea that by sidelining the proclamation of the law and the gospel and the celebration of baptism and Communion we could become more "missional"?

Calvin and other reformers argued that the Supper should occupy a central place alongside preaching each week. Yet its strange absence from the regular gathering of many churches today impoverishes the saints, weakens the diet and the sinews that connect us to our living Head and to each other as members of his body, and dampens the gratitude that feeds our missionary zeal. It is the Eucharist, along with preaching and baptism, that not only generates a church in the first place, but keeps its focus on Christ's presence in action as well as his absence in the flesh, generating our longing for his return.

Decades ago, Scottish minister H. H. William M. Cant argued, "Of course what our Lord has to say is not simply commands for another week, though worship will include these. . . . Yet before the imperatives . . . there must come the indicatives. He who is the risen One tells of what He has done for us."[2] Where in the service is this forgiveness and reconciliation given—even to lifelong believers? First of all, in preaching. Yet today, many ministers are suggesting that there are more meaningful ways of communicating the gospel, such as more "conversational" methods. But is this listening to the risen Lord or to the preacher and each other? Do we come to church expecting Christ to raise the dead and the weak and feeble? Cant asks.

> It is surely right, then, that the worshippers should come away from this worship, not only with a Gospel message for the individual, but with a strong sense of having been made a member again of the one Holy Catholic and Apostolic Church, with a new awareness of being joined once more to the joyful believing and committed company of the whole Church in heaven and upon earth in whose fellowship they

happily unite in the Lord's Prayer. If the transformation of life is a reality within the service of the Word through the presence of the risen Lord, how much more in the service of the Word *and* Sacrament.[3]

Remembering Christ's death is a key part of the sacrament. "Yet it has to be said that it is very easy along this memorialist road to become a Pelagian—we remember what Christ has done for us in the past, we recall the wonder of His dying love for our sins, and then we seek to make our human progress. We very easily forget that the ability to make the response of dying and rising again comes from the ascended Christ through the Spirit."[4] "This paschal mystery has two sides to it," Cant reminds us: "a descending and ascending movement, both *katabasis* ["down"] and *anabasis* ["up"] . . . . As we partake of the Table, we are lifted up into sharing in the glorified humanity of Christ, into sharing in the life of heaven."[5]

The Word that is preached, taught, sung, and prayed, along with baptism and the Eucharist, not only prepare us for mission; it is itself *the* missionary event *par excellence*, as visitors are able to hear and see the gospel that it communicates and the communion that it generates. To the extent that the marks define the mission and the mission justifies the marks, the church fulfills its apostolic identity. In a world filled with the old songs of racial division, niche marketing, generational segmentation, and other forms of group narcissism, we hear the strains of a heavenly choir:

> And they sang a new song, saying,
>   "Worthy are you to take the scroll and to open its seals, for you were slain, and by your blood you ransomed people for God from every tribe and language and people and nation, and you have made them a kingdom and priests to our God, and they shall reign on the earth." (Rev. 5:9–10)

The Promise-Driven Church

We cannot live without a script. Just as the judge tells defendants that if they cannot afford an attorney the court will appoint one, we must accept the fact that if we are not transformed by the renewing of our minds by God's Word, we will be conformed to the pattern of this world's thinking. Although its script is weak, its characters shallow, and its plot empty, the world has the advantage of powerful methods of indoctrinating us, complete with celebrities and surround sound. At least in democratic nations, this conformity is not enforced by armies but by the market, with its subdivisions of schools, entertainment, and advertising. It may not catechize us at gunpoint, but its relentless bombardment wears down our defenses.

Whoever we think we are or want to be, our identity and felt needs are often shaped by our consumer profile, which we mistakenly imagine that we have chosen all by ourselves. The world has its words of judgment and deliverance that it expects us all to embrace as universal truth. It also has its sacraments: the spectacles of national celebrations, the rituals of Wall Street's opening bell with its officials looking down from the balcony, the buzz of the mall, and the splendor of sporting events. Make no mistake about it: the world, like Christ, claims *our whole lives*. Every Sunday we have a pretty good idea of where—and what—people worship. If our churches are not bathing us in the unfading powers of the age to come, why should it surprise us when people assign greater reality and significance to the age that is passing away? If we think that we can sustain ourselves and our churches simply by trying to make things more user-friendly, we have not reckoned with the enormous power of this present age. Only when the powers of the age to come are allowed entrance through the ordained ministry of preaching and sacrament are the high places of the idols threatened and its prisoners liberated.

In his Pentecost sermon, Peter declared, "The promise is for you and for your children and for all who are far off, as many as the Lord our God will call to himself" (Acts 2:39). That is what it means to be missional!

First, *it is a promise that the church is called to deliver on God's behalf and in Christ's name.* Ambassadors do not send themselves, write up their own job description, and then formulate their own policies. God already has his plan figured out. He has already elected the citizens-to-be of his kingdom, sent his Son to redeem them, and poured his Spirit out on them and within them, so that they come joyfully to his feast. We do not bring our word, our promises, our threats and exhortations, but God's promise that Peter had just preached: Christ as the fulfillment of Israel's hope.

Second, *it is a promise "for you. . . ."* In faith, I embrace the amazing announcement that Christ not only died and rose again, but that he was crucified for *my* sins and was raised for *my* justification. The question, "How can I be saved?" is provoked by a sense of personal danger and it is answered by the promise.

Third, *the promise is also "for you and your children. . . ."* God has always been in the business of saving families. Of course, parents must first believe the gospel themselves. It's like the instruction given by the flight attendant: in the case of a loss of cabin pressure, parents are to put on their oxygen masks first and then fit them on their children. A parent who can't breathe is of little help to a child. The promise to which Peter refers was announced to our first parents after their sin and continued through the line of Seth all the way to Noah, then to Abraham, then to David, and finally to Jesus Christ. All along the way, God promised to be a God "to you and your children." The covenant of promise was to be passed down from generation to generation, as each person in each generation was circumcised, instructed in the faith, participated in the feasts, and embraced that promise in eager expectation of the groom's arrival for the wedding day.

The children of believers are often treated in the church as non-Christians who need to "get saved." I remember growing up asking Jesus to come into my heart on an almost daily basis, fearful that he might come back before I had really surrendered all. However, the new covenant no less than the old includes our children and this is what Peter assumes and pledges here. Each of us must embrace that promise for ourselves, but belonging to God visibly in his covenant of grace is ordinarily the means rather than the prerequisite for coming to faith and maturing in it.

It is a wonderful promise that God makes when he includes our children under his covenantal blessings. As I documented in *Christless Christianity*, we are losing the reached instead of reaching the lost. In the name of mission and outreach, we are failing to ground believers and their children in the promises of the gospel. One of the encouraging signs I see today is the growing recovery of family worship, including instruction from a catechism. Appalled by the biblical and doctrinal illiteracy of those under his care, Martin Luther wrote a *Small Catechism* and assumed the primary responsibility for teaching it to the children in his parish every day. Calvin and other reforming pastors followed his cue. The goal of Luther's catechism was to teach the basics of the Christian faith, following the outline of the Ten Commandments, the Apostles' Creed, and the Lord's Prayer. Other question and answer books, notably the *Heidelberg Catechism* and the *Westminster Shorter Catechism*, inculcated biblical faith and practice for generations down to the present day. And it was not something that was done just by pastors at church, but by parents at home each day. Parents saw their children not simply as unbelievers who would have a chance one day to be converted at summer camp or in their youth group, but as already belonging to the visible church, entitled to the promise, and therefore needing to learn the ABC's of the faith that they come to embrace for themselves.

In the book of Acts, converts believe and are baptized, but they bring their household with them to baptism. If we are going to be truly missional, we must treasure those whom God has already placed under our care. Over the last few generations, many of our young people have been pulled away from the common faith and practices of the church.

Recall the shape of apostolic church life and growth in Acts 2:42, where believers "devoted themselves to the apostles' teaching and fellowship, to the breaking of bread and the prayers." Often today, *devotion to the apostles' teaching* is subordinated to a wearying regimen of entertainment. If adults have come to believe that doctrine is unimportant and that nothing in the Christian life is worth investing in unless it can be measured in terms of fun, they may have learned this in their youth group.

Similarly, *fellowship* often takes the form of the niche marketing I have already described. We may still call it fellowship, but it may be closer to socializing. There is nothing wrong with socializing. Clubs are fine. There is a time and place for hanging out with people with similar tastes, interests, and hobbies. However, Christian homes and churches are the only institutions in which our children will learn to find themselves in God's story. When they are united more by the trends of pop culture than by the faith and practice of the whole church in all times and places, our youth become victims of our sloth. We should not be surprised that over half of those reared in evangelical homes and churches today do not join or even attend a church regularly when they go off to college. If we are going to see our children grow up into Christ instead of abandoning the church, our spiritual life at home and in the church must incorporate them into the teaching and fellowship of the apostolic faith. They can find "ministry opportunities" through United Way, the Peace Corps, or Habitat for Humanity. They can find friends at the fraternity or sorority. They can find intellectual stimulation in class. And they can find a sense of meaning and purpose in their vocations. If their home churches exchanged the ministry of preaching and teaching the apostles' doctrine for a variety of ministries and activities that they could find legitimate versions of in the world, then it is difficult to come up with a reasonable answer when they ask, "Why do I need the church?"

As they profess faith, embracing the promise that God made to them in their baptism, our children share in the *breaking of the bread*— Holy Communion. Through this meal, the word of promise is ratified and we find ourselves not only members of Christ but of each other as one body. As our children learn to join that body in *the prayers*, corporate worship becomes meaningful.

I tend to pray for the same things over and over again and these requests sound a lot like those of other Christians in my same age-group and demographic profile. Throw in some prayers from older and younger saints, from people who are richer and poorer, black, Latino, Asian, and European, and now my prayers become part of the prayers of the church. Once again, my narrow horizon of self-enclosed existence is opened up to a cross-centered and cross-cultural communion. The use of the definite article ("*the* prayers") underscores this point. Jesus quoted the Psalms from memory, not only because he learned them in catechism but because he sang them and prayed them in worship. The earliest Christians were raised with a prayer book in their synagogue liturgy. Just as Paul could speak of a formal creed—"the pattern of the sound words" (2 Tim. 1:13)—for confessing the same doctrine, there were patterns of sound prayer and singing. These were not opportunities merely for individual self-expression, but were part and parcel of being shaped and formed by God's Word even in the way we respond to God. Church becomes the place not only where individuals get together to share their experiences and express their piety, but where they become part of a cast in a plot of salvation history. It is no longer just "me and my personal relationship with Jesus," but a communion of saints to which we belong. Whether our prayers in the church are written down or not, they are public. That means that they are the prayers of the whole church for the whole world. We are saved together as one people and we come to God's throne of grace together in prayer and praise.

The promise is not only "for you and your children"; it is also "for all who are far off, everyone whom the Lord our God calls to himself." Some readers may never have been raised in a Christian home, but somehow heard the gospel. Yet they have been grafted onto the living

Vine. Now they too can be fathers and mothers in a dynasty of faith. Even one believing parent makes the children holy (1 Cor. 7:14). Single people have an important place in the body for sharing their gifts within the covenant family, including the children of the church. The gospel has a way of redefining "insiders" and "outsiders." Although the promise is "for you and your children," it cannot be defined simply as families. Even covenant families belong to the covenant family of which those without children or a spouse are full members.

There are perfectly good reasons to target a particular niche-demographic for a marketing campaign. It all depends on what one is trying to do. A quick return on an investment, with the recognition that the product will become obsolete and therefore lack long-term profits, is one way of doing business. In that case, you'll want to make the product as attractive as possible not only to a narrow slice of consumers, but to a narrow slice of consumers who will soon move on to other fashions. The covenant of grace, on the other hand, is passed on "from generation to generation." Selling a product to the hot prospects is different from receiving a heritage from a pervious generation and passing it down to the next. Everything that can be shaken will be shaken, the Scriptures remind us, and only the kingdom that God is building will remain (Heb. 12:27–28). The churches that become slaves of the market are made of hay, wood, and stubble, while those built on the apostolic foundation of gold, silver, and costly stones will remain (1 Cor. 3:5–17).

The Ministry and the Mission

It is easy to fall into a false choice between these fields of mission. Some churches focus on a personal relationship with Jesus to the point where the promise becomes focused on the inner subjectivity of the individual: private and mystical rather than public and outwardly focused on Christ, the fellowship of saints, and the world. Other churches focus on the covenantal nurture of their children, but often to the neglect of "all who are far off." They may provide richly for needs of the body, both spiritually and materially, but lack concern to bring the Good News to others and to care for their neighbors beyond their local church or denomination.

Still other churches concentrate so much on "all who are far off," that they fail adequately to feast at God's table themselves and to care for the spiritual and material welfare of fellow saints. When we begin to think that our job is to bring in Christ's kingdom through our own zealous—and often feverish—activity, we forget that God is the ultimate evangelist. He uses our witness, but God is the one who not only elects and redeems but gathers "all who are far off, *everyone whom the Lord our God calls to himself*." Our zeal, emotion, strategies, and efforts cannot raise those who are "dead in trespasses and sins" (Eph. 2:1), but when God speaks his promise through us and opens hearts by his Spirit through that gospel, a valley of dry bones becomes a living assembly (Ezekiel 37). The apostles proclaimed the gospel to Gentiles—those "who are far off." "And when the Gentiles heard this, they began rejoicing and glorifying the word of the Lord, and as many as were appointed to eternal life believed. And the word of the Lord was spreading throughout the whole region" (Acts 13:48–49). Now *that* is mission!

Today there is a lot of emphasis on the church as people rather than place: that is, focusing on the church as *the people who do certain things* rather than *a place where certain things are done*. However, this confuses law and gospel, our work and God's work. The preaching of the Word and the administration of the sacraments have (or at least should have) such preeminence in the church not because of the desire for clerical dominance over the laity; on the contrary, it is because of the unique and essential service that this ministry provides for the health of the whole body and its mission in the world. So instead of treating the formal ministry and marks of the church as one thing and the mission of the church as another, we should regard the former not only as the source but as in fact the same thing as the latter. The regular gathering of the saints for "the apostles' teaching and fellowship," "the breaking of bread," and "the prayers" is not treated in Acts merely as an exercise in spiritual togetherness but as itself the public sign that the kingdom had arrived in the Spirit. Mission in Acts is measured by the spread of the Word and the community it formed.

Furthermore, this gathering issued in a community that brought wonder and awe to its neighbors. Being built up into Christ, they realized a communion with each other that crossed the lines established by this present age. Richly fed with Christ and his gifts, they shared their gifts—spiritual *and* temporal—with each other and with outsiders, so that the Word of Christ continued to reverberate in ever-expanding rings from pulpit, font, and table to pew and then out into office buildings, homes, and restaurants as believers live out their existence in the world. Like a great dinner party where everyone is receiving and passing to others the rich food and drink prepared by a generous host, the communion established in Christ, by his Spirit, through the gospel sets in motion a truly alternative society to our individualistic, fast-food, self-serve culture.

The mission of the church is to execute the marks of the church, which are the same as the keys of the kingdom that Christ gave to his apostles (Matt. 16:19; cf. 18:18). Only because the church is a place where certain things happen—namely, God's act of rewriting us into his script—can there be a people who do certain things. Preaching, sacrament, and discipline are singled out in the Great Commission, in Acts 2:42, and elsewhere as the methods of mission. If these are missing, marginalized, or obscured, there is no office, no charismatic ministry, sense of community, social outreach, or innovative program that can build and expand Christ's kingdom. God may use many means, but he has ordained these and has promised to work the greatest signs and wonders through them.

Too Busy Serving to be Served?

There is a gathering—an *ekklesia*—because there is a work of God through preaching and sacrament called the gospel that does its work before we can get around to ours. In both traditional and contemporary forms of worship today, the emphasis seems to fall on our activity rather than on God's. Yet this fails to be genuinely evangelistic, either for Christians or others who might be present.

Look at the comparison between the sisters Martha and Mary in Luke 10. Mary "sat at the Lord's feet and listened to his teaching." "But Martha was distracted with much serving. And she went up to him and said, 'Lord, do you not care that my sister has left me to serve alone? Tell her then to help me.' But the Lord answered her, 'Martha, Martha, you are anxious and troubled about many things, but one thing is necessary. Mary has chosen the good portion, which will not be taken away from her'" (vv. 39–42). We have to be fed before we can feed. We cannot exchange and circulate gifts that we have not been given.

When Jesus insisted on washing the disciples' feet, Peter was indignant:

"Lord, do *you* wash *my* feet?" Jesus answered him, "What I am doing you do not understand now, but afterward you will understand." Peter said to him, "You shall never wash my feet." Jesus answered him, "If I do not wash you, you have no share with me." Simon Peter said to him, "Lord, not my feet only but also my hands and my head!" Jesus said to him, "The one who has bathed does not need to wash, except for his feet, but is completely clean. And you are clean . . . ." (John 13:6–10, emphasis added)

Only after the cross would Peter understand the meaning of Christ's humble service. Although we are clean—justified and holy in Christ—we still need to be served regularly by Christ through his public ministry. Before we can serve, we must be served.

We must therefore resist the false choice between the marks of the church (the preaching of the Word, administration of the sacraments, and discipline) and its mission. The faithful preaching of the Word means more than having our doctrinal ducks in a row; it includes taking the gospel to those who have not yet heard it. At the same time, there is no legitimate evangelism in the New Testament sense that does not add people to the church, baptizing and teaching them all that Christ delivered. The Great Commission does not allow us to choose between the ninety-nine sheep who are accounted for and the one that is missing. The same Word that brings conviction and conversion upon our first hearing of it continues convicting and converting us throughout our life. Therefore, if it is good enough for believers to be drawn perpetually to Christ, it will be good enough to draw in unbelievers for the first time. There is one ministry and it effectively serves believing and unbelieving sinners alike. The gospel is for those who are near and for those who are far off; for those who have heard it in various ways from innumerable passages for many years and for those who have heard it for the first time. The church not only *makes* disciples; it is the place where disciples *are made*, and not just once but throughout their Christian life. "For he is our God, and we are the people of his pasture, and the sheep of his hand" (Ps. 95:7). God is the focus, and the church is both his people and his pasture. The orderly worship of the saints gathered in weekly assembly for preaching, teaching, and witness *is* missional (1 Cor. 14:23–25).

Although it is easy for us to overlook, it is an empirical fact that most of the church's members over the last two millennia have been converted not through mass evangelism or revivals but through the ordinary means of grace in the church's public ministry. Most of these saints could not have told us when they came to believe the gospel; the Spirit worked through the weekly ministry of the church and the daily encounter with God's Word in the home. We may get tired of it. We may wonder if it is powerful, wise, and relevant in an era of impressive marketing and political campaigns. Yet in spite of its profoundly mixed record of faithfulness to its commission, this ordinary ministry of baptizing, catechizing, preaching, receiving the Supper, praying, singing, caring and comforting, admonishing and encouraging in fellowship, and finally, burying the dead in the hope of the resurrection has yielded the most effective results even when considered on purely empirical grounds. Those who are deeply rooted in the mysteries of the gospel will not only be more confident but more zealous to share their hope in the ordinary course of daily life. And they will also more eagerly encourage others to attend the public means of grace, where strangers are reconciled.

There is due place for doing the Word as well as hearing it, for serving as well as being served. However, when we know what we believe and why we believe it, fed richly on the indicatives of the gospel, we find ourselves filled with faith toward God and love toward our neighbor. Those who are properly suited with the belt of truth, the breastplate of righteousness, the shield of faith, and "the sword of the Spirit, which is the word of God," will also find themselves wearing "shoes for your feet" that "will make you ready to proclaim the gospel of peace" (Eph. 6:13–17). It is precisely by doing what it is commissioned to do for the people who have gathered in Christ's name that the church actually sets the stage for genuine conversation and conversion. While we certainly serve each other through our gifts in the body, the principal place where we *do* the Word is not in the church but in the world.

Dancing with Strangers

The ministry of John the Baptist is compared and contrasted with that of Jesus at various points in the Gospels. As the last prophet sent to prosecute the case of Yahweh versus Israel, preparing the way of the Lord, John's message concentrated on repentance and his baptism was typical of Jewish baptisms of repentance in the second temple period. Yet John himself pointed to the Lamb of God who would not only take away sin but baptize with the Spirit—fulfilling both aspects of the promise of the new covenant in Jeremiah 31 (John 1:26–34).

I mentioned previously that Jesus compared his generation to children playing the sad (funeral) game and the happy (wedding-reception) game, "and calling to one another, 'We played the flute for you, and you did not dance; we wailed, and you did not weep.' For John the Baptist has come eating no bread and drinking no wine, and you say, 'He has a demon'; the Son of Man has come eating and drinking, and you say, 'Look, a glutton and a drunkard, a friend of tax collectors and sinners!' Nevertheless, wisdom is vindicated by all her children" (vv. 31–35). John played the funeral dirge, but most of the people and religious leaders did not feel the sting of their guilt; Jesus brings the Good News of the gospel to sinners and he is rejected. "Now after John was arrested, Jesus came to Galilee, proclaiming the Good News of God, and saying, 'The time is fulfilled, and the kingdom of God has come near; repent, and believe in the Good News'" (Mark 1:14).

As in Jesus's day, the children of this age know neither how to mourn nor dance properly. Apart from God's grace, the gravity of our sin never reaches above the level of shame and our happiness never crosses the threshold of momentary pleasure. Christ's kingdom, however, is full of mirth, because of the joy of forgiveness. The funeral is prelude to the unending wedding reception. "Repent, and believe the Good News": this command forms the two aspects of conversion: repentance toward sin and faith toward God. After the funeral there is the wedding; after mourning, there is dancing. It is time to come to the feast. Now the Bridegroom has come and is even now filling the banquet hall with his guests. It is the gospel that makes us dance with strangers. The church is the world's largest news agency. The gospel created, preserves, and continues to create the church as it expands throughout and beyond every earthly empire.

So we do not really know who we are, much less who God is; we are confused even when we are confident that we know what we need. God just needs to take the microphone away from us. The one-man show simply is not working. Only when we come to this banquet do we really begin to understand the story of our own lives: its purpose, our failures to realize it, and the redemption that makes us forget our failures and join the celebration. We do not need better ideas and suggestions; we need to repent. We need to change our mind about everything that really matters. We need to burn our script and receive a new one. This does not happen when we just sit and reflect. It is not the result of introspection. It happens only when we enter another world: the theater of grace that God has established amid our comedy of errors—and hear something truly, wonderfully, and bewilderingly *new*.

In Psalm 72, Asaph confesses that his feet "almost stumbled" when he observed the way things seem to go in the world: the righteous often suffer, while the wicked seem to have it pretty good. Often, things do not seem ordered by a rational providence and it is cruel to expect sufferers to see God's foreordained pattern in their lives. It was only when he entered the sanctuary that Asaph says things fell into place. Undoubtedly, he saw the Table, with the Bread of Presence, Aaron's budding staff, the blood-soaked altar over the ark of the covenant with the tablets of the same Law he had broken. There he recognized the ultimate end of the wicked apart from the gospel and his faith in God's promise was renewed. He still may not have known why he was suffering, but now he had a sense of the bigger picture.

Something similar happens to us as we enter God's presence each week. God addresses us in his Word. We see his promise ratified in baptism and receive Christ's sacrifice afresh in the Supper. Paul reminds us that Communion links us to Christ's sacrifice in the *past* (1 Cor. 11:24–25). It also directs us to the *future*: "For as often as you eat this bread and drink this cup, you proclaim the Lord's death until he comes again" (1 Cor. 11:26). Even in the *present*, we feed on Christ's body and blood by faith: "The cup of blessing, which we bless, is it not a participation in the blood of Christ? The bread which we break, is it not a participation in the body of Christ?" (1 Cor. 10:16). Connected together to our Living Head in heaven, we are joined together as one body on earth: "For we, though many, are one bread and one body; for we all partake of that one bread" (v. 17).

Paul had also spoken of God's goodness, mercy, justice, and wisdom being supremely displayed in the mystery of the ages, as God's promise that Abraham's seed will lead to blessing for the nations as well as Israel was fulfilled. The prophets were given a vision of a world feast, with a radical recasting of the characters in the play. Israel's oppressors—Egypt, Assyria, and Babylon—are represented in this new age as fellow-heirs with Israel, with a highway connecting the ancient capitals as the nations bring their treasures into the New Jerusalem and are seated at the table with Abraham, Isaac, and Jacob.

In Luke 14 and its parallels, Jesus observes that we ordinarily invite only friends, relatives, and rich neighbors to grand banquets knowing that we'll receive such invitations in return. "But when you give a feast," Jesus tells his disciples, "invite the poor, the crippled, the lame, the blind, and you will be blessed, because they cannot repay you. You will be repaid at the resurrection of the just." This, after all, is the logic of the gospel: *We* are the poor and helpless, the outcasts, those who were once not a people but on the contrary were "children of wrath," and *God* has chosen, redeemed, and called those who cannot repay him. "When one of those who reclined at table with him heard these things, he said to him, 'Blessed is everyone who will eat bread in the kingdom of God!'" Immediately, Jesus tells his famous parable of the wedding banquet, where the invited guests make excuses. The no-shows in Jesus's parable are all caught up with the cares of daily life to such an extent that they cannot see the treasure held out to them. As C. S. Lewis writes, "It is not that our passions are too strong, but that they are too weak. . . . We are like children making mud pies in the slum because we cannot even imagine a holiday at the sea."[6] Jesus adds, "Then the master of the house became angry and said to his servant, 'Go out quickly to the streets and lanes of the city, and bring in the poor and crippled and blind and lame. And the servant said, 'Sir, what you commanded has been done, *and still there is room.*'" Here Jesus points up the liberal excess of the master's generosity: there is always room at his table. It is never crowded. There is always another place setting. So, Jesus continues, the master tells the servant to "go out to the highways and hedges and compel people to come in, that my house may be filled. For I tell you, none of those who were invited shall taste my banquet." The insiders are outsiders on that day, while the outsiders are insiders.

In both Psalm 34 and Jesus's parable, we are faced with a choice between the wisdom of the world, which is a logic of giving in order to get, and the wisdom of God, which is a logic of giving in order to give. The one gives rise to self-confident boasting—using others (even God) for our own happiness—the other to thanksgiving to God and love for our neighbor.

The real Thanksgiving dinner is not held once a year and it is not a national holiday, but an international banquet intended to confirm God's Word every time that it is preached. At this table we do not design our own guest lists but are servants of the master who holds it and commands us to bring in the other riffraff like ourselves. In fact, we get the word "Eucharist" from "thanksgiving." It is not a guilt offering that we offer for our sins, but a thanksgiving meal celebrating

God's gift that draws us out of the world and our common callings to share this feast. The message and the methods totally contradict the wisdom of the world and its logic of repayment, substituting instead the logic of the gift: a gift that we have been given together and which, together, we celebrate by exchanging gifts of fellowship, finances, love, and service. God's gift sets into motion a neverending exchange of gifts and no one is left out of anything. And through this event, we ourselves become a thank offering to God and an aroma to the world.

At this table, even the poor and humble leave filled, while those who think that they are rich, healthy, and well-off leave empty-handed. Here we have in this age a foretaste of the *marriage Supper* in the age to come. Let these two tables, so luxuriously supplied, fill our hearts with wonder and thanksgiving for God's goodness, justice, mercy, and wisdom. "My soul makes its boast in the LORD; let the humble hear and be glad. . . . Oh, taste and see that the LORD is good!" (Ps. 34:2, 8).

Recovering the Lord's Day

The Good News stops us in our tracks. Breaking up our ordinary news cycle of daily routines, we rest and become recipients of God's generous service. Christ's resurrection from the dead moved us from the end of the work week to the first day of his everlasting Sabbath, from Saturday to Sunday. Believers met regularly "on the first day of the week" (Acts 20:7; 1 Cor. 16:2). It is not insignificant that John received his revelation of the heavenly worship "on the Lord's day" (Rev 1:10). The Christian faith is not only a story. Nor is it just a system of doctrines. It includes concrete practices through which our lives are actually shaped by the reality of the new creation. But we have to break away from the powers of this fading age to be renewed by the powers of the age to come.

We cannot talk about the importance of discipleship and neglect public worship (Heb. 10:25). We cannot boast of belonging to the invisible church—"the assembly of the firstborn who are enrolled in heaven" (Heb. 12:23)—while treating lightly membership in the visible church and participating in its means of grace, fellowship, and discipline. The church *is* a concrete place, as well as a people. "Remember your leaders, those who spoke to you the word of God. . . . Obey your leaders and submit to them, for they are keeping watch over your souls, as those who will have to give an account. Let them do this with joy and not with groaning, for that would be of no advantage to you" (Heb. 13:7, 17). Christ's kingdom is indeed heavenly, but it takes a visible, earthly, and concrete form in the politics of the cross and resurrection. Its weapons are spiritual—that is, from the Holy Spirit—but they are heard and seen. Its head is ascended to the throne of all power, but his reign is administered on earth through deputized officers. We have been translated to the everlasting Sabbath, but we receive its foretaste on a particular day of the week.

It is not simply alone, in our hearts, that we receive Christ and respond in thanksgiving and worship. It is as members of Christ's body, in the concrete context of our corporate worship, that Christ draws us by his Spirit into his thanksgiving parade.

How we spend the Lord's Day is a register of our contentment in God's provision, both of daily bread and eternal life. On this day we are not consumers or producers, but coheirs of God's entire estate. On this day there is nothing to buy or sell; God himself has purchased everything for the feast. On this day the Shepherd beckons, "Come, everyone who thirsts, come to the waters; and he who has no money, come, buy and eat! Come, buy wine and milk without money and without price" (Isa. 55:1). The Lord of the Sabbath gives us rest in his victorious enthronement.

We may decry the stress, distractions, consumerism, and vocational ladder-climbing of everyday life, while nevertheless surrendering to the lordship of these rival claimants even on the day that God has given us to enjoy with him and his people. If we care so much for "taking time to be with the Lord," why have so many churches given up the evening service on Sunday? Why has Sunday become the most popular day for sports, entertainment, and shopping? God has not only served up breakfast, but dinner as well, and has summoned his guests. If believers are going to form a genuinely alternative community, a harbinger of the everlasting Sabbath, and a witness in the world to God's peace, we do not need more messages on stress relief and debt relief, but more faithful dedication of the Lord's Day to its proper use. God's politics must take priority over the politics of the present age. When God assembles us to receive his gifts each week, making us his own people, we are transformed. There is a time to work and a time to rest; a time to give and a time to receive. Only when we are saturated with God's Word on God's day does every day become different. Only then do we have something to give to those in need.

9

THE HEALTH PAGE

FEASTING IN A FAST-FOOD WORLD

According to Eric Schlosser's book *Fast-Food Nation*, only a generation ago in the United States three-quarters of its food expenses were spent on home cooked meals, while today half is spent on restaurants, and mostly fast-food chains.[1] This transformation has been referred to as "the McDonaldization of America." Ironically, in the wealthiest nations on earth, where we encounter famine victims primarily in pictures, the "Super Size Me" era has led to an epidemic of malnutrition by choice.

Yet in spite of our daily habits of consumption, we still know the difference when we sit down to a nice dinner with family or friends. I'll never forget an evening in Nicaragua many years ago, when a pastor and his wife prepared a dinner. Supporting his family as a local lobster fisherman, the pastor brought home the makings of a spectacular feast from his catch that day. Cooked over a grate on top of a fire, the lobster roasted as a pig scurried beneath our feet on the mud floor. We prayed, laughed, and shared our lives as we dined and it was nearly midnight before we felt compelled to call it quits. I discovered later that the pastor and his wife had traveled to the neighboring village to borrow chairs for the meal. Hospitality, not convenience, was their priority. Although this was the first time I had ever met this family and we struggled to understand each other's language, I felt closer to them than I have ever felt to my next-door neighbors. Ironically, the strangeness of the local setting, sharply contrasted with the banal familiarity of a McDonalds in Moscow, Nairobi, or my home town, was no match. It was even more than a great meal with terrific people; in Christ, we were family. The contrast between a drive-thru McDonalds "Happy Meal" and strangers whose souls become intertwined in the unfolding evening over a feast measures the lengths to which we will go in order to settle for a lot less than we should.

David Brooks has pointed out that American Boomers, lords of the suburbs, are part bourgeois, part bohemian.[2] The bourgeois part of us longs for vaguely traditional roots, nostalgic for Norman Rockwell scenes of hearth and home. But our bohemian side, crafted in the '70s, craves freedom from any and every constraint, anything that would remind us that our choices aren't limitless. If there is a line, we have to cross it. Transgression "authenticates" us, validating our supposedly unique identity, even if we're following the herd of our own demographic in doing so.

However, many of the Boomers' children cannot even remember enough Norman Rockwell moments to be able to re-create a nostalgic collage. They don't necessarily *want* to be endless drifters, transgressing every boundary. They just don't know quite where the boundaries are—or if such a thing exists. While their parents couldn't wait to *leave* home, many of them long to *have* one. Every generation has its quirks, but from the economy to the church it is evident that our narcissism has really made a mess in this party that we've been throwing for ourselves. And we've left it for our children and grandchildren to clean up.

The Worship Experience

One characteristic that seems to unite our generations is the way we experience the world as a shopping mall. Anonymous voyeurs of identities we might wish to assume, bodies that we imagine we have, and goods we imagine that we can afford, we long to be transported—even for a moment—from our banal but real existence to a manufactured pseudoreality. The amazing thing is that reality and simulation blur. We can have the "New York experience" at New York, NY, in Las Vegas. It's more manageable than the real New York. In Las Vegas, you are totally in control and anonymous—unaccountable to anyone or anything. "Your secret stays here."

Our local symphony advertises "a powerful musical experience"; evidently, the point isn't the music as such, but my transformed existence as a result of the event. At Disney's Epcot Center you can have the "China experience" without actually having to go to China. You can even take an appropriately hokey ride through the "Oxford Experience" when visiting the famous British university. Recently I learned of "The Army Experience Center." With branches popping up in malls across the United States, each Center promises visitors an "unparalleled interactive experience" through video games and simulators. I'm not saying these things are necessarily wrong. However, education as entertainment is pretty different from seeing a poster with a serious-looking Uncle Sam pointing his finger at you saying, "I want you," and sitting across from an officer who explains the Army and its opportunities and requirements. The more our decisions and commitments are determined by seductive images and prepackaged experiences, the more our reflective capacities are weakened. We can be taken almost anywhere by anyone when all that's necessary is a good "experience." Whatever one makes of the "experience economy" in the marketplace, the church is different.[3]

I suggested in the previous chapter that in spite of our rhetoric, our practice proves that we believe that we are the choosers, redeemers, and lords of the church and that we bring Christ's kingdom into existence by our decision and effort. Some of our phrases give this away. For example, referring to the public service as a "worship experience" makes us the object rather than God. Furthermore, it reflects the general tendency in our culture today to turn everything into an "experience," which usually means some form of entertainment. During the last general election, delegates at the two party conventions described their experience to reporters in the same euphoric terms that one might expect to hear from people on their way to the parking lot from a "worship experience." Like cruises and tours, these "experiences" are manufactured, packaged, and sold.

When God appeared and spoke from the top of Mount Sinai, delivering his commands, the Israelites were filled with terror: "Now when the people saw the thunder and the flashes of lightning and the sound of the trumpet and the mountain smoking, the people were afraid and trembled, and they stood far off and said to Moses, 'You speak to us, and we will listen; but do not let God speak to us, lest we die. . . . The people stood far off, while Moses drew near to the thick darkness where God was" (Exod. 19:18–19, 21). It was not something that they choreographed, manufactured, produced, or packaged. God simply showed up on the scene and started speaking. They were clearly not in control of the situation and they did not like the experience at all. However, it did create in them an urgent need that they did not feel before: namely, the need for a mediator.

Contrast this with the "worship experience" that they did manufacture, in which they were in control. While Moses was up on the mountain receiving the Law and mediating between the two parties, the people below were wondering why it was taking him so long. In his absence, they decided to make a golden calf. No longer disoriented by the real presence of God, they had this experience under control: "And the people sat down to eat and drink and rose up to play" (Exod. 32:6). They were not worshiping a different God than Yahweh; they just wanted a visible representation of their deity, just as the pagan tribes around them had theirs.

As it turned out, Moses' mediation was already being put to use, as God informs him that his people were already breaking the Law that he was giving Moses. "Now therefore let me alone," God told the mediator, "that my wrath may burn hot against them and I may consume them, in order that I may make a great nation of you" (Exod. 32:10). However, Moses reminded God that they were God's people, whom he had brought out of Egypt, and pleaded with God to relent for the sake of that unconditional promise that he swore to Abraham (vv. 11–13). "And the LORD relented from the disaster that he had spoken of bringing on his people" (v. 14). As Moses caught up with Joshua on his way down the hill, Joshua thought he heard the sound of war in the camp. But Moses knew better: "It is not the sound of shouting for victory, or the sound of the cry of defeat," he replied, "but the sound of singing that I hear" (vv. 17–18).

The sound of singing! It must be a "worship experience." And indeed it was: "And as soon as he came near the camp and saw the calf and the dancing, Moses' anger burned hot, and he threw the tablets out of his hands and broke them at the foot of the mountain. He took the calf that they had made and burned it with fire and ground it into powder and scattered it on the water and made the people of Israel drink it" (Exod. 32:19–20). All that his derelict lieutenant Aaron could say for himself was, "You know how the people are" (v. 22). Evidently, his acquiescence was calculated to keep them from more wide-scale mutiny, given Moses' absence. The natives were getting restless.

Moses was a servant, Jesus is God's Son. "He is the image [*eikōn*, icon] of the invisible God . . ." (Col. 1:15). God was saving his people for the incarnation—something far greater, far more "meaningful," than the worship experience that they could manufacture. But they would not wait. In the absence of Moses the mediator, the people barricaded themselves from the real God and his terrifying presence.

We find ourselves in a somewhat analogous situation. Although our mediator is no less than the incarnate Son, he is bodily absent from us for now, seated at the right hand of God. Like Moses' absence, our Lord's ascension to the Father is exactly what we need right now. That is where he is carrying out his mediatorial work even now. Instead of relying on the Spirit's work of delivering Christ and his gifts to his church through the means of grace—worshiping "in Spirit and in truth" (John 4:23)—we demand more immediate experiences that we can choreograph and control. In so doing, we are never terrified, never caught off guard, never put on trial. We sit down to eat and drink and rise up to play, settling for a Happy Meal that we can order right now, rather than a feast that God has prepared for us on his terms. But in this way we avoid the real presence of the actual God who not only judges but saves us through his sinless Mediator.

It is *our experience* that we find transforming and relevant, regardless of what or who it was that inspired us in this particular moment. But this is similar to the so-called Hedonistic Paradox: the more passionately we search for happiness as an end in itself, the less happy we actually are. Perhaps even more than others, we Christians tend to romanticize marriage and family, as if our spouse or children could satisfy our craving for total fulfillment. Of course, they can't, and idols soon become demons when they do not come through for us.

In the 2008 film *Wall-E* mass consumption has turned our planet into a vast trash heap and a giant superstore has relocated earthlings aboard the spaceship Axiom: a supermall, Times Square, and Las Vegas all rolled into one. Passengers, many of whom were raised on the ship, are all obese, attached to floating lounge chairs complete with TV monitors. Perpetually draining Big Gulps through a straw, their every whim is satisfied by robotic stewards at the touch of a button at their control panel. As if Axiom itself were not enough of an alternative reality, the passengers alternate between the TV and cell phone with which each gliding lounge is furnished. They have everything they want—until it is discovered that there is after all one living plant left on earth. Somewhere inside of each passenger there was still a longing for contact with something that was real.

Ironically, these manufactured and prepackaged "experiences" are incredibly short-lived. I cannot remember most movies I have seen. For whatever brief moments or even hours that I am wrapped in the cocoon of a space ride at Disneyland or am overwhelmed with intense emotion at a concert, the experience leaves as quickly as it came. However, my most enduring experiences are identified with events in which the goal was something other than having an experience. I will never forget hearing the minister say, "I now pronounce you husband and wife." Just words, right? They are words that change our life. "You have cancer." "We got all of the cancer—you're free and clear." "You're pregnant." "You got the job." Reports grounded in objective facts—outside of us and our experience—are the most significant experience generators in our lives.

Each week, as I join my brothers and sisters in a public confession of sin and our particular sins to God in silence, Christ's ambassador declares that I am forgiven in Christ's name and on the authority of his Word. Regardless of what I feel inside, God's external Word assures me that I have peace with God in his Son. This is not a subjective experience—a peaceful, easy feeling—but an objective announcement. And precisely because of its objectivity—the fact that it is announced to me even when I am not overwhelmed by it emotionally—I get the experience of forgiveness thrown in as well. Living for experiences is like chasing vapors. It is *sunsets*, not "the sunset experience"; *actual expressions of love*, not "the love experience"; *the Triune God*, and not "the worship experience," that turn out to deliver the most important and lasting experiences.

Headline: "Global Souls Come Home"

I observed in *Christless Christianity* that technology has now made it possible for us to consummate our Gnostic experience of transcending every restriction of our finitude and bodily existence. Online confessionals and now even Internet churches are growing in popularity. And why not? If the church is a mall or resource center for the things that we need for our spiritual makeovers, surely we can do our religious shopping online as well as anything else. But we were not created as disembodied souls and it is the fall rather than creation that has made us individuals turned in on ourselves in spiritual solitude. Christians confess their faith in Christ to raise their mortal bodies in immortal glory and in the gospel he calls us out of our narcissistic cave of private experience to join our fellow pilgrims in the royal procession to Zion's feast.

In his book *The Global Soul: Jet Lag, Shopping Malls, and the Search for Home*, Pico Iyer speaks for many of us today. An Indian born in England, moved to California as a boy, moved to Japan. "The Global Soul may see so many sides of every question that he never settles on a firm conviction; he may grow so used to giving back a different self according to his environment that he loses sight of who he is when nobody's around."[4] "Everywhere is so made up of everywhere else and our very souls have been put into circulation. Yet even global beings need a home." We live in "an anthology of generic spaces—the shopping mall, the food court, the hotel lobby—which bear the same relation to life, perhaps, that Musak does to music."[5] "The Global Soul is a ventriloquist, an impersonator, or an undercover agent: the question that most haunts him is 'Who are you today?'"[6] Iyer quotes Douglas Coupland: "I like hotels because in a hotel-room you have no history; you have only essence."[7] For his own part, Iyer prefers the anonymous space of airports: "part shopping mall, part border crossing."[8]

But precisely because this ethereal realm of simulated reality erases all sense of place, there cannot really be "border crossings" anymore. The same is true in the church. You used to know when you were in a Roman Catholic church as opposed to, say, a Presbyterian or a Baptist church. Today, it is sometimes difficult to tell when you are in a church rather than a mall, movie theater, or corporate headquarters. Of course, there is no divinely prescribed ecclesiastical architecture, but something's up when the pulpit, table, and font are less visibly dominant than the new means of grace, whether bands, organ pipes, choirs, or screens. It means something that what previous generations called a chancel we call a stage.

It is easy for us to settle for a drive-through meal, where one can order off of the menu but need not go through the rituals of dining with others and enjoying what God has set before us. In the movie, "The Big Night," two brothers from Italy open a restaurant. Down the street is a booming rival whose owner gives the customers what they want: an "Italian restaurant" with spaghetti, cheap Chianti, and the cheesy ambiance of an Old World experience. While the older brother insists upon quality and authenticity, even as the new restaurant struggles for customers, the younger is gradually drawn to the owner down the street who is only too happy to teach him the methods of success. In the climactic scene, however, the brothers—who have reconciled somewhat more out of filial bonds than agreement—provide the meal after which they have decided to close their restaurant. Inviting friends and neighbors at no cost, they provide a lavish feast of delicacies unknown on the rival's popular menu. Even though it took two days to prepare, all of the vegetables are fresh. Nothing is frozen or prepackaged. The diners, caught up in the delight of conversation, fall silent as they taste a meal that transcends anything that they have ever experienced or could have been ordered off of a menu.

A similar story is told in *Babette's Feast*, where a small community of rigorous pietists on a Danish island is treated to a sumptuous meal that brings delight beyond anything that the guests could have predicted. Babette, a famous Parisian chef who came to the island seeking isolation from her past life, had become a cook for two elderly sisters who had abandoned their promising careers to help their father guide his disciples. Much to Babette's surprise, an old lottery ticket had a winning number and she decided to spend all of her money on a shipment of fine French delicacies for the island's few inhabitants. Fearful of enjoying such worldly extravagance, the pious neighbors promised each other that they would respectfully pretend—but only pretend—to enjoy Babette's feast. Enclosed in their narrow world of unspoken doubts and desires, the neighbors were strangers to each other even though they met regularly for devotions and prayers. But the meal was too great to be mastered by their scruples and with every sip of Babette's fine wines and every morsel of each exquisite course, the faces of the guests turned from serious to tentative to smiling and laughing. Never told stories were shared in a swirl of newfound friendship. Who could imagine that a meal could revolutionize a community like that?

Snacking Is for Tourists

I suggested in chapter 1 that our world is filled with three types of people: masters, tourists, and pilgrims. The great figures of the modern era knew where they were going—and were determined to take the rest of the world with them. In fact, many of them believed that they had already arrived. The Enlightenment produced books with titles like Lessing's *The Education of the Human Race*, assuming that everything in the past represented childhood superstitions and dependence on authorities. Now, however, we have arrived at adulthood and can think for ourselves, he argued. Kant said the same thing, followed by acolytes of the new world order. Eventually, Marxists and capitalists, fascists and democrats asserted their mastery over the world, offering salvation from everything in the past. Starting from scratch, we would build a new world—a tower reaching to the heavens: this time, on the foundations of absolute reason, observation, and universal principles of morality. No longer would we need to rely on external authorities, whether the Bible or the church.

After successive programs for re-creating the world, the modern project has left widespread disillusionment, not to mention the slaughter of millions. We are less sure of ourselves than ever. Modern idolatry of the self, the state, ethnic blood, technology, and ideologies of the left and the right, have been diagnosed as pathological. Once upon a time, God's name was taken in vain (and still is) for these Promethean projects, but now, at least to many ears the invocation of "God" sounds like just another power grab. We have grown weary of sweeping narratives that promise to make sense of our lives and yet we long to be a part of something larger than ourselves.

If we are not *masters* of reality, fulfilling a supposedly divine destiny in our march from superstition to enlightenment (as modernity supposed), all that is left now is for us to be *tourists* who wander from nowhere to nowhere, creating reality as we go out of endless and random choices. It is still the sovereign will that lies at the heart of this pathology. The difference is that the master's will to power was guided by a "clear and distinct idea" of universal truth with blueprint and a concrete destination in mind, while the tourist's will to power is governed by whatever seems interesting along a path to nowhere in particular. In this respect at least "postmodernism" is not so much a radical departure from "modernity" as it is its completion. We no longer want to rule the world; we just want more space on our iPods and more opportunities for random, pointless, and fleeting choices in the supermarket of life.

The Feast Is for Pilgrims

In sharp contrast, we enter *God's* sanctuary as those who are summoned. We are neither masters nor tourists. God's electing grace, not the authentication of our supposedly autonomous will, brings us here and his gospel keeps us moving toward a destination of which we are certain and yet have only heard of, tasted, and glimpsed from a far off distance. He knows us by name. Through the lips of the minister, Christ announces his commands, which we know we have failed to keep. Together we confess that we all, like sheep, have gone astray, and together we confess our faith in God's Good News. And then God ratifies his promise to us in the Supper.

Psalm 78 recounts the whole history of God's relationship with Israel, reciting the familiar cycles of the people's unfaithfulness and God's faithfulness to his covenant. Included is the rebellion of the people in the wilderness: "They tested God in their heart by demanding the food they craved. They spoke against God, saying, 'Can God spread a table in the wilderness?' " Indeed, he can—and he did—even for his ungrateful people: "He struck the rock so that water gushed out and streams overflowed. Can he also give bread or provide meat for his people?" He even gave these gifts to sustain them, but "his anger rose against Israel, because they did not believe in God and did not trust his saving power." "Yet he commanded the skies above and opened the doors of heaven, and he rained down on them manna to eat and gave them the grain of heaven. Man ate of the bread of angels; he sent them food in abundance" (Ps. 78:18–24). In John 6, Jesus interpreted himself as the Bread of Heaven, whose flesh and blood nourishes his people with everlasting life. And Paul said that the Israelites in the wilderness "Drank from the spiritual Rock that followed them, and the Rock was Christ. Nevertheless, with most of them God was not pleased, for they were overthrown in the wilderness" (1 Cor. 10:4). God pledges his saving grace to us through his Word and sacraments. Again and again, he overwhelms our sin with his grace. Nevertheless, we must receive the promise that he preaches and ratifies, instead of demanding new experiences and the satisfaction of our immediate felt needs.

As Jesus taught, there is a time for fasting and time for feasting. John the Baptist and his disciples prepared the way: the somber news of imminent judgment was characterized by fasting, mourning over their personal and corporate unfaithfulness to the covenant, lying prostrate before God and his holy throne. But now Jesus Christ has arrived on the scene. When John's disciples asked Jesus why he and his disciples do not fast, the Savior replied, "Can the friends of the groom mourn as long as the groom is with them?" (Matt. 9:15). Now the Savior has come and his kingdom is full of joy and forgiveness. When John the Baptist sent his disciples to find out if Jesus was really the promised Messiah, Jesus told them to report back "what you have seen and heard: the blind see, the deaf hear, and the poor have the gospel preached to them" (Matt. 11:5). The lame dance, the outcasts are gathered from the dark alleys, and the feast is being prepared.

Christ returned to his heavenly throne to pour out his gifts (especially the Spirit) and to prepare the wedding feast for us. In the meantime, we are tasting that heavenly supper when we are gathered to hear and receive the gospel. Christ is the gift who keeps on giving and as our churches become more centered on the message and the methods that he has ordained for his gift giving, we will doubtless find a table spread in the wilderness. A feast in a fast-food world.

It's Like Watching Corn Grow

As a culture, we are losing our capacity to wait for things. We are not just a fast-food nation; we want everything quickly, results now. Convenience takes priority over quality. Eating dinner at home together used to be a family ritual. Who knows how many character traits, memories, and bonds were forged out of those communal practices? It takes time to make a good bottle of wine and the better reds may not reach their maturity for many years.

Take the example of the famous Stradivarius violin. Born in 1644, Antonio Stradivari became the greatest violin maker in history. The barely literate Italian craftsman developed an instrument distinguished by the quality of its rich resonance. Yet because they were hand-crafted, each violin had its own sound. Musicologists and violinists speculate to this day as to what exactly contributes to the uniqueness of a Stradivarius. The quality of the woods, the patches of wood placed strategically inside the belly of the instrument, and its shape are thought to play a major role. He made a little over a thousand violins, half of which survive today, and although Stradivari himself was not a mogul, they are coveted as national treasures by only the

wealthiest owners today. It is something that could not be mass produced on an assembly line in a factory.

For us, however, it is not the depth and richness of our experiences
and relationships, but the quantity and perpetual "zing" we get out
of them that matters. We are terrified of being bored. Educational
videos and lessons for children are advertised as "fun" and that is a
crucial criterion for everything from worship planning to evangelism
in the church.

Let's face it: a traditional Christian service of public invocation,
Bible reading, prayer, preaching, and sacraments is not ordinarily
fun. "It's like watching corn grow," as they say. There is no excuse for
pastors to be so aloof, lazy, or distracted from their congregation that
there is no connection. Nevertheless, on an average month of Sundays,
every believer *should* find church a little boring. I find marriage a little
boring. And raising four children. And going to work every day. I am
even bored by travel, although as a boy I went through the "I want
to be a pilot" phase. It's old hat now.

If we made all of our decisions based on how highly it scored today
on the fun meter, we would never commit ourselves to relationships
and processes that take a long time to see any results. Our culture is
falling apart over this one. The result is that we demand cargo ships
full of meaningful, life-altering, transformative, explosive, and unique
experiences every day and are losing our appreciation for the role that
a child's smile has in the grand scheme of things. Every date night has
to be the Love Boat, every family vacation must fill albums worth of
memories, and church can't be church; it has to be a "worship experience" that alters one's cell structure every time.

In what he calls "a short but self-important history of the Baby
Boomer Generation," Joe Queenan, writer for *The New York Times*
and *GQ*, makes sport of (among other things) his generation's "absolute inability to accept the ordinary."[9] A baseball game used to be
a baseball game, but now it replaces Bar Mitzvahs and First Holy
Communions, weddings and funerals, as a moment of eschatological
significance. He adds,

> Because Baby Boomers are obsessed with living in the moment, they
> insist that every experience be a watershed, every meal extraordinary,
> every friendship epochal, every concert superb, every sunset meta-
> celestial. Life isn't like that. Most meals are okay. Most friendships
> work until they don't work. Most concerts are decent. Sunsets are

sunsets. By turning spectacularly humdrum occurrences into formal rites, Baby Boomers have transmuted even the most banal activities into "events" requiring reflection, planning, research, underwriting and staggering masses of data. This has essentially ruined everything for everybody else because nothing can ever again be exactly what it was in the first place: something whose very charm is a direct result of its being accessible, near at hand, *ordinary*.[10]

Behind this exuberant cult of the immediate experience in the moment lurks a haunting nihilism. We came from nowhere and are going to nowhere, but somewhere in the middle of it all we have to make a big splash. Every moment must be orgasmic. "If the dead are not raised," Paul famously concluded by quoting a line from a Greek comedy, " 'let us eat and drink, for tomorrow we die' " (1 Cor. 15:32).

The technical term for this is *narcissism*. And the problem is that nobody can make us *that* happy, or even as happy as we think we deserve. Furthermore, the things that I think will make me happy are actually trivial distractions from the gift that God delivers. The fact is that in spite of what I can measure on the Richter scale in a given day, my marriage is a huge deal—for me, my wife, our children—and its impact is felt in the web of many other relationships. Over the long haul, you never know how many people are affected by it, but it is more significant than you think. Frankly, my children are sometimes a nuisance and an inconvenience, a constant threat to my selfishness, and precisely in that way they open me up to experiences that I would never have known in a daily routine of unhindered choices. It is precisely in our distraction from our immediate gratification that we discover hidden rooms filled with treasures.

Imagine what would happen if we determined what we would learn, teach, or endure on the basis of what William James called "its cash-value in experiential terms." Children would not learn the alphabet, the multiplication tables, primary colors, or the basic grammar of the Christian faith. School would be recess all day: filled with games and free play. There would be no great food, friendships, marriages, families, buildings, farms, athletes, or concerts. Ironically, the pursuit of instant gratification and perpetual amusement creates its own self-enclosed world of boredom. Spoiled children (of whatever age) are never satisfied.

The younger generations today have seen it all. They have been to every theme park, have every gadget, and know every band. The expression on a lot of their faces tells it all: "Been there, done that, got the shirt." And they are consummately bored. Now growing numbers of them tell us they are especially bored with the "contemporary worship experience." Our fear of God must become greater than our fear of boredom. Making disciples, like making crafts, great works of art, fine wine, a memorable dinner, and raising children, takes a long time. It *is* like watching corn grow and that's exactly what we are: a harvest whose firstfruits have already been raised and exalted.

Precisely because the Good News has been taken for granted, many churches today do not seem to realize that they have the best drama going. Demanding something extraordinary, novel, and exciting, we look away from what God is doing through ordinary preaching, water, wine, and bread, and focus on what we are doing to capture the headlines. Like a good parent, God knows that if we had all the cotton candy we wanted, we would not only be sick but would miss out on the dinner he has prepared.

Most people over the centuries have become Christians by being baptized, catechized, taking Communion, hearing sermons, talking to their parents, grandparents, and other elders in the faith, and then bringing others into this lifelong discipleship through their witness, until they are comforted by their pastor and other believers on their deathbed. However, this is too ordinary. We try to pull God down from heaven or bring Christ up from the dead by our feverish activity, assimilating God's story to the cult of immediate gratification. As with all forms of nihilism, this illness can be remedied only by rebuilding our connection to a significant beginning and future destiny, with our present moment as part of a pilgrimage instead of frantic zig-zagging from each exciting attraction at the carnival of death disguising itself as life. Only God's politics can accomplish this.

The Main Event: Eating and Drinking with God

The theme of eating and drinking in the presence of God is prominent from Genesis to Revelation. Instead of waiting for their host to give them the fruit from the Tree of Life, Adam and Eve wanted their Happy Meal here and ordered from their own menu. Like secular treaties, which were ratified by the great king (suzerain) sharing a state meal with his newly acquired servant-king (vassal), such events were rich with political overtones. After Abram's battle with God's enemies, he is treated to a covenantal meal of bread and wine with the mysterious Melchizedek, king of Salem, whom we are told was a type of Christ (Gen. 14:18, with Ps. 110:4 and Heb. 7:1, 17).

When God renewed his covenant, after the golden calf incident, God called Moses, Aaron and his sons (Nadab and Abihu), and seventy elders to ascend the mountain into the cloud of his presence. There the Lord ratified the covenant as his guests "beheld God, and ate and drank" (Exod. 24:11). Moses then received the tablets of the Ten Commandments and remained on the mountain, in the cloud with God, for forty days and forty nights (v. 18). For their continued unbelief, however, most of the desert generation were barred (along with Moses) from entering the Promised Land. Instead of enduring the trial and entering the land flowing with milk and honey, that generation died just short of the Jordan River. Significantly, God commanded the Bread of the Presence to be placed in the Holy of Holies, as a perpetual confirmation of his provision for his people (Exod. 25:30).

The theme of "eating and drinking in the presence of the LORD" is carried forward in the New Testament, beginning with Jesus's trial in the desert—for forty days and forty nights, recapitulating Israel's trial (and echoing Moses' mediation on the mountain with God for forty days and forty nights). This time, however, Jesus rebuffed the serpent's enticements for "glory now." Instead of demanding the food he craved, Jesus replied with the words of Scripture: "It is written, 'Man shall not live by bread alone, but by every word that comes from the mouth of God'" (Matt. 4:4).

It is striking how often in Scripture God, the stranger, meets us as we are on the way to somewhere else. Going about their daily work, with their own plans and expectations for the future, the disciples were confronted by Jesus and called out to join him on his journey to the feast.

Luke's Gospel particularly emphasizes the theme of Jesus as the journeying guest who is not received, even by his own (Luke 9:52–19:44). In fact, he is rejected in Jerusalem (19:45–23:49). *"Eating and drinking in the presence of the Lord"* (13:25, emphasis added) explicitly invokes the covenantal meals of the Old Testament. Only now, it is the "insiders" who, refusing the invitation, are cast out and the "outsiders" who are seated at the kingdom feast with Abraham, Isaac, and Jacob.

David P. Mossner explains,

In Deuteronomy the goal of all of Moses' journeying with the people to the Promised Land is to inherit the blessings of the covenant to Abraham, Isaac, and Jacob as summed up by "eating" and "rejoicing" before the Lord. . . . The first act upon entering the salvation of the land is to write the Law upon stones erected on Mt. Ebal, and there with a peace offering "eat and be filled and rejoice before the Lord" (Deut. 27:7). . . . The land itself is repeatedly envisioned as "flowing with milk and honey."[11]

It will be a place where only the best wine will be produced. In the wilderness, God says that apart from the miraculous provision, "You did not eat bread, you did not drink wine or strong drink" (Deut. 29:6). "In sum, to drink wine is to honor or fear the Lord by rejoicing in all of the gracious covenant blessings of the land (e.g., 14:23b)."[12] In Deuteronomy 12–26 the central theme is "eating and drinking before the Lord" in the *place* that he has appointed. There is also the appointed *time*, the major feasts: Passover (the "Feast of Unleavened Bread" and the "cup of salvation") and Pentecost, also known as Tabernacles or Booths (celebrating the final harvest in which the households are told to "rejoice in the feast") (6:13–15; cf 31:10–13).

Leading his people to the Promised Land, God spreads a table in the waterless desert. He gives them bread from heaven and water from the rock—and, as Paul reminds us, "that Rock was Christ" (1 Cor. 10:4). Yet even when the spies return with "first fruits" of the land they are about to enter, the people refuse these gifts and, with Moses, that generation dies just outside the boundaries of the land of promise. Everything else in the historical books and the prophets moves toward Jerusalem—Mount Zion, the place where God will dwell. No longer merely leading the journeying people, pitching his tent outside the camp, he will make his permanent dwelling "in their midst." "God with us." "Be silent before the Lord GOD! For the day of the LORD is near; the LORD has prepared a sacrifice and consecrated his guests" (Zeph. 1:7).

This history is recapitulated both in the life of Jesus and that of his contemporaries. John the Baptist comes announcing the nearness of the kingdom, but is beheaded (although some believed his report). His ministry is not one of jubilation in the Promised Land ("He came neither eating nor drinking"), but of serious judgment and a call to repentance, while the ministry of Jesus will be that of calling sinners, outcasts, strangers, and aliens to his festive banquet ("The Son of Man came eating and drinking and they say, 'Behold a glutton and a drunkard, a friend of tax-collectors and sinners'"). He feeds the five thousand, but they were there for a free meal, like that wilderness generation: "But can he give us *meat*?"

Rejected by his own, just as he was when the spies returned with their first fruits of the good land, he nevertheless sends his messenger "into the highways and byways" to gather guests for his banquet. Jesus moves toward Jerusalem, and as he does so, teaches the disciples to invite to the banquet those who cannot repay them (Luke 14:14). After all, isn't that what God does with us?

As we have seen, the disciples do not understand the meaning of the journey from Galilee to Jerusalem. Assuming that it will be a victory celebration, they vie for the best seat on either side of Jesus's throne on coronation day. Even after being on the road with Jesus for three years, they fail to understand that the feast awaiting them will be the body and blood of their Master, as he gives his life for their sins. Then, in the upper room, he spreads his banquet in the "wilderness" on the verge of the promised land—his own death and resurrection. Only in this case, unlike Moses, the mediator of *this* new covenant will not die with the disobedient generation on this dark side of the promised land, but as the Greater Joshua will, through his death and resurrection, lead his people across the Jordan. Jesus sends Peter and John ahead to find a place to celebrate this meal in Jerusalem, as Passover yields to Holy Communion (Luke 22).

Meeting a Stranger on the Way to Somewhere Else: Luke 24

It is dawn, on "the first day of the week"—the beginning of the new creation—as the women disciples brought fresh spices for their Master's dead body to the tomb, according to Jewish custom (Luke 24:1–12). However, when they arrived at dawn, there was no guard and the stone was rolled away, the tomb empty. Two angels appear "in dazzling apparel" and the women were "frightened and bowed their faces to the ground" (vv. 4, 23). A similar scene appears in Genesis 18, where two angels accompany a third, identified as Yahweh himself (v. 10), who later in the story returns to heaven to execute the judgment while the two angels continue on to the cities. The "two angels" motif appears again with the Transfiguration (Luke 9:30), as it will again with the ascension (Acts 1:10). This fits the pattern of legal testimony in court required in the law: "two or three witnesses."

These are witnesses *from heaven*. We have a similar scene here, complete with the themes of judgment and salvation as well as a covenant meal. However, the "third man" here, as in Genesis 18, is not another angel, but God himself—*Jesus Christ in their midst*.

Luke 24:6–7, like verses 26, 46, and 47, present a creedal statement with the formula of *crucifixion and resurrection on the third day*. The women at the tomb should seek Christ "among the living" rather than among the dead, say the angels. Crucial also is the fact that they are told that Jesus is risen *"as he told you"* (v. 6) and the women *"remembered his words"* (v. 8). Throughout this postresurrection appearance, the community is referred back to the *words* that Jesus had spoken. Everything now depends on recalling (reciting) Jesus's words, "hearing" it again for the first time! Faith not only moves from promise to fulfillment, but from fulfillment to promise.

Getting the plot of Scripture is crucial to the very existence of the church. Who is Jesus? We don't get to decide. The *story* tells us who Jesus is! He's not just anything and everything we want him to be in our lives. But even if everything else in your life seems to speak against this Jesus being the Christ, "the one who would redeem Israel," he *has* conquered your *greatest* enemy: the wages of sin, the sting of death, and the curse of the law. He is the one "about whom the scriptures spoke, that he should be crucified and rise again on the third day." Who is Jesus? Your substitutionary sacrifice for sin and your robe of righteousness and immortality. What is his kingdom—and thus the mission statement of the church? *The forgiveness of sins*. A kingdom of *grace* now, a kingdom of *glory* at the end.

The women ran to the apostles with the news, but their report "seemed to them an idle tale, and they did not believe them" (v. 11). Things changed when Peter went to the tomb for himself (v. 12). Standing this side of Easter, we often forget how disorienting, disruptive, and confusing this day was in the history of redemption. As Augustine reminded us, those who wish to attribute the fall to women (Eve), should recall that Christ was conceived and born in Mary's womb and women were the first reporters of the resurrection. Even Peter and the other men thought that the women were raving.

"That very day"—the day of Jesus's resurrection—two disciples were on their way to Emmaus, "about seven miles from Jerusalem," discussing the momentous events that they had just experienced in Jerusalem (vv. 13–14). This time, it is not an angel but Jesus Christ

himself who appears. "But their eyes were kept from recognizing him" (v. 16). There are no trumpets, no thunder or lightning, no voice from heaven; Jesus simply joins these two disciples on their journey and asks them what they are talking about with such vigor. "And they stood still, looking sad. Then one of them, named Cleopas, answered him, 'Are you the only visitor to Jerusalem who does not know the things that have happened there in these days?' 'What things?' Jesus asked.

> And they said to him, "Concerning Jesus of Nazareth, a man who was a prophet mighty in deed and word before God and all the people, and how our chief priests and rulers delivered him up to be condemned to death, and crucified him. But we had hoped that he was the one to redeem Israel. Yes, and besides all this, it is now the third day since these things happened. Moreover, some women of our company amazed us. They were at the tomb early in the morning, and when they did not find his body, they came back saying that they had even seen a vision of angels, who said that he was alive. Some of those who were with us went to the tomb and found it just as the women had said, but him they did not see." (vv. 19–24)

The two angelic witnesses from heaven announced the resurrection, while we have two witnesses below who are dejected and disillusioned when the stranger (Jesus) joins them on the road (v. 15). "Thy will be done *on earth* as it is *in heaven*": The goal is to get these covenantal witnesses to match up! Heaven knows what has happened; now it's time for the earth to receive the report.

The stranger is a guest (v. 29)

By drawing out the reasons for their disillusionment, Jesus was drawing out the misunderstandings of the kingdom that they had assumed. We have seen that throughout the narrative, the disciples have misunderstood the kingdom of heaven as an earthly, geopolitical kingdom: a restoration of the national theocracy, *a kingdom of glory*. Palm Sunday seemed so promising, yet the King was crucified by the same mob on Good Friday. They had forgotten Jesus's own teaching about the order of it all: crucifixion, resurrection, return in glory to judge and make all things new. They had forgotten that the most important need they and everyone else had was forgiveness of sin and victory over the tyranny of sin and death.

The kingdom of God had become for them a purely this-worldly regime here and now. They had gotten the "journey" wrong: a theology of glory versus a theology of the cross: first cross, then glory. Jesus was a mighty prophet. "But we had hoped that he was the one to redeem Israel," yet he was crucified and has been dead three days. The psalmist in Psalm 74, witnessing the destruction of Jerusalem, calls upon God to defend his cause and to "remember your sanctuary and your congregation." It is a lament for Zion, which was thought to be indestructible and yet the temple now lies in ruins. That is where these disciples are right now as well: with the death of their Master, their salvation lies in ruins. "We had hoped that he was the one to redeem Israel."

Remarkably, however, they stick to the facts: the witness of the women and the disciples to the empty tomb. Yet the empty tomb *by itself* did not establish the resurrection. They were confused by it all. Did someone steal the body? If so, who: the Romans, the Sanhedrin, some of the disciples? The disciples were walking along as dead men while the Lord of Life was walking beside them unrecognized. This Emmaus journey is like a recapitulation of the whole history of Israel. As Jesus interprets that whole history, "beginning with Moses and all the prophets," the hero of the epic is himself traveling at their side. He shows them that he not only is *with* them on the way, but is *himself* "the Way, the Truth, and the Life."

Gentiles might be expected not to get this; Israel surely should have, and the disciples are even more culpable, so Jesus rebukes them—not in wrath, but in gentleness, as he preaches himself from all the Scriptures. Instead of simply rebuking unbelief, Jesus preaches the gospel that creates faith. At this point, Jesus is still a stranger. Rather than referring first to his own teaching, he takes them to the Scriptures, which of course meant the Old Testament. Even before he reminds them of *his* words (v. 44), he reminds them of the words of *Scripture*.

Jesus knows the rules of hospitality and rather than lording it over them, as he could have (revealing himself as the Risen King all at once), he lets himself be a stranger, invited to dinner simply because "it is toward evening and the day is now far spent" (v. 29). Even after the resurrection, Jesus displays his humility, serving us in descending mercy. From their recollection in verse 32, these two disciples were no doubt pondering everything that the stranger had told them while the table was being set for dinner.

The stranger becomes the host (vv. 30–35)

Reversing the proper roles of hospitality, Jesus becomes the host. Just as the disciples had entered the upper room for one meal (Passover) only to receive in addition a new meal (the Lord's Supper), now Jesus takes over and transforms an ordinary meal into the first postresurrection Eucharist. In doing so, their sorrow is turned to joy, their unbelief is turned to recognition. The formula here, reminiscent of the words of the upper room in chapter 22, is unmistakable: "took . . . broke . . . gave." Not only in the *action* but in *the form of words* that Jesus repeated, the disciples recognized the one who had instituted this Supper.

The last day (Saturday) surrenders to the first day (Sunday) as the entrance of God's people into their everlasting rest. Tonight, and to the end of the age, Christ will host this meal from his Sabbath throne: "Where two or three are gathered in my name, I am there in the midst of them" (Matt. 18:20).

"And their eyes were opened and they recognized him. And he vanished from their sight" (v. 31). Again, the resurrection is something that happened to Jesus, and not simply a subjective experience of the disciples. It was not his memory or impact or influence or even his spirit that lived on, but Jesus of Nazareth the person himself! He was physically, bodily raised. Nevertheless, the *recognition* of this event is what happens to them. The same person, with the same physical characteristics, was present, but was not recognized. They had been *kept* from recognizing him until now, just as he "vanishes from their sight," not because *he* is a phantom but because *their senses* are being directed by him.

Roman Catholic interpreters often point to this as evidence that the Eucharist, rather than the preaching of the Word, is where Jesus makes himself known to us. However, although this meal brings about recognition, we read, "They said to each other, 'Did not our hearts burn within us as he talked to us on the road, while he opened to us the scriptures?' " (v. 32). Just as faith came to the women when the angels reminded them of what Jesus had said, it comes to these disciples through the word. Yet in this festive confirmation of that word, they recognize the stranger as none other than the Christ. The sacrament ratifies the words that they had heard the stranger speak on the road. Through the word *and* the Supper, the Spirit opens their understanding.

The strangers become the witnesses (vv. 33–49)

Now *everybody* is on the road again: back to Jerusalem, back to the upper room, but this time to get everybody on board to go spread the word to the world. The tables are turned: the preacher becomes the content of what is preached; the stranger becomes the host, and now the hosts are the strangers. Yet they too become recognized as witnesses and friends of the host. These two disciples on earth are now like the two angelic witnesses from heaven, returning to the disciples in Jerusalem with Good News. There they reunite with the disciples, who are already abuzz with the news of the empty tomb.

Now the church that had been scattered in denial, sorrow, and confusion is "gathered together" in joy, "saying, 'The Lord has risen indeed and has appeared to Simon!' There they told what had happened on the road and how he was known to them in the breaking of the bread" (vv. 33–35). Like the guests at Babette's feast, it is possible to be strangers even with neighbors on a tiny island who meet regularly for prayer and Bible reading. On the other hand, it is possible for complete strangers to embrace and dance together in the streets when the news is big enough. Apart from Christ, as he delivers himself to us through the public service of preaching and sacrament, "community" is a meaningless term. Other bonds (generational, socioeconomic, political, musical preferences, etc.) created by other affinities have no place here. In comparison with the risen Christ in our midst, dispensing his gifts, the decisions and activity of committees, leaders, and parishioners are no more significant than the march of ants from mound to mound. Through Christ's action among them, his disciples are not only made one with him but with each other.

Now at last, the "breaking of the bread" in the upper room made sense as the breaking of Christ's body for the life of his people. The Good News begins with the nucleus of this first band of Christians and then works itself out to "Jerusalem, Judea, Samaria, and the uttermost parts of the earth."

First things first: the *church* receives Christ (vv. 36–49). They cannot become witnesses until they themselves have been made recipients of the good news. "Jesus himself stood in the midst of them" (v. 36). Here is that covenantal language again: "Wherever two or three are gathered in my name. . . ." No longer *outside the gate* on the cross, nor *inside the tomb*, nor even *alongside the disciples* on the Emmaus road, but standing as the "pitched tabernacle" *in the midst of* his people, Jesus announces, "Peace to you!" A covenantal announcement, a benediction (or salutation), with which the liturgy is begun.

Again the story is made all the more credible by their all too human reaction: "But they were startled and frightened and thought they saw a spirit" (v. 37). Not until Jesus begins *speaking* his Word does the frightening stranger become the most welcome visitor. He is not a spirit, but resurrected flesh and bones (vv. 38–39). Jesus even condescends to their weakness by giving his hands and feet to their examination. The same body that had hung on the cross and lay dead for three days is now standing before them, resurrected but not yet glorified. "And *while they still disbelieved for joy and were marveling*, he said to them, 'Have you anything to eat?' They gave him a piece of broiled fish, and he took it and ate it before them" (vv. 41). Ghosts don't eat fish. Since he is the firstfruits of the whole harvest, this assures that our resurrection will be bodily: *restoring* and *glorifying* rather than *dispensing with* our earthiness. The death of Jesus belongs to the past age of sin and death which he conquered; his resurrection opens up a future for us all.

Even though they *see and examine* him, it is his *words* that they must *hear* if they are truly to recognize him for who he is (v. 44). And further still, they must have their minds *opened* (v. 45). These are passive verbs: they did not come with an open mind. They did not open their minds; their minds *were opened* by the Lord of the feast. Only as their minds are opened will they understand what he will say about himself and the next stage of the kingdom in verses 46–49. This witness, just as Jesus predicts, went out, "proclaimed in his name to all nations, beginning from Jerusalem."

Yet they are not ready. They are witnesses "*of* these things," but they are not yet empowered "from on high" to be *made* witnesses *to* these things throughout the earth. The ascension and Pentecost still lay ahead. Jesus will be with them for forty days (the period between the feasts of Passover—the feast of the "passing over" of God's wrath, and Pentecost—the feast of the harvest's first fruits). It's "40 Days of Preparation"—a little seminary, to turn disciples into apostles. It is a time to gather together in the upper room, awaiting the promised Spirit who will equip the witnesses for their mission. Micah had prophesied:

> It shall come to pass in the latter days that the mountain of the house of the LORD shall be established as the highest of the moun-

tains, and it shall be lifted above the hills; and peoples shall flow to it, and many nations shall come, and say: "Come, let us go up to the mountain of the LORD, to the house of the God of Jacob, that he may teach us his ways and that we may walk in his paths." For out of Zion shall go forth the law, and the word of the LORD from Jerusalem. (Micah 4:1–2)

The proclamation of Christ in Scripture in terms of promise and fulfillment becomes the substance of apostolic preaching in Acts, as Christ himself "stood in the midst" of his covenant people who gathered for the apostles' teaching, the breaking of the bread, fellowship, and the prayers.

Jesus told his disciples that he would not drink wine with them again until he returned in his kingdom of glory. Our Eucharistic table is not the heavenly wedding banquet. For now, it is the sacrificial meal in which Christ is the food and drink. Yet each time we gather, we not only proclaim Christ's death until he comes; we participate in the renewing powers of the age to come. We taste the morsels of that wedding banquet when the meal of Christ's sacrifice will become the feast of unending delight. For on that day, Christ will be the *host* rather than the *meal* and we will eat and drink *with* him in an everlasting exchange of gifts.

Conclusion

Each Lord's Day, we come to church with our problems. We imagined that the Christian life would be different than it is, perhaps even wondering why Jesus has not yet returned in glory and the world seems to go along as it always has, driven by ambition, greed, murder, war, sin, and death. Yet along our weekly journey, we are met by a stranger who expounds himself from all the Scriptures and opens our understanding by his Spirit. The stranger joins us for dinner and ends up making himself the host and the food of a heavenly banquet as a foretaste of that bread and wine we will share with him in *our* resurrected flesh when he comes again in glory. At last, the penny drops: we recognize again our risen Savior, knowing that he has conquered sin and the grave on our behalf. Hearing his words and feeding on his body and blood, we are assured of our own personal participation in his death and resurrection.

No longer as obsessed with the problems that we brought with us to church, we are gathered as this Eucharistic community in thanksgiving and joy. No longer filled with disillusionment and fear, our hearts are once again cheered with Good News to share with a needy world that still lies on the other side of Easter, in sin and death. As Frederick Buechner nicely summarizes,

> There is little that we can point to in our lives as deserving anything but God's wrath. Our best moments have been mostly grotesque parodies. Our best loves have been almost always blurred with selfishness and deceit. But there is something to which we can point. Not anything that we ever did or were, but something that was done for us by another. Not our own lives, but the life of one who died in our behalf and yet is still alive. This is our only glory and our only hope. And the sound that it makes is the sound of excitement and gladness and laughter that floats through the night air from a great banquet.[13]

Announced by his Word and sealed in his table fellowship "in the midst of us," this Good News, "Peace be with you!" wells up within us as a message to be proclaimed to others. "Gathered together in one place," we—on *this* side of Pentecost—are also scattered after the benediction out into the world as his witnesses to all that has been done. "The Lord is risen!" "He is risen indeed!" We are his people and he is our place, and that is Good News indeed.

10

TODAY'S HEADLINE

THE CHURCH IN EXILE

Jesus famously declared, "Render unto Caesar that which is Caesar's and unto God that which is God's" (Matt. 22:21). "Let everyone be subject to the governing authorities," Paul echoed. "For there is no authority except from God, and the authorities that exist are appointed by God." The secular officer "does not bear the sword in vain," but is in fact "a minister of God" in the secular sphere. "Render therefore to all their due: taxes to whom taxes are due, customs to whom customs, fear to whom fear, honor to whom honor" (Rom. 13:1–7). There are two kingdoms, each ruled ultimately by God, but through distinct institutions and political orders.

Because of the work that God is doing, "this present age" is not all that there is in the world. As Augustine argued in *The City of God*, there are two kingdoms or cities, each with its own ultimate loves, destinies, aims, and means.[1] Ultimately, the temporary city sets its gaze on the love of self, feeding this craving through domination and whatever methods are suited to the moment. This does not mean that the earthly city is not capable of being a house, where Christians live alongside non-Christians pursuing common tasks, but it cannot be a home. Believers are described in the New Testament in terms similar to Judah in her exile: strangers, aliens, and pilgrims.

A Letter to Exiles

Ever since Genesis 4, where Cain's family tree is noted for its distinguished cultural achievements and Seth's heirs are singled out as those who "began to call on the name of the LORD," God's people have been known more by their distinct creed and worship than by their contributions to civilization. The gospel is foolishness for proud hearts, trusting in the wisdom, power, and security of human resources. Hence, says Paul, God has chosen the weak things of the world—not many of noble birth (1 Cor. 1:29).

We must not overstate this, however. Daniel and other Jewish exiles studied at the most prestigious universities of Babylon and rose above their peers in the Babylonian court. In his letter to the exiles, the prophet Jeremiah wrote,

> Build houses and live in them; plant gardens and eat their produce. Take wives and have sons and daughters; take wives for your sons, and give your daughters in marriage, that they may bear sons and daughters; multiply there, and do not decrease. But seek the welfare of the city where I have sent you into exile, and pray to the LORD on its behalf, for in its welfare you will find your welfare. (Jer. 29:5–9)

This is exilic life. Basically, the prophet is telling them that when they are taken into captivity, they are not to live in tents, as if they are only passing through. "Build houses and live in them; plant gardens and eat their produce": be prepared for a long stay. Raise children— grow the covenant community—and "seek the welfare of the city where I have sent you into exile," even praying for it, because "in its welfare you will find your welfare." There is no call to subvert the wicked kingdom of Nebuchadnezzar who had carried them off in chains and destroyed their temple. At the same time, they will always be Jews first. Their ultimate identity will never be Babylonian.

Daniel and some of his fellow believers at court fell into disfavor when they refused to participate in idolatry, but in all other respects they honored the king. The same advice is found in 1 Thessalonians 4:9–12: no blueprint for a godly commonwealth or transformation of culture, but a call to faithful members of the church and "to live quietly and to mind your own business, so that you may live properly before outsiders and be dependent on no one." In other words, it is an era of participating in the common culture together with non-Christians and participating in the heavenly communion of saints that is made visible on earth only in the church.

Daniel clearly recognized the difference between honoring God and honoring Nebuchadnezzar, serving the city of God and the city of man. Like Abraham, he was looking to a better city than either Jerusalem or Babylon: "I will cleanse them from all the guilt of their sin against me, and I will forgive all the guilt of their sin and rebellion against me. And this city shall be to me a name of joy, a praise and a glory before all the nations of the earth who shall hear of all the good that I do for them" (Jer. 33:8–9). All of this will happen when God causes "a righteous Branch to spring up for David." "And this is the name by which it will be called: 'The LORD Our Righteousness'" (vv. 14–16).

This theme of exile is brought forward into the New Testament, marking the time between Christ's two advents. Peter exhorts new covenant believers to be "sober-minded" and "to set your hope fully on the grace that will be brought to you at the revelation of Jesus Christ." He calls them to "conduct yourselves, with fear *throughout the time of your exile*, knowing that you were ransomed from the futile ways inherited from your forefathers, not with perishable things like silver and gold, but with the precious blood of Christ, like that of a lamb without blemish or spot" (1 Peter 1:13–19, emphasis added). During this exile, believers are being "built up as a spiritual house, to be a holy priesthood, to offer spiritual sacrifices, acceptable to God through Jesus Christ" (2:4–5). Similar to Jeremiah's counsel to the exiles in Babylon, Peter adds, "Beloved, I urge you as sojourners and exiles to abstain from the passions of the flesh, which wage war against your soul. Keep your conduct among the Gentiles honorable, so that when they speak against you as evildoers, they may see your good deeds and glorify God on the day of visitation." Living as free people, he urges, believers are to submit themselves willingly to the secular authorities: "Fear God. Honor the emperor" (vv. 13–17).

Like Nebuchadnezzar, the Roman emperor was not exactly the church's best friend. But that was fine: who needs an ally in an earthly ruler when Christ has been exalted at the right hand of the Father? Caesar always knew how to handle an insurrection; he was befuddled by a church that continued to pray for him even as he sent them to their martyrdom.

Throughout the New Testament, converts go on in their ordinary earthly callings. Lydia went on serving her family and her neighbors by selling purple cloth, Cornelius continued to serve as a Roman centurion, and Paul even moonlighted as a tentmaker. However, the Josephs, Daniels, and Esthers—exiles who leave a major legacy upon their host culture—are relatively rare, at least from what we know in the Bible. One of the reasons that the covenant community has not distinguished itself in history by its contributions to civilization is that the Bible does not prescribe any distinct form of common life in the civic realm during periods of exile. Myriad architects, painters, poets, scientists, politicians, musicians, and engineers professed faith in Christ down to the present day. However, especially as heirs of the sawdust trail become upwardly mobile there is a danger of imposing on God's people an unbiblical burden to transform our cities into the city of God. Believers continue to share with unbelievers the original creation mandate to fulfill their cultural callings. Their motives may be different, but in most instances their daily work—its methods, tools, educational prerequisites, and standards—will be indistinguishable from that of their non-Christian co-workers.

Christians may be distinguishing themselves in the common realm of secular culture, but they are not doing this as part of the *church's* activity. They are not even doing "kingdom work." The church is not yet the realized kingdom of Christ on earth, but it is the only place where that kingdom becomes partially visible through the ministry of Word and sacrament. Even the work of Christians remains part of secular culture, where God sends sunshine and rain upon the just and the unjust alike. Their cultural endeavors are no more redemptive than those of their non-Christian neighbors, and yet the Spirit blesses all city building with his excellent gifts of common grace.

The kingdom of Christ, therefore, is not an earthly city, although believers are obviously in the world and even the church's worship exhibits similarities with secular culture. Known for its orators, the Greco-Roman world knew the value of public speaking, but in the covenant assembly the preaching of Christ introduced a foreign power into this world. Lavish public dinners were common, but at the Lord's Table believers tasted the powers of the age to come and not only became a society of friends but a communion of saints. Considering itself a commonwealth, Rome had an elaborate system of public welfare, but in the church each believer was to consider his or her goods and services as a common trust for the whole body. Christians were free to enjoy their own favorite music in common with unbelievers, but when they gathered together as God's colony, their calling was different: "Let the word of Christ dwell in you richly, teaching and admonishing one another in all wisdom, singing psalms and hymns and spiritual songs, with thankfulness in your hearts to God" (Col. 3:16).

Christ's kingdom is its own culture: holy rather than common. That does not mean that it is an alternative subculture. In other words, there is no such thing as Christian sports, entertainment, politics, architecture, or science. In these common fields, Christians and non-Christians are indistinguishable except by their ultimate goals and motivations. Ironically, many of the statistics we read today show that professing evangelicals do not differ from non-Christians in their core beliefs and ethics, while an elaborate "Christian" subculture flourishes. In contrast, the second-century *Epistle of Diognetus* reported that Christians are distinguished from others "neither by country nor by language nor by customs." They do not live in their own ghettos or "use a strange form of speech." They do not differ in cultural customs of their respective lands or in dress and food. Yet in their ordinary lives "they show forth the remarkable and admittedly strange order of their own [heavenly] citizenship." "They live in fatherlands of their own, but as aliens. They share all things as citizens, and suffer all things as strangers. Every foreign land is their fatherland, and every fatherland a foreign land. . . . They pass their days on earth, but they have their citizenship in heaven."[2]

The churches freely shared their earthly resources as well as their spiritual gifts, but they did not advocate a redistribution of wealth in the empire. They established their own church courts for dealing with strife, division, and heresy, but did not call for the temporal sword of the civil magistrate to enforce physical punishments. They sang psalms, but did not turn the worship of God into a concert hall or theater. They shared love feasts and the Lord's Supper, but when the Corinthians allowed the social customs of their pagan culture to determine their celebration, Paul rebuked them sharply. The ministry of Word and sacrament—God's politics—creates a distinct culture within the cultures of this age. When this culture breaks down and the methods of this passing age are allowed to smother the in-breaking of the age to come, the passing of the covenant from generation to generation and outreach to those who are far off is threatened. The salt loses its savor.

The City of God after Christendom

With the political recognition of Christianity under Constantine in the fourth century, "Christendom" was born. According to Lactantius, Constantine and his soldiers had a vision telling them that they would win the battle at the Milvian Bridge (AD 312) if they would emblazon Christ's name on their shields. Instead of signifying the martyr's participation in Christ's suffering, the cross was now an imperial symbol: "With this sign conquer." Jumping the eschatological gun, the announcement that the kingdoms of this world (at least one of them) had now become the kingdom of Christ was not only premature but of lasting consequences for both church and state. "Babylon" was now "Christendom" and Christians no longer saw themselves as exiles but as masters.

At least in Rome, this celebration was interrupted, at least for the moment, by the sacking of Rome by the Goths and Vandals in AD 410. Pagans blamed Christians for the collapse of the empire and many Christians wondered if the church would survive. Where the secular culture becomes so intertwined with the kingdom of Christ, the collapse of the former leads to despair. The church father Jerome lamented, "What is to become of the church now that Rome has fallen?" It was in this context that Augustine wrote his masterpiece, *The City of God*. God has brought the mission field to the missionaries, he said. Reflecting two distinct eschatologies as well as the nature and relationship of the kingdom of God and the kingdoms of this world, Jerome and Augustine continue to provide the two dominant answers to cultural crisis.

In *The City of God*, Augustine explains,

> These are the two loves: . . . the first is social, the second selfish; the first consults the common welfare for the sake of celestial [heavenly] society, the second grasps at a selfish control of social affairs for the sake of arrogant domination; the first is submissive to God, the second tries to rival God; the first is quiet, the second restless; the first is peaceful, the second, trouble-making; the first prefers truth to the praises

of those who are in error, the second is greedy for praise, however it might be obtained. . . . Accordingly, two cities have been formed by two loves: the earthly by the love of self, even to the contempt of God; the heavenly by the love of God, even to the contempt of self.[3]

Accordingly, the earthly kingdoms establish diverse laws and customs that will engender earthly peace—no small accomplishment for humanity after the fall. But the heavenly city is always different in its ambitions, seeking heavenly peace and calling people out of the nations into the kingdom of God.

This does not mean that believers are no longer citizens of the earthly city, but that they do not derive their *ultimate* comfort, satisfaction, security, vindication, or hope from it. Secular society is a gift of God before and after the fall and it must be cultivated by Christians as well as their non-believing neighbors. In fact, "God can never be believed to have left the kingdoms of men, their dominations and servitudes, outside of the laws of His providence."[4] But the earthly city is always Babylon—it is never converted, as are many of its inhabitants, into the dwelling-place of God. The kingdom of God advances through the proclamation of the gospel, not through force: "This city is therefore now in building; stones are cut down from the hills by the hands of those who preach truth, they are squared that they may enter into an everlasting structure."[5]

Needless to say, the identification of Christ's kingdom with the temporal city regained its steam with the "Christianization" of the barbarians in a renewed Holy Roman Empire. Throughout the middle ages, the empire often played out its identity as the fulfillment of the Old Testament theocracy, the true Israel of God. The emperor was a blend of King David (hence, the *Holy* part of the name) and Caesar (hence, the *Roman* bit). The whole empire and, in fact, all Christian states, composed the *corpus Christianum*, the body of Christ. And this one kingdom of God would grow and spread its unified cult and culture, its worship and its civilization, to the ends of the earth.

With the Reformation, Luther revived Augustine's insights. The kingdom of Christ advances exclusively through the spiritual sword: the Word of God. It is embraced by faith, rather than being coercively imposed by force. In earthly affairs, unbelievers often excel believers. We build temporal cities by our works, but receive the kingdom of Christ through preaching and sacrament.

Trained in some of the most distinguished circles of French humanism, John Calvin was familiar with a wide range of literature and subjects. Far from repudiating this heritage, he continued to appreciate its strengths even as he came to recognize more clearly the weaknesses in secular thought. "Whenever we come upon these matters in secular writers," he pleaded, "let that admirable light of truth shining in them teach us that the mind of man, though fallen and perverted from its wholeness, is nevertheless clothed and ornamented with God's excellent gifts." He continues:

> What then? Shall we deny that the truth shone on the ancient jurists who established civic order and discipline with such great equity? Shall we say that the philosophers were blind in their fine observation and artful description of nature? . . . Shall we say that they are insane who developed medicine, devoting their labor to our benefit? What shall we say of all the mathematical sciences? Shall we consider them the ravings of madmen? . . . Those men whom Scripture calls "natural men" were, indeed, sharp and penetrating in their investigation of earthly things. Let us, accordingly, learn by their example how many gifts the Lord left to human nature even after it was despoiled of its true good.[6]

Just as God, in his common grace, preserved Cain so that he could build a city, God cares for the "Babylons" in which we are exiles. However, the kingdoms of this age never become the kingdom of Christ until the return of the King in the flesh at the end of the age.

Opposing what Calvin called the "contrived empire" known as "Christendom" was not popular in the sixteenth century. And, like Augustine and Luther, Calvin's practice was not always consistent with his theory. Nevertheless, he insists, we must recognize that we are "under a two-fold government, . . . so that we do not (as commonly happens) unwisely mingle these two, which have a completely different nature." Just as the body and soul are distinct without being necessarily opposed, "Christ's spiritual kingdom and the civil jurisdiction are things completely distinct." But he continues:

> Yet this distinction does not lead us to consider the whole nature of government a thing polluted, which has nothing to do with Christian men. That is what, indeed, certain fanatics who delight in unbridled license shout and boast. . . . But as we have just now pointed out that this kind of government is distinct from that spiritual and inward Kingdom of Christ, so we must know that they are not at variance.[7]

Because of God's goodness in creation and providence, the secular kingdom could not be renounced without incurring divine displeasure, but because of sin and rebellion against God the cities of this world would never be reconciled to God apart from his final judgment at the end of history.

If the medieval church wanted to rule the world, Anabaptist communities wanted to separate entirely from it. The Schleitheim Confession (1527) of the Anabaptists urged that all true believers must refuse to participate in the common life of the wicked. Since they are "a great abomination to God, it is not possible for anything to grow or issue from them except abominable things." Ironically, these separated communities became a new confusion of kingdoms: the secular and spiritual governments were regarded as one and the same, just as they had been in Christendom.

While some Anabaptists withdrew, others sought to overthrow existing governments and institute the kingdom of God by force, as in Thomas Müntzer's ill-fated revolution. The problem with the Anabaptists on this point, Calvin argued, was that they would not distinguish properly between creation and fall or between the two kingdoms instituted by God. In this way, justification before God was confused with moral, social, and political righteousness, undermining both civility between Christian and non-Christian as well as the gospel. So, Calvin writes, "How malicious and hateful toward public welfare would a man be who is offended by such diversity, which is perfectly adapted to maintain the observance of God's law! For the statement of some, that the law of God given through Moses is dishonored when it is abrogated and new laws preferred to it, is utterly vain."[8] After all, Calvin says, "It is a fact that the law of God which we call the moral law is nothing else than a testimony of natural law and of that conscience which God has engraved on the minds of men."[9] Even unbelievers can rule justly and prudently, as Paul indicates even under the more pagan circumstances of his day (Rom. 13:1–7).

Calvin had been expelled from Geneva precisely because he and the other ministers had insisted on the liberty of the church in the spiritual affairs of the people. In other cities where the Reformation was embraced, the city council or the prince determined the confession and the outward form and government of the church in their realm. However, Calvin insisted upon the independence of the church from secular lordship. In earthly things, we obey our rulers; in heavenly things, we hear only the voice of our risen King.

When, after much pleading from the city council, Calvin returned to Geneva after his exile, he picked up exactly where he had left off in his exposition of Scripture. Fueled by the ministry of Word and sacrament, the diaconate became a thriving office, caring for the refugees who were streaming into Geneva from everywhere.

Having been raised in churches where programs seemed sometimes to attract more of the leadership's attention than people, one of the things that I have found striking as a newcomer to confessional Reformed churches is the extent to which the diaconate plays a prominent role in caring for the physical welfare of the saints. Geneva was not a utopia, but the culture of Christ's kingdom had an immense influence—precisely to the extent that the church was enabled to pursue its own distinct calling. It is easy for us—especially in comfortable suburban churches—to send missionaries and money to far off fields to preach the gospel and relieve suffering, but what if each local church in the United States became a model of genuine fellowship, love, and mutual care in body and soul among its own members and in the local community?

Modern Triumphalism and Disillusionment

Much like in Augustine's day, the triumphalism of Constantinian "Christendom" was bound to lead to disappointment. The last quarter of the nineteenth century witnessed the clash of two eschatologies, or views of history and creation's destiny: triumphalism and disillusionment.

1. Triumphalism

Much like Constantine's conversion experience in the Battle of the Milvian Bridge in 312, the surprising defeat of the Spanish Armada by Britain in 1588 signaled for many Protestant states the beginning of the end of Antichrist's reign. Christ's thousand year reign (millennium) was identified with the progress of the kingdom of Christ through the progress of earthly empires.

Ironically, Protestant nations shared with their Roman Catholic adversaries the Constantinian and medieval ideal of Christendom, appealing to Old Testament passages to reinforce their status as God's favored empire. This is the myth behind the Crusades, the Inquisition, and such American institutions as slavery and the doctrine of "manifest destiny" which gave narrative justification for the slaughter of native Americans. Needless to say, the confusion of the two kingdoms has yielded the lion's share of blame for the atrocities committed in the name of God and his Messiah.

In the nineteenth century, most Protestants were optimistic. The evangelist Charles G. Finney (1792–1875) sharply rejected the Augustinian and Calvinistic doctrines of original sin and the radical need for grace. Conversion, both of the individual and of the nation, was entirely in our hands. The kingdom of Christ would come through radical social and moral reform. Temperance societies emerged as one of many movements organized around the vision of a Christianized America. "The kingdoms of this world will not have become the kingdoms of our Lord," Strong opined, "until the money power has been Christianized."[10] Long before the conservative-liberal polarizations, American evangelicalism had championed the so-called "social gospel," as one notices in the following comment from Horace Bushnell:

> Talent has been Christianized already on a large scale. The political power of states and kingdoms has been long assumed to be, and now at last really is, as far as it becomes their accepted office to maintain personal security and liberty. Architecture, arts, constitutions, schools, and learning have been largely Christianized. But the money power, which is one of the most operative and grandest of all, is only beginning to be; though with promising tokens of a finally complete reduction to Christ and the uses of His Kingdom. . . . That day, when it comes, is the morning, so to speak, of the new creation. Is it not time for that day to dawn?[11]

The American version of the Holy Roman Empire regarded the proliferation of Protestant hospitals, colleges, women's societies, and men's societies as signs of God's approval and, indeed, of the advancement of the kingdom of God. The American Social Gospel movement was in large measure the result of progressive evangelical revivalism. Social progress (including the expansion of the American way of life overseas) was seen as a harbinger of Christ's kingdom.

2. Disillusionment

American Protestantism had already experienced upsurges of disillusionment with the notion of progress throughout the nineteenth century. Not surprisingly, these eruptions of what we would now call premillennialism occurred among the marginalized sects of Protestantism. It is difficult to join in the celebration when one is left out of the preparations. Various groups—like the Millerites—insisted that nothing short of Christ's return would change things, and they even set dates that many frontier Americans expectantly awaited. But the prophesied day came and went. American historians call it "the Great Disappointment."

However, premillennialism began to gain strength in mainstream Protestant circles. In the last quarter of the eighteenth century, fellow evangelicals Josiah Strong and D. L. Moody would represent the growing cleavage between the triumphalistic postmillennialists and the pessimistic premillennialists. Although initially quite representative of Charles Finney's social activism, Moody became increasingly pessimistic about the extent to which earthly empires could become the kingdom of God. "I look upon this world as a wrecked vessel," he would later write. "God has given me a lifeboat and said to me, 'Moody, save all you can.' "[12] Whereas revival was usually regarded as an instrument of Christianizing society through evangelism and social action, Moody saw it as a means of converting individuals.

Things turned sour, especially as the United States was drawn reluctantly into World War I. President Woodrow Wilson, a postmillennial Presbyterian, called it "the war to end all wars," but, of course, it didn't. World War II provided the perfect climate for an eschatology of despair, separation from the world, and apocalyptic visions of imminent disaster.

Both the Christian Right and the Christian Left derive from this late nineteenth-century evangelicalism. It is this quite recent train of thought (or, more precisely, activism), rather than the profound reflection of Augustine and the reformers that guides contemporary evangelical activism. Ironically, even staunch premillennialists like Jerry Falwell sound a good deal like the postmillennialists of yesteryear. In fact, in conversations both Jerry Falwell and Jerry Wallis have told me that they consider Charles Finney to be a leading model for their vision of Christianity in American life.

Looking to Jesus

It is easy for us to look away from Jesus, or at least to look away from him as the one who was crucified for our sins and raised for our justification. Like his contemporaries, we want a Messiah we can use:

someone who will make all of our dreams come true, here and now, and make his kingdom visible in power and glory in our world. It is easy to take our eyes off Jesus Christ in heaven, at the Father's right hand, interceding for us and dispensing his gifts. It is easier to focus on what we are doing to make his absence in the flesh less obvious.

Brad Kallenberg probably speaks for many evangelicals today when he writes, "No longer is the belief in God or the deity of Christ or the authority and inspiration of Scripture standard. In other words, we need to do as missionaries do: become students of the host culture so we can discover how God's Spirit intends the Gospel to become embodied in the new era. Missiologists call this contextualization."[13] However, this is not what missionaries did or do, at least when they are faithful to their calling. Right where Kallenberg says, "become students of the host culture," we must say, "become students of the Word." Right where he switches the tracks from Jesus Christ to our own "incarnation" of the gospel, we need to switch them back to the only one who embodies the gospel. If people do not know the gospel, we need to proclaim it, teach it, administer it, and allow our lives to be shaped by its declarative power. Implied in Kallenberg's appeal is the possibility that the Spirit works differently, either in the content or methods employed (or perhaps both), depending on the "host culture." However, the Spirit has no other word than the unchanging gospel and no other means than those ordained by Jesus Christ. I am all for understanding our context, but this must include a theological analysis deeply grounded in Scripture, which names all of our "contexts" as hostile to the Good News and the reign of Christ.

Christ's bodily absence in this time between his two advents is neither unproductive nor indefinite. He is right now doing something in heaven that is more important than anything that the church could conceive or do by its own clever machinations. And he has sent his Spirit to communicate the riches of his reign to a world in bondage to sin and death. It is that same Spirit who engenders within us the longing cry for Christ's return.

Christ is Lord of all. Already, with his triumphant resurrection, Jesus has been given the name that is above every name in heaven and on earth. Even now, his kingdom is present, advancing amid the rubble of this passing evil age. Nevertheless, he is presently reigning in grace, not yet in glory. His kingdom is visible now in ways that the world does not recognize: in the proclamation of the gospel, which the world considers foolish; in baptizing, teaching, administering

Communion, prayer, the spiritual and physical care of elders and deacons, and the fellowship of the saints. None of this is likely to elicit the interest of the media, but through this ministry a tiny seed is growing into a tree whose branches spread around the earth. By this ministry the Spirit brings the blessings of the age to come into this present age, fixing our eyes on Christ, who has come for our redemption, now dispenses the spoils of his victory, and will return in glory to consummate his kingdom.

In the meantime, believers belong to two cultures. They share together with non-Christians the blessings of common grace and the common curse of the fall. Believers and unbelievers alike enjoy the warmth of a dinner with close friends and equally suffer from personal and natural catastrophes. Our release from this captivity to the common curse is assured in the resurrection and ascension of Christ, our Living Head, who is "the firstfruits" of the whole harvest (1 Cor. 15:20; see also Heb. 2:5–9). "For our citizenship is in heaven, from which we also eagerly wait for the Savior, the Lord Jesus Christ, who will transform our lowly body that it may be conformed to His glorious body, according to the working by which He is able even to subdue all things to Himself" (Phil. 3:20–21). "If then you were raised with Christ, seek those things which are above, where Christ is, sitting at the right hand of God. Set your mind on things above, not on things on the earth. For you died, and your life is hidden with Christ in God. When Christ who is our life appears, then you also will appear with Him in glory" (Col. 3:1–4).

Even Abraham longed for a better piece of real estate than Canaan, which was only a type of the heavenly rest (Heb. 11:10). Like Christ in his humiliation and death, "let us go forth to [Christ], outside the camp, bearing His reproach. For here we have no continuing city, but we seek the one to come" (13:12–14). It is not yet time for the church to rule in this world with Christ, but to suffer for his gospel. For now, the work of the church—as the church—is distinct from the work of individual believers in their common citizenship with unbelievers. The expansion of Christ's kingdom is a cultic rather than a cultural activity, holy rather than common.

The New Testament is not asking us to accept the pagan myth of the flight of the soul from the body at death in some uncreated realm. The antithesis that it offers is not one between material and spiritual existence, but against "this age" (dominated by sin and death) and "the age to come" (dominated by God's sabbath reign, which has already received its first installment in Christ's resurrection). In the heavenly worship anticipated in the book of Revelation, it is not culture in general but Babylon (symbolic of the City of Man) that is left behind in God's judgment of the old order. In the New Jerusalem, the riches of the nations—the cultural goods with which God has endowed particular nations—will be brought with Zion's liberated captives into the City of God forever.

In the meantime, just as God blesses believer and unbeliever alike, so Christians are to love and serve rather than judge and condemn their neighbors (Matt. 5:43–48; see also 7:1–6). The wheat and the weeds are to be allowed to grow together, separated only at the final harvest (13:24–30). When James and John, the "sons of thunder," presume to invoke God's judgment on a Samaritan village that rejected the preaching of Jesus, Jesus "rebuked them sharply" and they went to another town (Luke 9:51–56). This is not the age of holy wars against the ungodly, as were the old covenant campaigns that God commanded as a foretaste of the last judgment, but the "day of salvation" before the dreadful "day of the LORD." We are not riding the war chariots of the hosts of the Lord and his Anointed, as the saints of old and the saints on the last day. Rather, we are to be giving cups of cold water to our enemies, loving those who persecute us, and proclaiming the kingdom of Christ whose universal power is hidden under suffering and the cross.

Not having arrived in the promised land (as both Christendom and modernity would have it, in their own ways), and yet far from aimless wanderers (the inclination of postmodernism), we are "aliens and strangers," "pilgrims," with a set course and a destination to which we are constantly pressing. Rather than being able to point to a set location of God's presence, such as the temple or an earthly land or city, and say, "Here it is" or "There it is," the kingdom is among us in the power of the Spirit who unites us to Christ through Word and sacrament, knitting us together in bonds of love deeper than our natural ties. The water of baptism is thicker than the blood of race and kinship.

The Only Power for a *Cross*-Cultural Community

The church is a *cross*-culture—the double entendre is intentional. Do we believe that the gospel really has the power to create not only saved individuals but a saved culture? That is, a new humanity "from every tribe, tongue, people, and nation" as redeemed saints, "a kingdom of priests to our God" (Rev. 5:9)? Before we answer too quickly, we need to realize that it is going to cost us—all of us—something, even perhaps some things that we value highly, even though we might not even be aware that we value them or why. It will involve difficult questions that may never receive an adequate theoretical answer, but at least a more explicit practice: such as, to what extent does our catholicity—that is, our location "in Christ" together—*eliminate* and to what extent does it *incorporate* the specific characteristics of our diverse cultural, ethnic, socioeconomic, and generational mix?

A while ago a pastor told me that his church, predominantly white and suburban, was merging with an inner city black church. Both churches were Presbyterian, but they had been defined by something other than the cross. Widely reported in the local press, the merger was a marvelous testimony to the power of the gospel and this pastor was filled with joy and anticipation about the ministry that lay before him and his new copastor. There is no blueprint in the Bible for how every church must accommodate itself to this new creation reality. It may look different in various times and places. However, we must transcend our cultural loyalties and step outside of our social comfort zones if we are to realize in concrete terms what it means to find our ultimate location in Christ.

Think again of that *Life* cover photo, and the announcement of victory in Europe that turned anonymous passersby into a communion of ecstatic fellow citizens. The gospel is far greater news, of a far greater victory, achieved with everlasting results. It takes a lifetime of preaching, teaching, prayer, feasting at the Lord's Table, home visitations from pastors and elders, sharing in baptisms, funerals, and fellowship with fellow saints to shape our identity as citizens of the new creation.

The Christian churches do not have any power—at least the kind of power that the world considers powerful. At least it shouldn't. Aside from the doubtful thesis that there ever was a truly Christian civilization, the very idea is a bad one. The only weapon that the church really has is the gospel. This Good News—foolishness to Gentiles but the power of God for salvation to everyone who believes—is all that we have. And, attended by the work of the Spirit, it is more than enough to create the world of which it speaks.

As I have argued, by drawing together drama, doctrine, doxology, and discipleship, we cannot choose between thinking, feeling, and acting as Christians. The word "orthodoxy" itself means *right belief and praise*. It has been said frequently that the church is to be "in the world, but not of it." In all sorts of ways, the churches in the West, particularly in the United States, seem to be "of the world, but not in it." Having built our own subculture complete with sanitized knock-offs of nearly anything in the world, we can be cajoled, entertained, flattered, pampered, and praised without having to justify what we believe and why we believe it to the rest of the world.

Dinesh D'Souza is right on target when he observes that some professing Christians—especially pastors and theologians—"have assumed a reverse mission: instead of being the church's missionaries to the world, they have become the world's missionaries to the church."[14] He calls this a "yes-but" Christianity. Although we cannot believe in miracles any longer or in a God of sovereign authority and holy wrath, there may still be something worth salvaging—usually a few moral maxims. "This yes-but Christianity is full intellectual withdrawal, and it is also becoming less relevant," empirically verifiable by mainline Protestantism's precipitous loss of members. D'Souza is right: retreat is no way to win a war.[15]

As careful as we must be to avoid resorting to hostile rhetoric, there is a war going on right now and it's the biggest one we have ever had. It is not fought with guns, or even with marketing campaigns and political power plays. It is fought with loving, patient, well-informed, and well-argued testimony to Jesus Christ. It is no time to surrender our confidence in the one thing that has the power to liberate both the church and the world from its captivity to alien gods. The gospel is not a comfort for the heart if it cannot be embraced by the mind. Lots of people give their lives for all sorts of worthy and unworthy things. The ancient church flourished in a pagan environment not only because its members were willing to die for their faith but because they were willing to argue for it. When Paul says that the gospel is foolishness to those who are perishing, he is not saying that faith is an irrational leap in the dark. His point is that for those who are looking for their best life now and seek to ascend to the heavens through speculative metaphysics, mysticism, and their own efforts, the message of God's descent in the flesh, his crucifixion for our sins, and resurrection in the flesh are beside the point. They do not answer the questions with which the Gentile mind is obsessed. The gospel is counterintuitive to our moral reasoning as sinners, not to reason itself.

Paul reminds us, "For the weapons of our warfare are not of the flesh but have divine power to destroy strongholds. We destroy arguments and every lofty opinion raised against the knowledge of God, and take every thought captive to obey Christ . . ." (2 Cor. 10:4–5). The teachings of Jesus Christ and his apostles have occupied some of the greatest intellects in history, even in our day, and to the extent that the church or its leaders—embarrassed by this message—imagine that they have something more interesting or more compelling to say, they become irrelevant.

Lazy minds breed lazy hearts and hands. Presupposing the naturalistic worldview of their neighbors, liberalism assumed that religion inhabits the realm of inner mystical experience and universal morality. Why would anyone feel compelled to consider Christian claims if their would-be defenders either denied them or denied intellectual access to them? The greatest threat to Christianity is never vigorous intellectual criticism but a creeping senility that transforms truths into feelings, public claims into private experiences, and facts into mere values. Christianity is either true or false, but it is not irrational. If its claims are not objectively true, then they are not subjectively useful. If our only reason for believing that Jesus is alive is that "he lives within my heart," then, as Paul said, "our preaching is in vain and your faith is in vain." "We are even found to be misrepresenting God, because we testified about God that he raised Christ. . . . And if Christ has not been raised, your faith is futile and you are still in your sins. . . . If in Christ we have hope in this life only, we are of all people most to be pitied" (1 Cor. 15:14–19). We must recover our distinctively biblical commitment to rigorous, inquisitive, and persuasive thinking before there can be a genuine renewal of Christian conviction, faith, repentance, and discipleship. It is time once again to love God with our minds.

Dorothy Sayers pleaded with her British audience in the 1950s,

> Let us, in Heaven's name, drag out the Divine Drama from under the dreadful accumulation of slipshod thinking and trashy sentiment heaped upon it, and set it on an open stage to startle the world into some sort of vigorous reaction. If the pious are the first to be shocked, so much the worse for the pious—others will pass into the Kingdom of Heaven before them. If all men are offended because of Christ, let them be offended; but where is the sense of their being offended at something that is not Christ and is nothing like Him? We do Him singularly little honour by watering down His Personality till it could not offend a fly. Surely it is not the business of the Church to adapt Christ to men, but to adapt men to Christ.
>
> It is the dogma that is the drama—not beautiful phrases, nor comforting sentiments, nor vague aspirations to loving-kindness and moral

uplift, nor the promise of something nice after death—but the terrifying assertion that the same God who made the world lived in the world and passed through the grave and gate of death. Show that to the heathen, and they may not believe it; but at least they may realize that here is something that one might be glad to believe.[16]

As Paul's comment above reminds us, if this story is not true, it is not even useful—at least in any serious, ultimate sense. So there is no going around the doctrine. "We can, as we cheerfully say, 'agree to differ.' 'Never mind about theology,' we observe in kindly tones, 'if we just go on being brotherly to one another it doesn't matter what we believe about God.' "[17] Dispensing with the difficult questions and the potential for offense, we turn the most public announcement on earth into a private affair of the soul.

"But no good whatever will be done by a retreat into personal piety or by mere exhortation to a 'recall to prayer,' " Sayers observes. " 'Take away theology and give us some nice religion' has been a popular slogan for so long that we are apt to accept it, without inquiring whether religion without theology has any meaning. . . . And however unpopular I may make myself I shall and will affirm that the reason why the Churches are discredited today is not that they are too bigoted about theology, but that they have run away from theology."[18] Take away theology and you take away any reason to bother with God. At a time when evangelical leaders sometimes call for "deeds over creeds," Sayers's point is especially pertinent:

> But if Christian dogma is irrelevant to life, to what, in Heaven's name, is it relevant?—since religious dogma is in fact nothing but a statement of doctrines concerning the nature of life and the universe. If Christian ministers really believe it is only an intellectual game for theologians and has no bearing on human life, it is no wonder that their congregations are ignorant, bored, and bewildered.[19]

Of course, there are parts of the story that are difficult, even downright offensive. Nevertheless, "If people will not understand the meaning of judgment, they will never come to understand the meaning of grace. If they hear not Moses or the Prophets, neither will they be persuaded, though one rose from the dead."[20]

Today, orthodoxy is often confused with a cultural and even political conservatism. This has not always been so (and still is not in other parts of the world). Frequently, America's antagonists in the culture wars are identified as "orthodox" and "progressives," which is to define orthodoxy again in terms other than Christian doctrine. Similarly, in the church, worldliness comes in the form of both conservatism and progressivism, where commitment to cultural values (either of uncritical traditionalism or an equally uncritical attachment to novelty and innovations) undermine the culture of the cross and resurrection.

Setting its sights on the plotline of God's mighty acts in history "for us and for our salvation," orthodoxy defines faithfulness by how well we not only conserve this faith but by how well we correct our faith and practice to conform to its rule. That's why orthodoxy has given rise as often to reformations as to conservations. It is a living faith—in fact, the only part of what calls itself Christianity that is actually alive. From this Archimedean point, William Wilberforce was able to stand almost alone in bringing down the British slave trade. Christian orthodoxy has no personal stake in progressivism or conservatism; its instincts are *evangelical* in the deepest sense: oriented to the gospel that creates and sustains the church in all times and places.

Conservatism and progressivism are easy paths. Just go on parroting whatever you've been told and doing what you have done or follow the spirit of the age wherever it may lead. *Orthodoxy is the challenge.* Orthodoxy forces us to set sail for ever new and distant harbors, beyond the comfort of our cherished assumptions and practices. It is orthodoxy that is adventuresome, refusing to allow us to stew in our own juices. We are not allowed to reduce our horizon to the dimensions of our own experience in our own time and place but must become "catholic" creatures: opened up to the church in all times and places. Implicit faith—that is, unthinking assent—characterizes conservatism and progressivism. Christians, however, do not believe in the past, the present, or the future, but in the Triune God who is Lord over all times and places.

Because Christ is Lord, there is a church in exile, receiving everything from heaven, and on earth witnessing to, loving, and serving their neighbors. For a new reformation in the church and renewed witness in the world, we need not only to re-arm ourselves with the drama and the doctrine, but allow the greatest story ever told to shape us into a cross-cultural community—a light set upon a hill.

We can find resources for our religious therapy online, but we cannot become part of the communion of saints apart from God's sovereign act of gathering us together with his flock as recipients of grace. There is a circulation of gifts that is set in motion by God's grace through preaching and sacrament. Receiving God's good gifts from the Father, in the Son, by the Spirit, we become part of the exchange of gifts in the communion of saints. Here are all of those strangers I may not have chosen for my closest relations, but God chose me—and them— together. Books have been written by historians and economists on the enormous social impact of the Reformation churches as they recovered the genuine proclamation of the gospel, instruction in the common faith, fellowship in common prayer, and the meaning and frequent celebration of Communion. Gifts came down from God, generating a new order in this passing age, and the results included energetic diaconal ministry as well as the ordinary vocations of individual believers in their secular callings as parents, co-workers, and neighbors.

A friend recounted to me his experience as a pastor during the Vietnam War. Since he proclaimed the Scriptures rather than his own political views, the church consisted of believers who held various positions on the Vietnam War. In the parking lot one day, he noticed two parishioners—a veteran and an anti-war protester—arguing to the point of fisticuffs. Calling them into the service, my friend wondered what might happen once they were brought under the same roof. Sitting on opposite sides of the church, they heard the pastor greet them in Christ's name. As they heard the law, they were visibly moved—and even more so, as they participated in the corporate confession of sin and heard Christ's absolution through the lips of the minister. After the sermon, he noticed that they not only came to the rail for Communion, but they knelt there together with their arms around each other, sobbing, as they held out their empty hands for the bread.

There is an important place for the world's politics. The issues we vote on and that some of us adjudicate as public servants are not unimportant. God cares a great deal about the daily welfare of everything that he has created. He calls us to love and serve our neighbors in our secular callings and politics is a part of that. Nevertheless, on the Lord's Day we are made citizens of another kingdom. There are no flags marking national boundaries, no banners signaling a particular ethnic, socioeconomic, generational, or gender identity. There is a pulpit, table, and font, where we gather as one people around the cross, "called out of darkness into his marvelous light." There, the "no-people" become "the people of God," recipients of God's mercy (1 Peter 2:9–10).

The mountain of Zion trumps all other hills, towers, and high places. No temporal government, cultural movement, or market niche can bring together a remnant "from every tribe, kindred, tongue, people, and nation" and make them into "a kingdom of priests to our God" who "will reign forever" (Rev. 5:9). We are building our earthly kingdoms, but Zion is the city that *God* is building. We are made recipients together of this kingdom, rather than architects and builders of our own interest groups. All other kingdoms will be shaken on the last day and finally collapse in rubble, but this kingdom—despised as weak and foolish in the eyes of the world—will endure forever.

Everything that is in Christ is alive, while outside of him life withers and dies, blown away like the chaff that is finally burned. Instead of trying to make God and his Christ a part of our story of personal fulfillment, consumer tastes, national pride, or ethnic empowerment, we are given a new script, with a new plot that defines our ultimate identity, hopes, longings, and experience. Instead of asking for the blood of his sons and daughters, this King gives his own blood for them. Rather than grasping for power and domination, "the Son of Man came not to be served but to serve and to give his life as a ransom for many" (Matt. 20:26) and calls us to become servants rather than lords (vv. 20–27).

At last there is an identity politics that unites people from many races, cultures, classes, generations, and tastes. At the mall, they may be builders, boomers, or busters. In the voting booth, they may be Republicans, Democrats, Libertarians, or Independents. They may join their neighbors at a rock concert or the symphony, at a football game or on the ski slopes. However, at Christ's font, in the pew, and at the table, they become a new people. Here we are made citizens of the holy city "coming down from heaven from God, prepared as a bride adorned for her husband," an anticipation and foretaste of the marriage feast of the Lamb, when we will hear finally and forever, "Behold, the dwelling place of God is with us" (Rev. 21:2–3). It is this Good News that dismantles Satan's dreadful kingdom and fills the world with the faint but growing laughter of a heavenly feast.

NOTES

Chapter 1 The Front-Page God: Checking the Headlines

1. Michael Horton, *Christless Christianity: The Alternative Gospel of the American Church* (Grand Rapids: Baker, 2008).

2. Quoted by Mark C. Taylor, *Erring: A Postmodern A/theology* (Chicago: University of Chicago Press, 1987), 66.

3. G. K. Chesterton, *Orthodoxy: The Romance of Faith* (New York: Doubleday, 1990), 75.

4. Ibid.

5. Ibid., 75–76.

6. Ibid., 76.

7. Immanuel Kant, *Political Writings*, ed. Hans Reiss, trans. H. B. Nisbet (Cambridge: Cambridge University Press, 1970), 43.

8. G. K. Chesterton, *Orthodoxy*, 157–58.

9. Ibid., 31.

10. Ibid., 32.

11. Ibid., 74.

12. Mark C. Taylor, *Erring*, 155.

13. Ibid., 53.

14. Ibid., 66.

15. Ibid., 20–30.

16. Ibid., 97.

17. G. K. Chesterton, *Orthodoxy*, 157.

Chapter 2 The Real Crisis

1. Stanley Hauerwas, "A Pacifist Response," in *Dissent from the Homeland: Essays after September 11*, ed. Stanley Hauerwas and Frank Lentricchia (Durham, NC: Duke University Press, 2003), 188.

2. H. Richard Niebuhr, *The Kingdom of God in America* (New York: Harper, 1959), 193.

3. *Westminster Shorter Catechism*, Q. 1.

4. Augustine, *Confessions*, trans. Henry Chadwick (Oxford: Oxford University Press, 1991), 3.

5. Michael Wyschogrod and R. Kendall Soulen, eds., *Abraham's Promise: Judaism and Jewish-Christian Relations* (Grand Rapids: Eerdmans, 2004), 53ff.

6. Ibid., 70.

7. George Lindbeck, "Justification and Atonement: An Ecumenical Trajectory," in *By Faith Alone: Essays on Justification in Honor of Gerhard O. Forde*, ed. Joesph A. Burgess and Marc Kolden (Grand Rapids: Eerdmans, 2004), 205.

8. Ibid., 205–6.

9. Ibid., 211.

10. George Hunsinger, *Disruptive Grace: Studies in the Theology of Karl Barth*, rev. ed. (Grand Rapids: Eerdmans, 2000), 16–17.

11. Ibid., 21.

12. Ibid.

13. C. Fitzsimons Allison, "Pastoral Care in the Light of Justification by Faith Alone," in Joseph A. Burgess and Marc Kolden, eds., *By Faith Alone*, 308.

14. Ibid., 312.

Chapter 3 The Big Story

1. Dorothy Sayers, *Creed or Chaos?* (New York: Harcourt, Brace and Company, 1949), 3.

Chapter 5 Don't Just *Do* Something, *Sit* There! Finding Yourself in the Story

1. See Walter von Loewenich, *Luther's Theology of the Cross* (Minneapolis: Augsburg, 1976).

2. Neal Gabler, *Life, the Movie: How Entertainment Conquered Reality* (New York: Alfred A. Knopf, 1998), 8.

3. Robert Jay Lifton, "The Protean Style," in *The Truth About Truth: De-confusing and Re-constructing the Postmodern World*, ed. Walter Truett Anderson (New York: Tarcher, 1995), 130–35.

4. Karl Barth, *The Göttingen Dogmatics: Instruction in the Christian Religion*, ed. Hannelotte Reiffen, trans. Geoffrey Bromiley (Grand Rapids: Eerdmans, 1991), 1:273.

5. G. K. Chesterton, *Orthodoxy: The Romance of Faith* (New York: Doubleday, 1990), 157.

6. Martin Luther, "Ninety-Five Theses," in *Martin Luther's Basic Theological Writings*, ed. Timothy Lull (Minneapolis: Fortress Press, 1989), 21.

7. See *The Catechism of the Catholic Church* (New York: USCCB, 1995), 364–67. "Christ instituted the sacrament of Penance for all sinful members of the Church: above

all for those who, since Baptism, have fallen into grave sin, and have thus lost their baptismal grace and wounded ecclesial communion. It is to them that the sacrament of Penance offers a new possibility to convert and to recover the grace of justification. The Fathers of the Church present this sacrament as 'the second plank [of salvation] after the shipwreck which is the loss of grace' " (363).

8. Ibid.

9. John Calvin, *Institutes of the Christian Religion*, trans. Henry Beveridge (Grand Rapids: Eerdmans, 1990), III.ii.7, emphasis added.

10. Ibid., III.ii.15.

11. *Heidelberg Catechism*, Q. 21, emphasis added.

12. *Westminster Larger Catechism*, Q. 155.

13. C. S. Lewis, *The Problem of Pain* (New York: HarperSanFrancisco, 2001), 124–25.

Chapter 6 The Promise-Driven Life

1. Richard Foster, "Spiritual Formation Agenda: Three Priorities for the Next Thirty Years," *Christianity Today* 53.1 (January 2009).

2. Thomas Finger, *A Contemporary Anabaptist Theology* (Downers Grove, IL: InterVarsity Press, 2004).

3. See George A. Lindbeck, *The Church in a Postliberal Age* (Grand Rapids: Eerdmans, 2003).

4. John Calvin, *Commentary on the Gospel According to John*, trans. William Pringle (Grand Rapids: Baker, 1996), 179–80.

5. Ibid., 180–81.

6. Ibid., 183.

7. Gerhard Forde, *On Being a Theologian of the Cross: Reflections on Luther's Heidelberg Disputation, 1518* (Grand Rapids: Eerdmans, 1997), 56–57.

8. *Epitome* III.11; cf. *Solid Declaration* III.23, 26, 36, 41.

9. Ibid., 58; *Luther's Works* 36:39.

10. Ibid., 59.

11. C. S. Lewis, *Mere Christianity* (New York: HarperSanFrancisco, 2001), 224.

12. Ibid., 161.

13. Ibid., 225.

14. Lewis, *The Problem of Pain*, 127–28.

15. Etiènne Gilson, *The Spirit of Medieval Philosophy* (London: Sheed and Ward, 1936), 421.

16. G. C. Berkouwer, *Faith and Sanctification* (Grand Rapids: Eerdmans, 1952), 29.

17. *Smalcald Articles* III.iii.44, quoted in Edmund Schlink, *The Theology of the Lutheran Confessions* (St. Louis: Concordia Publishing House, 2003), 160.

18. Richard Foster, "Spiritual Formation Agenda."

Chapter 7 News of War and Peace: God's Politics for a New Creation

1. Robert Payne, *The Dream and the Tomb: A History of the Crusades* (New York: Stein & Day, 1985), 34.

2. *Orat.* 1.6–2.5, cited in Douglas Farrow, *Ascension and Ecclesia: On the Significance of the Doctrine of the Ascension for Ecclesiology and Christian Cosmology* (Grand Rapids: Eerdmans, 1999), 115.

3. David Van Biema and Jeff Israely, "The Passion of the Pope," *Time*, November 27, 2006, 46.

4. Jon D. Levenson, *Sinai and Zion: An Entry into the Jewish Bible* (New York: HarperCollins, 1985), 19.

5. Ibid., 91.

6. Ibid., 137.

7. Ibid., 172.

8. Ibid.

9. Andrew Lincoln, *Ephesians*, Word Biblical Commentary (Dallas: Word, 1990), 243.

10. Ibid.

11. Ibid.

12. Ibid., 226.

Chapter 8 How the Good News Creates a Cross-Cultural Community

1. Martin Luther, "Second Sermon on Monday after Invocavit, March 10, 1522," in *Luther's Works*, ed. John W. Doberstein and Helmut T. Lehmann (Philadelphia: Fortress Press, 1958), 51:75–76.

2. William M. Cant, "The Most Urgent Call to the Kirk: The Celebration of Christ in the Liturgy of Word and Sacrament," *Scottish Journal of Theology* 40.1 (1987): 110.

3. Ibid., 115.

4. Ibid., 117.

5. Ibid., 120–21.

6. C. S. Lewis, *The Weight of Glory* (New York: HarperCollins, 2001), 26.

Chapter 9 The Health Page: Feasting in a Fast-Food World

1. Eric Schlosser, *Fast-Food Nation: The Dark Side of the All-American Meal* (New York: Penguin, 2001), 4–5.

2. David Brooks, *Bobos in Paradise: The New Upper Class and How They Got There* (New York: Simon & Schuster, 2000).

3. James Pine and James Gilmore, *The Experience Economy: Work Is Theater and Every Business a Stage* (Cambridge, MA: Harvard Business School Press, 1999). See also the interview with James Gilmore in *Modern Reformation* 18.4 (July/August 2009): 12–13.

4. Pico Iyer, *The Global Soul: Jet Lag, Shopping Malls, and the Search for Home* (New York: Alfred A. Knopf, 2000), 25.

5. Ibid., 43.

6. Ibid., 140.

7. Ibid., 145.

8. Ibid.

9. Joe Queenan, *Balsamic Dreams: A Short but Self-Important History of the Baby Boomer Generation* (New York: Henry Holt and Company, 2001), 23.

10. Ibid., 24.

11. David P. Mossner, *The Lord of the Banquet: The Literary and Theological Significance of the Lukan Travel Narrative* (Minneapolis: Fortress Press, 1989), 264.

12. Ibid., 264–65.

13. Frederick Buechner, *Magnificent Defeat* (New York: HarperOne, 1985), 89.

Chapter 10 Today's Headline: The Church in Exile

1. Augustine, *City of God,* in *The Essential Augustine,* ed. Vernon J. Bourke (Indianapolis: Hackett, 1983), 201.

2. *The Epistle to Diognetus* (c. 170–80) in Ray C. Petry, ed., *A History of Christianity,* vol. 1, *The Early and Medieval Church* (New York: Prentice Hall, 1962), 19.

3. *Essential Augustine,* 201.

4. Ibid., 222.

5. Ibid., 208.

6. Calvin, *Institutes,* II.ii.15.

7. Ibid., IV.xx.1–2.

8. Ibid., IV.xx.8, 14.

9. Ibid.

10. Josiah Strong, "Our Country," in William G. McLoughlin, ed., *The American Evangelicals, 1800–1900: An Anthology* (Gloucester, MA: Peter Smith, 1976), 196.

11. Cited in ibid.

12. Cited in George Marsden, *Fundamentalism and American Culture* (New York: Oxford University Press, 1980), 38.

13. Brad J. Kallenberg, *Live to Tell: Evangelism in a Postmodern World* (Grand Rapids: Brazos, 2002), 13.

14. Dinesh D'Souza, *What's So Great About Christianity?* (Washington, DC: Regnery Publishing, 2007), 3.

15. Ibid.

16. Sayers, *Creed or Chaos?,* 5.

17. Ibid., 24.

18. Ibid., 26–27.

19. Ibid., 29–31.

20. Ibid., 45.

A Prophetic Wake-Up Call for the American Church

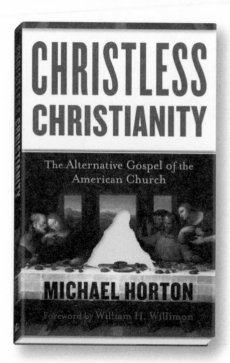

Christless Christianity:
The Alternative Gospel of
the American Church

by Michael Horton

9780801013188   272 pp. $19.99c

Is it possible that we have left Christ out of Christianity?

Is the faith and practice of American Christians today more American than Christian? These are the provocative questions Michael Horton—Professor of Systematic Theology and Apologetics at Westminster Seminary California, host of *The White Horse Inn* radio broadcast, and editor-in-chief of *Modern Reformation* magazine—addresses in this thoughtful book.

> "Horton confronts modern evangelicalism in terms reminiscent of J. Gresham Machen's challenge to liberalism in the 1920s."
>
> —PARKER T. WILLIAMSON, editor emeritus and senior correspondent, *The Presbyterian Layman*

BakerBooks
a division of Baker Publishing Group
www.BakerBooks.com